ENCYCLOPAEDIA OF INDIA, PAKISTAN AND BANGLADESH

ENCYCLOPAEDIA OF

INDIA, PAKISTAN AND BANGLADESH

(In 9 Volumes)

(Volume 4)

OM GUPTA

ISHA

ISHA BOOKS

Delhi-110033

Encyclopaedia of India, Pakistan and Bangladesh
(In 9 Volumes)

ISBN : 81-8205-389-7 (Set)
ISBN : 81-8205-393-5 (Vol. 4)

Rs. 6300 (Set)

Published in 2006 in India by
Isha Books
D-43, Prithviraj Road,
Adarsh Nagar, Delhi - 110033
e-mail : ishabooks@hotmail.com

Laser Typesetting : Vinayak Printers, Delhi
[illegible] : Salasar Imaging [illegible]

Preface

According to Oxford dictionary Encyclopaedia is a book or aset of books that gives information on many subjects or many aspect of one subject. This encyclopaedia does that on India, Pakistan and Bangladesh. It is the first work of its kind. There have been anthologies on India but there is no compendium of information in an alphabetical order. Even Britannica could go as far as four-volume encyclopaedia on Indian history.

Encyclcpaedia is an extension of a dictionary. The latter gives you meanings of words while the former gives facts about people, places and events. No one can claim to compile all the facts and that of a sub-continent called India. But then it is the prerogative of the editor to pick up his entries that he considers would be useful to his reader. Generally we soon find our comfort levels in a language. And rarely consults a dictionary and lesser an encyclopaedia. But those who dare, find the experience worth it. lt can be easily compared to a human body. In our daily life we tend to be our own quacks and medicate on the basis of common sense. If we refer to a doctor we come to know the actual cause of the symptom and get relieved on knowing the gravity of the situation or the absence of it. One would realize that encyclopaedia reveals the fundamentals of any situation, person or the event and we feel at home with that information.

A dictionary and an encyclopaedia can easily enlarge the process of learning even to an uninitiated person. It is truer in case of humanities. Popular myth about encyclopaedia is that it is meant to be referred to in a library only. The librarians, the world over keep encyclopaedia in such zealously guarded protection that the generally refrain from asking for it. Since the advent of internet in our life, the bulkiness of encyclopaedias has disappeared. That is why we have divided this enterprise in nine volumes. Encyclopaedias are generally global in its expanse. Even subject-related encyclopaedias give the global perspective.That is why country-specific encylopaedias have never been seriousy attempted. We hope that this effort will fill that volume. Traditionally encyclopaedias don't deal with factual data e.g. Indian exports, population figures, GDP. That is the job of annual reference books. They are also different from alamans in as much as that they don't give dated entries. That will become texts on history. Encyclopaedias need to be updated. A country is alive and kicking. People and events continue to play role in various aspects of life. Hence they need to be added. That is why either annual supplements or updation needs to be done in encyclopaedias. We would strive for that.

Regarding its contents only those entries have been included that continue to influence the life of a nation. There are historical figures who might have played a significant role in their times but if those deeds have no relevance to the present they have been excluded. Another example is literary awards. They always create controversies because their selection at times is subjective. Hence only universally accepted meritorious work has found place in these volumes. In this context a debatable point need to be stated. Who is more important book or the author. Conventionally work is an end product and only that is a measure of the author's importance but then a prolic writer might have produced a large body of creations. Hence to save space the author is entered with all his important work.That is also an international practice.

Lastly, why India, Pakistan and Bangladesh have been clubbed together. Before India's independence they were one nation. They share a common heritage and composite culture. Their post-independence history is different but 22their foundation is undivided. In order to appreciate the historical context better it is necessary to cross-refer and that was possible when they are juxtaposed.

Om Gupta

G

Gadchiroli District : Gadchiroli District is an administrative district in Maharashtra, India. It is one of the most underdeveloped districts of India. The town of Gadchiroli is the administrative headquarters of the district. The district is situated in the southeastern corner of Maharashtra, and is bounded by Chandrapur District to the west, Gondiya District to the north, Chhatisgarh state to the east, and Andhra Pradesh state to the south and southwest.

The district is categoried as a tribal and undeveloped district, and most of the land is covered with forest and hills. Forests cover more than 79.36 % of the geographical area of the district. This district is famous for bamboo and Tendu leaves. Paddy is the main agricultural product of the district. The district is divided into three sub-divisions, Gadchiroli, Aheri and Desaiganj, and each sub-division has four talukas. The district has three Legislative Assembly constituencies, Gadchiroli, Armori and Sironcha. The district has 12 Panchayat Samitis. Only two municipalities, Gadchiroli and Wadsa, exist in the district. The main river basin of the district is the Godavari, which flows west to east and forms the southern boundary of the district.

Gadiara : Gadiara is a village in Howrah District of West Bengal, India. This place is the point of convergence of the Damodar, the Rupnarayan and the Hoogli rivers. Gadiara in the lap of nature is a popular spot with the localities as well as the tourists.

Gahirmatha Beach : Gahirmatha Beach is a beach in the Indian state of Orissa. The beach separates the Bhitarkanika mangroves from the Bay of Bengal, is the world's most important nesting beach for Olive Ridley Sea Turtles. The beach is part of Gahirmatha Marine Wildlife Sanctuary, which also includes the adjacent portion of the Bay of Bengal.

Gahma Purnami : In Orissa, this festival is celebrated as a merry festival of 'Ĝahma Pumei', on the full moon day of the lunar month of Shravana and is especially auspicious to agriculturists. On this day, cattle, especially plough cattle, are colourfully decorated and given special offering and are worshipped as 'Go-Lakshmi'. That is the day of rest for the cattle. This festival has much attraction for some tribal groups like the Hill Bhuiyan of Orissa that in these lean months of semi-starvations.

Gair : Originally a dance of Southern Rajasthan, it is another Holi dance performed only by men. This becomes Dhandia Gair in Jodhpur and Greendad in Shekhwati.

Gair Ghumar : This is typical of the Bhil tribals and is performed during the Holi festival together by men and women dressed in traditional costumes.

Gairsen : Gairsen is a village in Uttaranchal, India which is being built as the state's future capital. The site was chosen due to its central location in the state. The current provisional capital is Dehradun.

Gakhars : Gakhars or Ghakkar (who hold the title Kayani), are a clan that today forms the aristocracy of the (Rawalpindi) district. From the moment where oral traditions give way to the more authentic records of the historian, the history of the (Rawalpindi) district becomes that of the Gakhar clan, who, brought into a prominent position at the time of the early Muslim invasions, maintained their rule over Rawalpindi and parts of the Hazara and Jhelum districts, more or less independent of the sovereign powers at Delhi and Agra, until being annihilated at the beginning of the present (19th) century by the Sikhs.

Galyat : The Galyat region is an area in Pakistan centered on the hill station of Murree. It is a popular summer-holiday destination in Pakistan. Many of the towns in the area have the word gali (valley) as part of their names. Galyat is a plural of gali.

Gama Pehalwan : Ahmad Baksh Gama was born in Datiya (MP). He was fond of wrestling since his childhood. By 20, he had defeated all most all the national level wrestlers.

"Rustam-e-Hind" Gama pehalwan, who brought the Indian style of wrestling to international sports and lend it credentials, had tricks of the trade running in his blood. In 1910, a wrestling match was organized for the award of the title "Rustam-e-Hind", Gama defeated all the wrestlers and earned the title. Gama's last match was with J.C Peterson whom he defeated in 45 seconds.

Gama wrestled for many years and always emerged victorious. One of his greatest quality was that he had not only a sense of self respect but was very friendly in nature. Indian wrestling owes its popularity to Gama. He died in Lahore on 22nd May in 1960.

Gambhir River : Gambhir River originates in the hills near Karauli village in Sawai Madhopur District. It flows from south to north up to Kanjoli village (Toda Bhim), then towards northeast up to village Mertha of Roopbas

Block, before entering Uttar Pradesh. The river again enters Rajasthan near Catchapaura village in Dholpur District and forms the boundary between UP and Rajasthan. It then enters Mainpuri District in UP to finally joins River Yamuna.

Gambhira Dance : This dance accompanies gambhira songs and used to be quite popular in the Maldah district of undivided Bengal. Though not as popular today as it was in the past, it continues to be performed in Rajshahi. The dance is performed by a pair of artistes, one acting the role of a nana (maternal grandfather) and the other that of his nati (grandson). Through their dancing and singing, they critique contemporary social, political, economic and moral problems. The dialogue is in both prose and verse. There is a chorus which repeats the refrain of the song. The main musical accompaniments are the harmonium, flute, drum and judi. The gambhira dance, with its mixture of dialogue, dance, songs and music, resembles a folk play. While the chorus sings the refrain, the nana and nati dance, with the nati wearing a string of bells round his ankles. In Maldah, the artistes wear masks.

Gambhira Gan : Gambhira Gan is a type of folk song popular in the northwestern region of Bangladesh. Gambhira songs are assumed to have originated from the worship of the god shiva, who is also known as 'Gambhir'. In ancient times, gambhira used to be celebrated as puja (worship) only. In the medieval period, most Hindu communities celebrated the puja of dharma thakur (a popular god of the Hindus) on the last three days of the Bengali year; this came to be known as the gajan of Shiva later on. In the past Shiva was imagined to be present at the performance.

Initially, gambhira was of two kinds: the primary gambhira and the narrative gambhira. The primary gambhira would address gods and goddesses and describe human joys and sorrows, and, sometimes, important events of the year. In the narrative gambhira, every character would represent a social problem.

Gambhira songs originated among the Hindu community of Maldah in west bengal. After the creation of Pakistan, Chapai Nawabganj in rajshahi became the main centre of gambhira songs, which underwent major changes in theme and mode of presentation. Muslims became the custodians of this song and made it an integral part of their social life and their culture. Apart from Rajshahi, gambhira songs are also popular in nawabganj and naogaon.

At present the main characters of a gambhira are a maternal grandfather and his grandson. The performance is structured as a dialogue, interspersed with songs. Both prose and verse are used for the dialogue. The gambhira reflects contemporary social problems through witty dialogue, songs, dances and jokes. Both the actors wear lungi. The grey-bearded grandfather wears a mathal (straw hat) on his head and holds a stick in his hand. The grandson wears a torn jersey and has a gamchha (local checked towel) tied round his waist.

In the past gambhira songs were sung in the measures of ektal, trital, dadra, khemta, kaharba etc. Today the tunes are influenced by songs from popular Bangla and Hindi movies. Kutubul Alam, Rakibuddin, Biren Ghosh and Mahbubul Alam of Nawabganj have made the gambhira song popular in Bangladesh by introducing new subjects and characters and interesting and witty dialogue.

Gana-forum : Gana-forum Kamal Hossain, an eminent lawyer and a former leader of Awami League, floated Gana-forum in 1992. It was established as a political party in August 1993. It is a left-liberal party, which works for a stronger civil society and a rule based egalitarian society.

Ganamukti Parishad : Tripura Rajaer Upajati Ganamukti Parishad (Bengali for 'Tripura State Tribal People's Liberation Council') is a leftwing movement working amongst the tribal peoples of Tripura, in north-eastern India. In 1948 the Mukti Parishad (Liberation Council, later renamed Ganamukti Parishad) was formed as a struggle front against the despotic rule of the monarchic leadership of Tripura. The predecessors of the Mukti Parishad were the Janamangal Samiti (People's Welfare Association), the Tripura Rajya Prajamandal (Tripura State Popular Assembly) and especially the Janasiksha Samiti (People's Educational Association). All these organizations had a some influence from the local cell of the Communist Party of India. Also the Mukti Parishad was closely associated with the Communist Party, even though there were only two card-holding communists within its ranks at the time of the foundation of movement.

Gandak : The Gandak is a tributary of the Ganges River. It starts in the Himalayas in Nepal where it is known as the Narayani. It then flows through India in Bihar, eventualy merging with the Ganges near at Hajipur Patna.

Gandhara : Gandhara (also Ghandara, Ghandahra, Chandahara, and Persian Gandara) is the name of an ancient kingdom in eastern Afghanistan and north-west province of Pakistan. Gandhara was located mainly on northern side of Kabul River. In the east, it extended beyond Indus River and included within its boundaries parts of the valley of Kashmir (Political History of Ancient India, 1996, p 151). Kingdom of Gandhara lasted from 6th Century BC to 11th Century AD. It attained its height from 1st century to 5th Century AD under Buddhist Kushan Kings. After it was conquered by Mahmood of Ghazni in 1021 AD, the name Gandhara disappeared. During Muslim period the area was administered from Lahore or from

Kabul. During Mughals time area was part of Kabul province.

Gandhara Grave Culture : Gandhara grave culture emerges from ca. 1600 BC, and flourishes in Gandhara ca. 1500 BC to 500 BC. Relevant finds, artifacts found primarily in graves, were distributed along the banks of the Swat and Dir rivers in the north, Taxila in the southeast, along the Gomal river to the south. The pottery finds show clear links with contemporary finds from southern Central Asia (BMAC) and the Iranian Plateau. Simply made terracotta figurines were buried with the pottery, and other items are decorated with simple dot designs. Horse remains were found in at least one burial. The Gandhara grave people have been associated by some scholars with early Indo-Aryan speakers, and the Indo-Aryan migration into India, that, fused with indigenous elements of the remnants of the Indus Valley Civilization (OCP, Cemetery H), gave rise to the Vedic civilization.

Gandhi Sagar Dam : The Gandhi Sagar dam is the first of the four dams built on the Chambal river. It is located in the Mandsaur district of Madhya Pradesh. It is a 64 metre high masonry gravity dam, with a live storage capacity of 6,920 Mm^3 and a catchment area of 22,584 km^2. The dam was completed in the year 1960. The hydro-power station comprises five generating units, four of 23 MW each and one 27 MW capacity. The water released after power generation is utilised for irrigation through Kota Barrage.

Gandhidham : Gandhidham, is a city in the Kutch district of the Indian state of Gujarat. This well-planned rich city was established in 1960s for Sindhi immigrants. It is 12 kilometers from Kandla, one of India's largest ports and only free trade zone. Thus, most of businesses in Gandhidham are shipping related. After the 2001 earthquake devastated the area, the Government declared the Kutch district as a tax exempt district for next 5 years; as a result, many businesses were established in Gandhidham.

Gandhinagar : Gandhinagar is the capital of Gujarat State, India. It is a planned city similar to Chandigarh. It is also the headquarters of Gandhinagar District. The new city is spread on either banks of Sabarmati river. The main city is designed on the west bank of the river on 42.9 km^2 of land. The site is gently sloping, from north-east to south-west. Fine landscape lies along the west bank of the river Sabarmati.

Gandhism : Gandhism is an informal reference to the vision, core inspirations, principles, beliefs and philosophy of Mohandas Karamchand Gandhi, who was a major political and spiritual leader of India and the Indian Independence Movement. It is a body of ideas and principles that best describe not only the inspiration, vision and the life work of Mahatma Gandhi, but what Gandhi's ideas, words and actions meant to common Indians and human beings around the world, and how they used them for guidance in building their own future. Gandhism also permeates into the realm of the individual human being, non-political and non-social.

Ganeriwala : Ganeriwala is an Indus Valley civilization site of an urban center in the Punjab, Pakistan. It is located near the border to India which was discovered by Pakistani archaeologist M.R. Mughal in 1975. It is near a dry bed of River Hakra (also known as Ghaggar or Sarasvati River). The Harappa Culture of Indus Valley grew out of the earlier Village Culture of Baluchistan, NWFP, Sind, Punjab and Western India. By 3000 B.C., hundreds of farming communities sprang up in Indus Valley. Helped by the annual flooding of the Indus and its tributaries, communities grow different crops in the rich soil. The result of this development was the more advanced urban center than the Pre Harappa Towns of Kot Diji or Rehman Dheri. Until now five urban centers of Harappa Culture have been discovered; Harappa, Mohenjo Daro, Ganweriwala in Pakistan, Rakhigarhi and Dholavira in India.

Ganesh Chaturthi : Ganesh Chaturthi is the birthday of Ganesh - the elephant headed son of Lord Shiva and Parvathi. It is the birthday of Ganesh—the elephant headed son of Shiva and Parvathi. Ganesh is believed to be the harbinger of good luck who removes all obstacles to success. He brings prosperity and keeps natural calamities at bay in the lives of those who worship him. This ten day festival begins with the installation of the deity, who is then worshipped daily till the immersion on the final day. Small Ganesh idols are installed in homes. Idols can tower 10m high and weigh several tonnes. On the tenth day, serpentine processions fill the streets and with the accompaniment of drumbeats and music the image of Ganesh is immersed in the water. Devotees chant 'Ganapati Bappa Morya' which means Ganesh, Daddy, please come back soon next year.

Ganga Lake (Gyaker Sinyi) : Ganga a natural Lake locally known as Gyaker Sinyi (confined water), 6km away from Itanagar situated on the foothills of the Himalayas, is a beautiful spot for outings, boating and picnics. This green forest lake surrounded by primeval vegetation, orchids masses on tall trees, tree ferns provides an insight to the magnificent forests of the state.

Gangabal Lake : The famous Gangabal lake of Haramukh is regarded as sacred by Kashmiri Hindus to the same extent as Haridwar is held in India. Here also Saussurea Sacra grows in plenty. Another remarkable peak in the east seen all over the city is Mahadev (13,000 ft.). in Summer pilgrims climb this peak. On the lower sides of this mountain, one comes across a herb Macrotomia

Benthami in wild profusion. This herb is well known as Kah zaban or Gaw Zaban. It is frequently prescribed by the local physicians to ailing persons.

Ganges Delta : The Ganges Delta is a river delta in the south Asia region of Bengal, consisting of Bangladesh and the state of West Bengal, India. It is the world's largest delta, and empties into the Bay of Bengal. The delta, also known as the Ganges-Brahmaputra Delta, stretches from the Hugli River on the west to the Meghna River on the east. It is approximately 220 miles across at the Bay of Bengal. Kolkata, India (formerly Calcutta), and Chittagong, Bangladesh are the principal seaports on the delta. The Ganges Delta arises from the confluence of the following rivers: Padma (Lower Ganges) (Pôdda) Jamuna (Lower Brahmaputra) (Jomuna) and Meghna.

Ganges River : The Ganges River (Ganga in Indian languages; Ganges is the Latin form) (Devanagari) is the major river in northern India and Bangladesh. The river has a long history of reverence in India and is often called the 'holy Ganga'. It originates as the Bhagirathi from the Gangotri Glacier in the Uttaranchal Himalayas and joins the Alaknanda near Deoprayag to form the Ganga. Then on, the Ganga flows across the large plains of North India (called the Gangetic Plains) and empties into the Bay of Bengal after dividing up into many distributaries. One of them is the Hoogli River near Kolkata, another major distributary being the Padma River that enters Bangladesh and merges with Jamuna River, a branch of the Brahmaputra River.

The total length of the river is about 2,510 km (1,560 mi). One of the densest human population belts on earth is built around the Ganga. The region encompassing the delta near the Bay of Bengal coast is known as The Sundarbans (Beautiful Forests) — a region of thick mangrove forests, and one of the major habitats of the

Royal Bengal tiger. The Ganges Basin is incredibly fertile and, at present, about one in every 12 people in the world (8.5%) live in its catchment area. However, due to this incredible concentration of population, pollution and destruction of habitats is increasing at an alarming rate in the region.

The Yamuna River — a major river in its own right, and nearly as sacred — is a tributary of the Ganga, and their confluence is near what is the site of the traditional holy Hindu city of Prayag, now known as Allahabad. Two species of dolphin can be found in the Ganges, the Ganges River Dolphin and the Irrawaddy Dolphin. The Ganges is also notable in that it contains a rare species of freshwater shark, Glyphis gangeticus about which little is known.

Ganges River Dolphin : The Ganges River Dolphin (Platanista gangetica gangetica) and Indus River Dolphin (Platanista gangetica minor) are two sub-species of freshwater or river dolphins found in India and Pakistan. From the 1970s they had commonly been regarded as separate species. The Ganges River Dolphin is primarily found in River Ganges and its tributaries in India while the Indus River Dolphin is found in the Indus river in Pakistan. However in 1998, a seminal work on cetacean taxonomy listed them as a single species once again

Ganges-Padma River System : Ganges-Padma river system is one of the three major river systems of Bangladesh. The Bengal delta occupies a unique position among the larger deltas of the world for its varied and complex river and drainage system. The whole delta is criss-crossed by innumerable large and small channels of which some are decaying, some are active, while some others are being drained only by the tidal flow. In the northeastern part of the delta there are some abandoned or partially abandoned courses of decaying rivers while the eastern and southeastern delta is characterised by the flow of active rivers with heavy discharges.

The southwestern portion of the Ganges delta, which includes the world's largest mangrove forest, the Sundarbans, is completely a maze of tidal creeks and channels. The river system's channels however carry a substantial amount of water through its various distributaries which join these tidal channels and estuarine creeks. Almost the whole delta is dotted with numerous lakes, marshes and low-lying swamps. In recent years, the area of these marshes and swamps has gradually shrunk owing to the encroachment of human habitations and reclamation of land for agriculture.

Gangolihat : Gangolihat is a small Himalayan hill town in the Pithoragarh district of Uttaranchal, India. It is 44 km from Pithoragarh. It is tehsil and sub divisional headquarter of the district. Gangolihat is famous for its Hatkalika temple of goddess Kali. Nearby at 'Patal Bhubneshwar', underground caves are major tourist attraction.

Gangor-Puja Dance : This dance is performed in villages bordering on Rajasthan. It is ceremonial dance of woman in connection with puja ceremony of Iswar and Gangor *(Lord Shiva* and *Pravati)* dressed in colourful costumes and Jewellery, with brass jars on their head, the woman move in circle, the movements and the pattern of the dance changing according to the music. The smiles of the dancers are important element in the performance. It is devotional dance to invoke the blessings of the gods for good harvest and is usually performed in the months of palghun and Chait. Sometimes the dance takes the form of a *Kirtan,* associated with the love of Lord Shiva and Parvati. The girls enter the circle one by one, dancing and singing devotional songs. The dance continues for hours.

Gangotri : Gangotri is a Hindu pilgrim town on the banks of the river Bhagirathi, in the Indian state of Uttaranchal. It is on the Greater Himalayan Range, at a height of 10,100 ft. This small town is centered around a temple of the goddess Ganga, which was built by the Gurkha General Amar Singh Thapa in the 18th century. It is one of the four sites in the Char Dham pilgrimage circuit. The Gangotri temple can be reached in one day's travel from Rishikesh, Haridwar or Dehradun, or in two days from Yamunotri, the first site in the Char Dham circuit. More popular and important than its sister site to the east, Gangotri is also accessible directly by car and bus, meaning that it sees many more pilgrims than Yamunotri.

Several guesthouses and restaurants in the town serves the pilgrim community. Ritual duties are supervised by the Semwal family of pujaris. The aarti ceremony at the Gangotri is especially impressive, as is the temple, a stately affair that sits on the banks of the rushing Ganga. Adventurous pilgrims can make an overnight 17 km trek to Gaumukh, the actual current source of the Ganga.

Gangotri Glacier : Gangotri Glacier is located in Uttaranchal, India in a region bordering Tibet. The glacier is about 30 km long and 2 to 4 km wide. The source of the Gangotri Glacier is said to resemble a cow's mouth, and the place is called Goumukh (gou, cow + mukh, face). Goumukh, which is about 18 km from the town of Gangotri, is the precise source of the Bhagirathi river, an important tributary of the Ganga. Goumukh is situated near the base of a mountain called Shivling. The Gangotri glacier is a traditional Hindu pilgrimage site. Devout Hindus consider bathing in the icy waters near Gangotri town to be a holy ritual, and many make the trek to Goumukh. The Gangotri glacier is roughly 30 km long. In recent times, it has been pointed out that the retreat of the glacier has quickened significantly.

Gangotri National Park : The park is situated in Uttarkashi District is a vast area1553sq.km. in extent. The airport and rail head is Dehradun. The nearest town is

Harsil 30 km away from Gangotri. The park provides majestic beauty of coniferous forests and grandeur of glacial world combined with lush green meadows. The forests of the park are Himalayan moist temperate type. Vegetation consist of chirpine deodar, fir, spruce, oak and rhododendrons.

Gangotri Temple : The shrine of Gangotri is situated at an elevation of 3200 m amidst charming surroundings of deodars and pines. The original temple was constructed by the Gorkha General Amar Singh Thapa. Every year people from all around the world visit this shrine. A number of ashrams and dharamshalas are located on the other side. It is believed that Raja Bhagirath used to worship Shiva on a slab of rock "Bhagirath Shila" situated near the temple. Submerged in the river there is a natural rock shivling where according to mythology Lord Shiva sat when he received the Goddess Ganga in his matted locks.

Gangtok : Gangtok is the capital and largest town of the Indian state of Sikkim. It is situated in the lower Himalayas, located at 27.2° N 88.4° E. Known for its clean surroundings and temperate climate, this hill station of about fifty thousand people is the centre of Sikkim's tourist industry.

Gangtok was a small hamlet until the construction of the Enchey Monastery in 1840 made it a pilgrimage center. It became a major stopover between Tibet and British India at the end of the 19th century. Following India's independence in 1947, Sikkim became a nation-state with Gangtok as its capital. In 1975 the monarchy was abrogated and Sikkim became India's twenty-second state, with Gangtok remaining as its capital.

The precise meaning of the name Gangtok is unclear, though it is generally held to mean "lofty hill". Gangtok is also a centre of Tibetan Buddhist culture and learning with numerous monasteries and religious educational institutions.

Gangubhai Hangal : Gangubhai Hangal (born on March 5, 1912) is one of the greats of the Hindustani classical music. She is a vocalist and an exponent of the Kirana Gharana. She learnt her music under the tutelage of Sawai Gandharva. Gangubhai lives in the town of Hubli in Karnataka.

She is known to let herself drift in the melody of the raga she renders. She believes that Music helped her have a communion with God. In 2002, she was awarded the Padma Vibhushan, India's second highest civilian award.

Ganjam : Ganjam is a district in the Indian state of Orissa located on the border of Andhra Pradesh. Ganjam is known for its beaches bordering the Indian Ocean, the most famous ones being Gopalpur (a famous tourist destination) and Dhavaleshwar. The most populous city in Ganjam, Berhampur, is famous for silver filigree and silk sarees woven with gold and silver threads

Garaga Dance : Garaga means a pot or vessel. The dance performed with a vessel on the head is known as Garaganrityam. This is very popular in Karnataka and Tamil Nadu. This dance was performed as a ritual by Asadis during propitiating ceremonies of village goddesses. In Andhra this is popular in the coastal districts and the border districts of Karnataka and Tamil Nadu.

In olden days the priest in trance known as Ganachary used to dance without any make up for himself, with a decorated earthen pot on his head in-front of the temple of a village goddess or along with her retinue in procession to the beats of Dappu. It is a strong percussion instruments. In course of time the Garaga dance has acquired many attractive adjuncts in make up and dance styles. Brass vessels covered with colourful cloths, decorated with vermilion and turmeric are held on the heads by the artistes when they dance. The mouth of the brass vessel is covered with a five hooded serpent made in brass or bronze.

The dancers put on colourful clothes and hold a bunch of margosa leaves symbolic of Shakti worship. The adept Dappu players produce varying beats in Trisara, Caturasra and other Gatis and the Garaga dancers dance and produce the same sounds with the jingling bells tied to their ankles. The artistes maintain the balance of the vessels on their heads by without moving their heads though their bodies and limbs move very fast. They have introduced many nuances and acrobatics in their dance styles for attracting the spectators. They lie down on their bellies and pick up coins and sticks with their lips. They stand facing each other on one leg and make a knot with each others leg and dance to the drum beats. They also play Kolatam striking at each others stick. All these while maintaining the balance of the vessels on their heads.

Garam Masala : Garam masala is a blend of dry-roasted ground spices common in Pakistani/Indian cuisine, whose literal meaning is 'hot spices'. There are many variants: most traditional mixes use just cinnamon, cloves, nutmeg (and/or mace), black pepper and green cardamom seed or black cardamom pods. Many commercial mixtures may include more of other less expensive spices and may contain dried red chili peppers, dried garlic, ginger powder, sesame, mustard seeds, turmeric, coriander, cloves, black pepper, cardamom, cinnamon, bay leaves, cumin, nutmeg, and fennel. While commercial garam masala preparations can be bought ready ground, it does not keep well, and soon loses its aroma. It is much better to buy the whole spices, which keep fresh much longer, and to grind them when needed using a pestle or electric coffee grinder.

Garam masala can be used during cooking, but unlike many spices, it is often added at the end of cooking, so that the full aroma is not lost. Garam masala is not "hot" in the sense that chilis are, but is fairly pungent.

Garba Dance : Garba Dance is a popular folk Dance of Gujarat. It is a circular form of dance performed by ladies on the Navaratri days, Sharad Purnima, Vasant Panchami, Holi and such other festive occasions. The word Garba is derived from the word Garbha Deep meaning a lamp inside a perforated earthen pot. The light inside the perforated earthen pot symbolised the embryonic life. In this folk dance, ladies place the pot with the lamp on their heads and move in circles, singing in time measure by clapping their palms or snapping their fingers, to the accompaniment of folk instruments. The actual performance begins at night after the women finish their house hold work. All gather at street corners. A photograph of the goddess or a lamp is kept in the centre and around it the circle is formed. The dancing begins with slow tempo and reaches a fast tempo. The rhythm is kept by a Dholi or drummer who sit in the centre. Some times, women carry on their heads 'Mandavali' a small canopy made of bamboo chips covered with a red silk piece of cloth. They dance with it and later put it in the centre.

Mandavali symbolises the temple of the goddess. Women wear sari in the Gujarati style. Each community wears different clothes. In Saurashtra, women wear embroidered petticoats (Ghaghara), a backless choli (Kapdu) and a head cover (odhani) with lots of silver and head ornaments. Males wear Kediyum (shirt) Vajani (trouser) and Rumal a printed head piece with silver ornaments on the waist, neck and hands. The musical instruments used for Garba are mainly the drum or Dhol and Nal. But Rasa has Pavo (a double flute) Vansali (flute) Zanza (Discs)etc. The drummer ties his drums around the neck and moves inside the circle beating it.

Garbhadhanam : It is a ritual for women in Kerala to get a blessing from god to conceive. This is the first sacrament which followed immediately on every matrimonial union.

Garbhama Samkranti : This festival is celebrated on the first day of the solar month of Karthika. This is the time when the paddy plants or the ears of corn are forming. This is compared to pregnancy and hence the name 'Garbhma'. These pregnant rice plants represent Lakshmi the Goddess of wealth and fertility and are worshipped with offerings in the paddy fields. They believe that through supernatural intervention a huge quantity of corn will thus harvested. All the family members eat to their heart's content.

Garhwal : Garhwal, or Gurwal, is a region and administrative division of Uttaranchal state, India, lying in the Himalayas. It is bounded on the north by Tibet, on the east by Kumaon region, on the south by Uttar Pradesh state, and on the west by Himachal Pradesh state. It includes the districts of Chamoli, Dehradun, Haridwar, Pauri Garhwal, Rudraprayag, Tehri Garhwal, and Uttarkashi. The administrative centre for Garhwal division is the town of Pauri.

The region consists almost entirely of rugged mountain ranges running in all directions, and separated by narrow valleys which in some cases become deep gorges or ravines. The only level portion of the district was a narrow strip of waterless forest between the southern slopes of the hills and the fertile plains of Rohilkhand. The highest mountains are in the north, the principal peaks being Nanda Devi (25,661 feet), Kamet (25,413 feet), Trisul (23,382 feet), Badrinath (23,210 feet), Dunagiri (23,181 feet) and Kedarnath (22,853 feet). The Alaknanda River, one of the main sources of the Ganges, receives with its affluents the whole drainage of the district. At Deoprayag the Alaknanda joins the Bhagirathi, and thenceforward the united streams bear the name of the Ganges. Cultivation is principally confined to the immediate vicinity of the rivers, which are employed for purposes of irrigation.

Garhwali : Garhwali is a term that refers to people belonging to the hilly Garhwal subdivision of Uttaranchal. It is also the language spoken by natives of Garhwal. Garhwali dialects are basically spoken in the Garhwal Division of Uttaranchal and belongs to the Indo-Aryan language group. Bhotiyas living in the north speak Tibeto-Burman dialects that is unintelligble to other Garwhali dialects and Tibetan. The closest language is Kumauni or Kumaoni to its immediate east in the Central subgroup of the Pahari chain of dialects stretching from Himachal Pradesh to Nepal. Garhwali, like Kumauni has many regional dialects spoken in different places in Uttaranchal. The Script used for Garhwali is Devanagari.

Garo Hills : Garo Hills known for its abundance of wildlife in Meghalaya, should interest naturalists and photographers to capture the variegated facets of life of a unique range of flora and fauna Two mountain ranges-the Arabella range and the Tura range, pass through the Garo Hills, forming the great Balpakram Valley in between. The headquarters town of Tura 323 kms via Guwahati, at an altitude of 657 metres. The highest point is Nokrek Peak with elevation of 1,412 metres.

Garo Hills known for its abundance of wildlife should interest naturalists and photographers to capture the variegated facets of life of a unique range of flora and fauna. Two mountain ranges—the Arabella range and the Tura range, pass through the Garo Hills, forming the great

Balpakram valley in between. The headquarters town of Tura is 323 Kms via Guwahati, at an altitude of 657 Kms. The highest point is Nokrek Peak with elevation of 1412 metres.

Garos : The Garos are a tribe in Meghalaya, India, and Mymensingh, Bangladesh, who call themselves Achik. They are the second-largest tribe in Meghalaya after the Khasi and comprise about a third of the local population. The majority of Garos are Christian. There are a large number of Baptists and Roman Catholics. There is also a sprinkling of Seventh-day Adventists, Anglicans and others belonging to some new denominations.

The Garo language belongs to the Bodo branch of the Bodo-Naga-Kachin family of the Sino-Tibetan phylum. They are mainly distributed over the Kamrup, Goalpara and Karbi Anglong Districts of Assam, Garo Hills in Meghalaya, and substantial numbers, about 200,000 are found in Mymensingh district of Bangladesh.

Gasherbrum I : Gasherbrum I (also known as Hidden Peak or K5) is the eleventh highest peak on Earth. Gasherbrum I is part of the Gasherbrum massif, located in the Karakoram region of the Himalaya. Gasherbrum is often claimed to mean "Shining Wall", presumably a reference to the highly visible face of the neighboring peak Gasherbrum IV; but in fact it comes from "rgasha" (beautiful) + "brum" (mountain) in Balti, hence it actually means "beautiful mountain."

Gasherbrum I was designated K5 (meaning the 5th peak of the Karakoram) by T.G. Montgomery in 1856 when he first spotted the peaks of the Karakoram from more than 200 km away during the Great Trigonometric Survey of India. In 1892, William Martin Conway provided the alternate name, Hidden Peak, in reference to its extreme remoteness.

Gasherbrum II : Gasherbrum II (also known as K4) is the thirteenth highest mountain on Earth. Gasherbrum II is the third highest peak of the Gasherbrum massif, located in the Karakoram range of the Himalaya. The standard route is via the SW ridge as it is relatively free of objective hazards such as ice fall and avalanches. A typical expedition lasts 7 to 8 weeks with climbing permits costing about $7,500 USD for five climbers.

Gasherbrum III : Gasherbrum III, situated between Gasherbrum II and IV of the Gasherbrum massif, is the fifteenth highest mountain in the world. It was the highest unclimbed peak up to 1974. Gasherbrum III was first climbed in 1975 by Wanda Rutkiewicz, Alison Chadwick-Onyszkiewicz, Janusz Onyszkiewicz and Krystof Zdzitowiecki of a Polish expedition.

Gasherbrum IV : Gasherbrum IV is one of the peaks in the Gasherbrum massif. Gasherbrum IV was first climbed on August 6, 1958 by Walter Bonatti and Carlo Mauri

Gateway of India : The Gateway of India is a monument located in Mumbai, India. Located on the waterfront in South Mumbai, the Gateway is a basalt arch 26 metres high. The Gateway is traditionally the first thing visitors arriving by boat would see of Bombay. Behind the Gateway steps lead down to the waterfront, where boat trips can be had to locations such as Elephanta Island.

The Gateway is built from yellow kharodi basalt and reinforced concrete. While Indo-Saracenic in architectural style, elements are derived from the Muslim architectural styles of 16th century Gujarat. The central dome is 15 metres in diameter and 26 metres above ground at its highest point. The whole harbour front was realigned in order to come in line with a planned esplanade which would sweep down to the centre of the town. The cost of the construction was Rs. 21 lakhs, borne mainly by the Government of India. For lack of funds, the approach road was never built, and so the Gateway stands at an angle to the road leading up to it.

The Gateway of India was built to commemorate the visit of King George V and Queen Mary to Bombay, prior to the Darbar in Delhi in December 1911. The foundation stone was laid on March 31, 1911 by the Governor of Bombay, with George Wittet's final design sanctioned in August 1914. Between 1915 and 1919 work proceeded on reclamations at Apollo Bunder for the land on which the gateway and the new sea wall would be built. The foundations were completed in 1920, and construction was finished in 1924. The Gateway was opened on December 4, 1924 by the Viceroy, the Earl of Reading. The last British troops to leave India, the First Battalion of the Somerset Light Infantry, passed through the gate in a ceremony on February 28, 1948.

Gatka : Gatka is a traditional Sikh martial art. There are two (or more) conflicting theories on how it came to be. One is that it was created from the remnants of an earlier and more complete Sikh martial system called Shastar Vidiya after the British overran and subjugated the Sikh kingdom in the two Sikh wars of the mid-1800s. The other is that it is an authentic system handed down from the times of the 6th Guru of the Sikhs, Guru Hargobind Sahib (early 17th century) who learned and instructed his Sikhs to learn the martial art. Both theories have their strong and vocal advocates.

Gaudiya Math : Shortly after Srila Bhaktisiddhanta Sarasvati Thakura took the renounced order of Sanyasa in 1918, the Gaudiya Math was organized. Its purpose was to spread Gaudiya Vaishnavism throughout India through preaching and publishing work. Eventually, sixty-four (64) branches of temples, ashrams, and mathas were established, with the Caitanya Gaudiya Math as the flagship math of Bhaktisiddhanta Sarasvati Thakura. An effort was made to preach to European countries by the Gaudiya Math in the 1930's, but only reaped a handful of longtime adherents, such as E.G.Schulze of Germany, who became Sadananda Swami, and later, Walther Eidlitz of Austria, who became Vamana dasa.

With Bhaktisiddhanta's passing in 1937, the maths and disciples lost the cohesiveness and unity that they once enjoyed during his life of preaching. The disciples of Bhaktisiddhanta founded their own mathas and organizations and became Acharyas. The most famous organization created by a disciple of Bhaktisiddhanta was ISKCON by Srila A.C. Bhaktivedanta Swami Prabhupada, who spread Gaudiya Vaishnavism worldwide like no other. Other prominent Mathas are Sri Krishna Chaitanya Mission founded by Srila Bhakti Vaibhava Puri Maharaj, Sri Chaitanya Saraswat Math founded by Srila Bhakti Raksak Sridhar Maharaja and Sri Gopinath Gaudiya Math founded by Srila Bhakti Promode Puri Maharaja.

Gaudiya Nritya : Gaudiya Nritya is the revived form of a forgotten dance form of West Bengal. It was revived as a result of the efforts of Dr. Mohua Mukherjee. Hundreds of exquisite dancing figures, painstakingly carved in terracotta on the pillars and panels of the 17th century Hansheshwari temple situated in Bansberia in the Hoogly district of West Bengal, are responsible for reviving this classical dance form which had been lost and forgotten. 'Gaudiya Nritya' is characterized by soft, sensual and graceful movements, combined with bold ideas full of conviction and a sense of power. Gaudiya Nritya depends heavily on a blend of the folk - classical music tradition.

Gaudiya Vaishnavism : Gaudiya Vaishnavism, (Bengal) Vaishnavism, is a sect of Hinduism founded by Chaitanya Mahaprabhu. Brahma-Madhva-Gaudiya sampradaya is the disciplic succession following this particular type of Vaishnavism (and Vaishnava Theology), which worships Krishna as God or the Supreme Personality of Godhead, as ISKCON terms it.

Gaudiya Vyakaran : Gaudiya Vyakaran is the first complete Bangla grammar written by a Bengali. It was authored by raja rammohun roy and published by the calcutta school-book society in 1833. The grammar was based on an earlier text that Rammohun had written in English: Bengali Grammar in the English Language. Gaudiya Vyakaran has twelve chapters, with the first chapter touching on sounds, letters, pronunciation, words, syllables etc, with examples. Other chapters deal with gender, inflection, parsing, syntax, prosody etc.

Gaur : Gaur, or Laknauti is a ruined city, in the Malda district of West Bengal, India, on the west bank of the Ganges 40 km downstream from Rajmahal. It is said to have been founded by Lakshman, and its most ancient name was Lakshmanavati, corrupted into Lakhnauti. Its known history begins with its conquest in 1198 by the Mahommedans, who retained it as the chief seat of their power in Bengal for more than three centuries. When the Afghan kings of Bengal established their independence, they transferred their seat of government (about 1350) to Pandua, also in Malda district, and to build their new capital they plundered Gaur of every monument that could be removed.

When Pandua was in its turn deserted (1453), Gaur once more became the capital under the name of Jannatabad; it remained so as long as the Mahommedan kings retained their independence. In 1564 Sulaiman Kirani, a Pathan adventurer, abandoned it for Tanda, a place somewhat nearer the Ganges. Gaur was sacked by Sher Shah in 1539, and was occupied by Akbars general in 1575, when Daud Shah, the last of the Afghan dynasty, refused to pay homage to the Mughal emperor. This occupation was followed by an outbreak of the plague, which completed the downfall of the city, and since then it has been little better than a heap of ruins, almost overgrown with jungle.

Gaur Dance : The most popular among the Madhya Pradesh dances, is the Gaur dance of the Sing Marias or Tallaguda Marias (bison-horn Marias) of South Bastar. This spectacular dance symbolizes the hunting spirit of the tribe. The word 'Gaur' means a ferocious bison. The invitation for a dance is given by sounding a bamboo trumpet or a horn. Wearing head-dresses frilled with stringed 'cowries' and plumes of peacock feathers fastened to them the men folk with flutes and drums make their way to the dancing ground. Women adorned with brass fillets and bead necklaces over their tattooed bodies soon join the assemblage. They carry dancing sticks called Tirududi in their right hands and tap them to conform with the drum-beats.

They dance in their own groups by the side of the male members. But they also take the liberty to cross and re-cross in between the groups of male dancers and drummers. Their jingling anklets correspond to the songs of their lips as they move. The men beat the drums, tossing the horns and feathers of their head-gears to the rising tempo that gives the dance a wilder touch. The men with drums usually move in a circle and create a variety of dancing patterns when they are spirited. In the bison dance (Gaur) they attack one another and chase the female dancers. The Marias imitate a number of bison movements. Most of them perform like frisky bulls, hurling wisps of grass into air, charging and tossing horns.

Gaur Palace : Gaur Palace was built by successive rulers during the Sultanate period and lies within the citadel to its south-western part. Now in ruins, and almost obliterated, it is surrounded by the popular baishgaji wall, so named because of its great height, literally 'twenty-two yards'. The wall now stands in four segments—three on the east and one on the north-pronouncing its great strength in width and height, and showing the general character of mediaeval fortification in Bengal.

Gautama Buddha : Gautama Buddha was a spiritual teacher who was born in Lumbini, a place situated in modern Nepal. He spent most of his time in Northern India, approximately 563 BCE to 483 BCE, preaching his knowledge. Born as Siddhartha Gautama he became "the Buddha" after embarking on a quest for spiritual meaning. He is universally recognised by Buddhists as the Supreme Buddha (literally Enlightened One or Awakened One) of our age. He is also commonly known as Shakyamuni or Sakyamuni ("sage of the Shakya clan") and as the Tathagata ("thus-come-one").

Gautama is the key figure in Buddhism, and accounts of his life, discourses, and monastic rules were summarized after his death and memorized by the sangha. Passed down by oral tradition, the Tripitaka was committed to writing about four hundred years later. Some Hindus regard Gautama as an avatar of Lord Vishnu.

The Buddha emphasized that he was not a god, he was simply enlightened. He stated that there is no intermediary between mankind and the divine; distant gods are subjected to karma themselves in decaying heavens; and the Buddha is solely a guide and teacher for the sentient beings who must tread the path of Nibbana themselves to attain spiritual awakening and see truth and reality as it is. The Buddhist system of insight, thought, and meditation practice was not revealed divinely, but by the understanding of the true nature of the mind, which could be discovered by anybody.

For the remaining 45 years of his life, the Buddha traveled in the Gangetic Plain of Northeastern India, teaching his doctrine and discipline to an extremely diverse range of people— from nobles to street outcaste sweepers, including many adherents of rival philosophies and religions. The Buddha founded the community of Buddhist monks and nuns (the Sangha) to continue the dispensation after his Parinibbana or complete Nibbana, and made thousands of converts. His religion was open to all races and classes and had no caste structure. On the other hand, Buddhist texts record that he was reluctant to ordain women as nuns: he eventually accepted them on the grounds that their capacity for enlightenment was equal to that of men, but he gave them certain additional rules (Vinaya) to follow. The death of the Buddha, or parinirvana, Gandhara 2-3rd century.

Gawilghur : Gawilghur (also Gawilgarh) is the name of well-fortified stronghold of the Maratha Empire. It was popularly considered impregnable at the time but was successfully assaulted by Arthur Wellesley (later the First Duke of Wellington) in 1803. The remains of the fortress are located in the vicinity of Melghat Tiger Reserve in Amravati District of Maharashtra. In popular culture, the campaign to take Gawilghur forms the background of the novel Sharpe's Fortress by Bernard Cornwell.

Gaye Holud : Gaye Holud is a ceremony part of the marriange related festivities. This ceremony is observed mostly in Bangladesh, and to some extent, in West Bengal, India. The Bengali name "Gaye Holud" literally means "yellowing the body". The ceremony takes place one or two days prior to the actual wedding ceremony. For the bride's Gaye Holud, the groom's family - minus the groom himself - go in procession to the bride's home. They carry with them the bride's wedding outfit, wedding decoration including turmeric paste and henna, sweetmeats and gifts.

They also take a large fish cooked and decorated. The procession traditionally centers on the (younger) female relative and friends of bride, and they are traditionally all in matching clothes, mostly yellow, orange or red in colour.

The bride is seated on a dias, and the henna is used to decorate the bride's hands and feet with elaborate abstract designs. The turmeric paste is applied by the bride's friends to her body. This is said to soften the skin, but also colours her with the distinctive yellow hue that gives its name to this ceremony. The sweets are then fed to the bride by all involved, piece by piece. There is, of course, a feast for the guests. The groom's Gay Holud comes next, and has the same form as the bridal ceremony.

Gedrosia : Gedrosia is the ancient name of an area that corresponds to the southernwestern part of today 's Pakistan, from the Indus River to the areas of Baluchistan or Balochistan and Makran. It is directly to the south of the ancient provinces of Arachosia and Drangiana, and to the east of Carmania. In 325 BCE, Alexander the Great crossed this desert on his way back to Babylon after campaigning in the east. Historians say he lost three-quarters of his army along the way. John Prevas, in his book "Envy of the Gods : Alexander the Great's Ill-Fated Journey Across Asia", says that Alexander wanted to punish his army for refusing to conquer more of India.

Gee's Golden Langur : Gee's Golden Langur (Trachypithecus geei) or simply the Golden Langur is an Old World monkey found primarily in the foothills of the Himalayas along the Assam Bhutan border. Although considered sacred by many Himalayan peoples, the Golden Langur was first discovered by scientists in the 1920s.

The Golden Langur is known for its rich golden to bright creamish hair, a black face and a very long tail measuring up to 50 cm in length. For the most part, the langur is confined to high trees where its long tail serves as a balancer when it leaps across branches. During the rainy season it obtains water from dew and rain drenched leaves. Its diet is herbivorous, consisting of ripe and unripe fruits, mature and young leaves, seeds, buds and flowers. It generally lives in troops of about 8 (but sometimes up to 50) with several females to each adult male.

The Golden Langur is currently endangered, the total population being about 10,000, with the relative dearth of infants and juveniles indicating a declining population and the habitat being degraded by human activity.

Geet Sethi : Geet Sethi (born April 17, 1961) is an Indian billiards player who has dominated the sport of snooker throughout much of the 1990s.

Born in New Delhi, India, he rose to prominence by winning the World Amateur Billiards Championships in 1985 and 1987. The next year he completed a 147 break in snooker, the first amateur to complete an official maximum. In the 1992 World Professional Billiards Championship, he constructed a world record break of 1276 under the three-pot rule. He won the title in this year and would go on to win it again in 1993, 1995, 1998 and 2001.

A major sporting hero in India, Geet has recently set up a number of Internet web sites such as the portal Kheladi.com. He is a recipient of India's highest sporting award, the Rajiv Gandhi Khel Ratna in the year 1992-1993. He presently stays in Ahmedabad, Gujarat.

Geeta Zutshi : Geeta Zutshi was a famed Indian athlete. She established several national and Asian running records in 800 m and 1500 m track events. She was coached by the unconventional Mohammad Ilyas Babar. She won the women's 800 m gold metal in the 1978 Asian

Games in Bangkok and won silver medals for the 800 m in 1982, and for the 1500 m in both 1978 and 1982. As the top Indian woman athlete at the 1982 Asian Games in New Delhi, she swore an oath on behalf of all the competitors during the opening ceremony. For her achievements she has been awarded the Arjuna award and the Padma Shri.

She has inspired other Indian women, such as Bachendri Pal, the first to climb Mount Everest. As a child, Pal began to aspire to national fame after seeing a newspaper photograph of Zutshi with Prime Minister Indira Gandhi. After 17 years in the USA, she returned to India in July, 2002, and took over as coach of the Indian junior athletics team (800m and 1500m).

Gegong Apang : Gegong Apang (born July 8, 1949) is the chief minister of Arunachal Pradesh. He was born to parents of Adi descent. He has served as chief minister since August 3, 2003 and also served as chief minister from January 18, 1980 to January 19, 1999.

His most cherished dream was to surpass West Bengal patriarch Jyoti Basu's record as the longest surviving chief minister of any state in the country. This was shattered, when he had no other alternatives but to resign after losing a trial of strength in the Arunachal Pradesh assembly. He resigned as Chief Minister after a stint of 19 years in 1999. He was elected leader of the newly formed United Democratic Front, a coalition of his own political party Arunachal Congress and several others, in 2003. Only a few months later, Apang and his supporting MLA's merged with the Bharatiya Janata Party, making Arunachal Pradesh the first BJP-ruled state in India's Northeast.

A few months after the BJP-ruled National Democratic Alliance lost power at the center during 2004 elections,

Apang merged with the Indian National Congress. In October, the Congress won a majority in state assembly elections and Apang continues as Chief Minister today.

General Gul Hassan Khan : General Gul Hassan Khan was the Chief of Army Staff, Pakistan. General Gul Hassan was born in Quetta, was educated at the Royal Indian Military College (now the Rashtriya Indian Military College), Dehra Dun. In 1933 he was commissioned in the British army. After Partition, he served the Pakistani army for 25 years. He was ousted as army chief on March 3, 1972 by Pakistani prime minister Zulfikar Ali Bhutto. He was allegedly hudled up in a car and taken to Lahore by road by Ghulam Mustafa Khar, a crony of Bhutto and a politician.

He had three brothers and a sister. He has relatives still residing in Pabbi near Peshawar, Pakistan. General Gul Hassan Khan passed away in 1999 and was buried in Pabbi. In the last few years of his life he was dividing his time between Vienna, Austria and Rawalpindi, Pakistan. He wrote a book Memoirs of Lt. Gen. Gul Hassan Khan.

General Muhammad Zia-ul-Haq : General Muhammad Zia-ul-Haq (August 12, 1924–August 17, 1988) ruled Pakistan from 1977 to 1988. Zia-ul-Haq was the third person in the history of Pakistan to enforce martial law and halt civilian rule in the country.

He was born in Jalandhar in 1924 as the second child of a school teacher named Mohammad Akbar. He completed his initial education in Simla and then at St. Stephen's College in Delhi. He was commissioned in the British Army in 1943 and served during World War II. At independence, Zia joined the Pakistani Army as a major. He trained in the United States 1962–1964 at the U.S. Army Command and General Staff College Fort Leavenworth, Kansas. Zia was stationed in Jordan from 1967 to 1970, helping in the training of Jordanian soldiers. On 1 April 1976, Prime Minister Zulfiqar Ali Bhutto appointed Zia-ul-Haq as Chief of Army Staff, ahead of a number of more senior officers.

On July 5, 1977, Zia led a coup against Bhutto's government, and enforced martial law. He promised elections within three months. Zia released Bhutto and said that he could contest new elections in October 1977. However, after it became clear that Bhutto's popularity had survived his government, Zia postponed the elections and began criminal investigations of the senior PPP leadership. Bhutto was sentenced to death. Despite international appeals, Bhutto was hanged on April 4, 1979.

In the mid 1980s, Zia decided to fulfill his promise of holding elections. Before handing over power, however, he decided to secure his position. A referendum was held in December 1984, and the option was to elect or reject the General as the future President. The question asked in the referendum was whether the people of Pakistan wanted Islamic (Shari'a) laws enforced in the country. An affirmative answer also meant that Zia would be elected as President for five years. The people of the predominantly Muslim Pakistan voted for Zia-ul-Haq's Islamization, thereby inadvertently also electing Zia-ul-Haq as President for five years.

In early 1988, rumours about the differences between the Prime Minister and Zia-ul-Haq were rife. The president, who had enjoyed absolute power for eight years, was not ready to share it with anybody else. On May 29, 1988 Zia-ul-Haq finally dissolved the National Assembly and removed the Prime Minister under article 58(2) b of the amended Constitution.

After eleven years, Zia-ul-Haq once again promised the nation that he would hold fresh elections within next ninety days. With Benazir Bhutto back in the country and his popularity at an all time low, Zia was trapped in the most difficult situation of his political life. The only option left was to repeat history and to postpone the elections once again. Before he had made a decision, however, Zia-ul-Haq died in a plane crash on August 17, 1988, after leaving the town of Bahawalpur in the Punjab province. His death is still a contentious topic in Pakistan. Many people do not believe that it was a simple accident, and hold either the United States or the Soviet Union responsible for Zia-ul-Haq's death. But no evidence has yet come to light to prove either hypothesis. Zia-ul-Haq's remains are housed in a small tomb outside the Faisal Mosque in Islamabad. Recently, John Gunther Dean, a former US ambassador to India, blamed Mossad, the Israeli intelligence agency, for orchestrating the assassination of Zia-ul-Haq, though he offered no proof for his allegation, made to the World Policy Journal.

General Reginald "Rex" Edward Harry Dyer : Brigadier-General Reginald "Rex" Edward Harry Dyer CB (October 9, 1864 – July 23, 1927) was a British Indian Army officer remembered for his role in the Amritsar Massacre. Dyer was born in Murree, then in India, now in Pakistan. He grew up in Shimla and attended the Bishop Cotton School there. In 1885 he was commissioned into the Queen's (Royal West Surrey) Regiment, and served in riot control duties in Belfast (1886) and the Third Burma War (1886-87). He then transferred to the Indian Army, initially joining 39th Bengal Infantry then transferring to 29th Punjabis. He served in the latter in the Black Mountain campaign (1888), the Relief of Chitral (1895)and the Mahsud blockade (1901-2). He transferred to 25th Punjabis then served in the Zakha Khel Expedition (1908). He commanded 25th Punjabis in India and Hong Kong. During World War I (1914-18) he commanded the Seistan Field Force, for which he was mentioned in despatches and awarded the Companion of the Bath (CB). In 1919, over a month after the Amritsar incident, in the Third Anglo-Afghan War, his Brigade relieved the garrison of Thal, for which he was again Mentioned in Dispatches. 5th Brigade at Jamrud was his last command posting for a few months in 1919.

Under his command, 90 troops (25 Gurkhas of 1st/9th Gurkha Rifles, 25 Pathans and Baluch of 54th Sikhs and 59th Scinde Rifles, all armed with. 303 Lee-Enfield rifles; another 40 Gurkhas armed only with kukris) killed over 379 (probably 530 or more) unarmed Indians and injured over 1000 (though many Indians claim a death toll in the thousands) in the Amritsar Massacre of April 13, 1919. The totals of dead and wounded were never ascertained. The crowd was assembled in the Jallianwala Bagh, an enclosure of 2.4-2.8 ha (6-7 acres) in the centre of the city, some participating in a banned political rally protesting against the Rowlatt Acts, some going about their daily business or resting in the public place. The enclosure was walled, and had only five narrow entrances, one of which the troops blocked, others of which were barred. The crowd was unable to comply with commands to disperse.

Dyer was in command of the 45th (Jullundur) Brigade at time of the massacre. Although some praised his ruthlessness, he was widely condemned internationally, and, in 1920, after the publication of the report of the Hunter Committee, which enquired into the Punjab Disturbances, and which heavily censured Dyer, the Government of India removed him from his post and sent him back to England. After debates on his case in Parliament, one of which censured him (the Commons), the other of which supported him (the Lords), Dyer resigned in 1920.

Geo TV : Geo TV or GEO Television is a Urdu language Pakistani television television network. Its broadcast facilities are based at Dubai Media City in the United Arab Emirates (UAE) and its Uplink Teleport station is Samacom the monopoly uplink provider in the UAE.

Geological Survey of India (GSI) : Geological Survey of India (GSI), established in 1851, is one of the oldest of such organizations in the world, and is a premier organization of India for conducting geological surveys and studies. Currently an organization under the control of the Union Ministry of Mines, Government of India, and the roots of the Geological Survey of India may be traced to 1836 when a Committee, named Coal Committee, followed by more such committees, was formed by the East India Company to study and explore availability of coals in the eastern parts of India. The phrase "Geological Survey of India" was first used in a report by one of such committees in a report in the year 1848-49. On 4th February 1848, Sir David Williams was appointed the Geological Surveyor of the Geological Survey of India. After his demise in 1848, McClelland took over as the "Officiating Surveyor" until his retirement on 5th March 1851.

At around the same time, in 1852, Sir Thomas Oldham, the-then Governor of Bengal, a province under the British India, mooted the idea of broadening the ambit of the scope of functioning of the Geological Survey of India, and consequently, the activities of the GSI was expanded to cover a broader geological study and studies of the Earth sciences of the territories of the Undivided India.

Geosynchronous Satellite Launch Vehicle : The Geosynchronous Satellite Launch Vehicle or GSLV was developed by India (Indian Space Research Organization) to launch INSAT-type satellites into geostationary orbit to make India less dependent on foreign rockets. The GSLV improved on the performance of the PSLV with the addition of liquid strap-on boosters and a cryogenic upper stage. It is a three-stage launch vehicle with the first stage being solid-propelled, the second liquid-propelled and the final stage being cryogenically propelled. The solid first and liquid second stages are carried over from the PSLV. The GSLV used cryogenic upper stage supplied by Russia, having ordered 7 upper stages. India originally tried to buy the technology to build a cryogenic upper stage from Russia, but under pressure from the United States, that technology was not provided. Therefore, India, has been working on developing a cryogenic upper stage for the past eleven years.

The first two flights of the GSLV were developmental. The first, partially successful, flight was in April 2001 which launched GSAT-1. The second, which was fully successful, was in May 2003 launching the experimental communication satellite GSAT-2. The first operational flight was the launch of the EDUSAT communications satellite on 20th September 2004.

The three flights of GSLV so far have used Russian cryogenic engine for the last stage. The next flight is expected to use an Indian cryogenic engine. The GSLV uses four L40 liquid strap-on boosters and can place approximately 5000 kg (11,000 lbm) into an easterly LEO orbit. Using the Russian KVD-1 cryogenic upper stage, GSLV can place 2200 kg (4,850 lbm) into an 18 degree Geosynchronous Transfer Orbit(GTO) orbit.

Gersoppa Falls : The Gersoppa Falls a cataract on the Sharavathi River near Mumbai, India, but present day Karnataka. The river descends in four separate cascades called the Raja or Horseshoe, the Roarer, the Rocket and the Dame Blanche. The cliff over which the river plunges is 830 ft. high, and the pool at the base of the Raja Fall is 132 ft. deep. The falls are reached by boat from Honavar, or by road from Gersoppa village, 18 miles distant. Near the village are extensive ruins (one of which is a cruciform temple) of Nagarbastikere, the capital of the Jam chiefs of Gersoppa. Their family was established in power in 1409 by the Vijayanagar kings, but subsequently became practically independent. The chieftaincy was several times held by women, and on the death of the last queen (1608) it collapsed, having been attacked by the chief of Bednur. Among the Portuguese the district was celebrated for its pepper, and they called its queen Regina da pimenta (queen of pepper).

Gettuvadyam : It is a rare stringed instrument of South India. It is like tambura which is supported at the neck and has four strings. The performer strikes all the four strings simultaneously with the help of two light bamboo blades held in both hands. While the left hand strikes the strings with regular rhythmic beats, the right hand plays intricate patterns that are reminiscent of the mridangam.

It is used rarely as a secondary instrument along with the mridangam in concerts. Only very few masters of gettuvadyam are found. This instrument belongs to south India.

Geyzing : Gyalshing or Geyzing is the capital of the district of West Sikkim in the Indian state of Sikkim. The town is connected to the capital Gangtok by a metalled road. Geyzing is also connected to the West Bengal towns of Darjeeling and Kalimpong via Jorethang. A few kilometres north is the town of Pelling. The town has a large Nepali population and the Nepali language is the predominant language of the region. The town is situated at an altitude of about 6500 feet (1900 m). The town enjoys a temperate climate for most of the year and snow sometimes falls in the vicinity.

Near Geyzing is the ancient town of Yuksom, the ancient capital of Sikkim built in 1642. Other attractions include Pemyangtse monastery built in 1640, reputed to be Sikkim's oldest and Khecheopalri Lake which as legend has it not a leaf is allowed to float on the surface. The town is the base for trekking in the Himalayas and professional expeditions to Mount Kanchenjunga. Geyzing has a couple of English medium schools including a convent school and a major hospital. It also has the district's only three star hotel.

Ghadar Party : The Ghadar Party was a predominantly Sikh party formed in the United States and Canada in June 1913 with the aim to liberate India from British rule. The first issue of the Ghadar, their paper was published from San Francisco in November 1, 1913. The party rose to prominence in the second decade of the 20th century, and grew in strength owing to Indian discontent over World War I and the lack of political reforms. Ghadar activists undertook what the British described as political terrorism, but what was revolution to most Indians. Ghadar activists were responsible for bombs planted on government property, and targeted assassinations of British and police officials. The Ghadar party commanded a loyal following the province of Punjab, but many of its most prominent activists were forced into exile to Canada and the United States. It ceased to play an active role in Indian politics after 1919.

Ghaggar-Hakra River : The Ghaggar-Hakra River is a dried out river, now consisting of the seasonal Ghaggar River in India and the Hakra riverbed in Pakistan. It is often identified with the Vedic Sarasvati River, but it is disputed if all Rigvedic references to the Sarasvati River refer to this river.

Estimates of the date at which the river dried up range, very roughly, from 2500 to 2000 BC, with a further margin of error at either end of the date-range. This may be precise in geological terms, but for the Indus Valley Civilization (2800 to 1800 BC) it makes all the difference whether the river dried up in 2500 (its early phase) or 2000 (its late phase). Similarly, for the Gandhara grave culture, often identified with the early influx of Indo-Aryans from ca. 1600 BC, it makes a great difference whether the river dried up a millennium earlier, or only a few generations ago, so that by contact with remnants of the IVC like the Cemetery H culture, legendary knowledge of the event may have been acquired.

Ghaghara River : Ghaghara also called the Gogra, is a river in Northern India, one of the largest affluents of the Ganges. It rises in the Southern slopes of the Himalayas in Tibet, at an altitude of about 13,000 feet (3962 metres) above sea level. The river flows South through Nepal as the Karnali River. In Uttar Pradesh State the Ghaghara flows in a Southeast direction to the town of Chapra, where, after a course of 570 miles (917 Kilometres), it joins the Ganges. The river is one of the most important commercial waterways of Uttar Pradesh.

Ghaghat River : Ghaghat river is a distributary of the Tista river originating at Jaldhaka in Nilphamari district. It takes a meandering course from north to southeast and after passing through Gaibandha town, joins the Brahmaputra a few kilometres north of Fulchhari Ghat. The Ghaghat has a distributary named the Bangali that flows from the east of Gaibandha town, moves south and meets the Karatoya south of Sherpur sadar upazila of Sherpur district. It is a sluggish stream for most of its course and choked with weeds. In ancient times, the Ghaghat was an important distributary of the Tista but at present it is separated from the Tista and has become a small channel. Total length of the Ghaghat is 236 km. Its flow varies from 50 to 2,500 cusec, whereas the Bangali has a flow varying from 400 to 21,000 cusec.

Ghani Khan : Ghani Khan (1914-1996) is widely considered the best Pashto language poet of the 20th century,along with Amir Hamza Khan Shinwaray, and stands on a par with Khushal Khan Khattak and Rahman Baba. He was also a respected writer and artist.

He was born in Hashtnagar, modern day Charsadda, the son of the Red-Shirt Leader Khan Abdul Ghaffar Khan, aka Bacha Khan and The Frontier Gandhi. He studied at Rabindranath Tagore's Shanti Niketan Art Academy and developed a liking for painting and sculpture. Largely owing to his father's influence, he was also involved in politics, supporting the cause of the Pashtuns of Pakistan. He was arrested by the Government of Pakistan in 1948 – although he had given up politics by then – and remained in prison till 1954, in various jails all over the country.

It was during these years that he wrote his poem collection Da Panjray Chaghaar, which he considered the best work of his life. His contribution to literature (often unpublished) was ignored by the Pakistan government for much of his life although near the end of his life his works did receive much praise and as well as an award from the Government of Pakistan. For his contributions to Pukhto literature and painting, the President of Pakistan, General Muhammad Zia-ul-Haq, conferred on him the prestigious award of Sitara-e-Imtiaz.

Ghanshyam Das Birla : G.D. Birla was a great architect of India's industrial growth. He started his career in Calcutta at the beginning of this century. He entered the field of business during the days of the First World War and established himself after the war years. He established a cotton mill in Sabzi Mandi, Delhi followed by Keshoram Cotton Mills and Birla Jute Mills around 1920. In 1919, with an investment of 50 lacs, the Birla Brothers Limited was formed and thereafter a mill was set up in Gwalior.

In the decade of the 30's he set up Sugar and Paper mills. From 1943 to 1946, Birla Brothers ventured into the area of cars. He had also established Ruby, Asiatic Insurance Co and Inland Air Service. After independence, the Birlas expanded their business and started production in many fields. Near Mirzapur, he, in collaboration with Caesar, an American friend, set up an Aluminum Plant 'Hindalco'. He also started many educational Institutions. To his credit go many temples, planetariums and hospitals. During the decades of 70's and 80's, Birla brothers were among the topmost Industrial Houses of India. G.D. Birla award for scientific Research has been established to encourage scientists for their contribution in the various fields of scientific Research.

Ghantasala : Ghantasala, is a village in the state of Andhra Pradesh in India, is in the Krishna district, 21 km west of Machilipatnam. It is a rare and reputed centre for Buddhist sculptures. Here the remains of an important Buddhist stupa and sculptural slabs were found in 1919-20. Ghantasala was once a flourishing Indo-Roman trade as well as an important religious centre. The Buddhist relics and the Hindu structures at the place reveal its past glory. Carved limestone columns belonging to pillared halls associated with 2C-3C Buddhist monastic establishments have been discovered. The ruined Maha Chaitya or stupa that was excavated here is of a unique design. A cube of solid bricks is set in the centre, inscribed with 12 constellations of zodiac. Some of the carved slabs have found their way to museums in Paris.

Gharana : Gharana is an exclusive tradition, or school, of music centring on a maestro. The Urdu word gharana means a family. Fellow practitioners and learners of a particular genre of music constitute a gharana. In this sense, the disciples of a particular guru are also identified as a gharana. When a talented maestro begins to present songs or instrumental music in his own style and starts teaching his disciples, his own style becomes in due course a gharana. It is believed that well-organised gharanas began to develop early in the 14th century, although there already existed two principal gharanas- kalavanta and kawal-and some rules and disciplines of music. Each gharana is identified by an individualistic style of singing or playing of instruments. A gharana is named after its founding guru or after the place of its growth: for example the Amir Khasru gharana and the Bishnupur gharana. Each gharana trains up its disciples according to its own curriculum, and it takes generations to develop a reputed gharana. The devoted practitioners of a gharana thus enrich it, adding new resources to the gharana's culture of music.

Gharanas suffered a decline due mainly to the abolition of the zamindari system and the modern communication system. Music, like other branches of knowledge, is no longer regionalised. The music of one region now travels almost instantly to others. Inclusion of music in the curriculum of different educational institutions has also reduced the exclusiveness of the gharanas. Now the emphasis is on the universality of music, not on its narrow confines.

Ghatam : A ghatam is a percussion instrument, used in South Indian Carnatic music. It is nothing but an earthenware pot; the artist uses both hands, wrists, fingers and nails to hit the outer surface of the walls of the ghatam.

An airy low-pitch sound is created by hitting over the hole. The artist sometimes uses his belly to cover the mouth of the pot, controlling the tuning, but the instrument can also be held mouth upwards or facing the audience. Different volumes and tonal colors can be produced by hitting different parts of the surface. Ghatam is usually accompanied by a mridangam.

Ghatu Dance : This dance accompanies ghatu songs. It has no religious or social basis, its object being solely to entertain the audience. One or more teenaged boys dressed as girls form its main attraction. The songs are usually based on the story of radha and krishna. One person sings while the others dance. Dances are also based on popular love stories. The drum, cymbals, the flute and the sarinda are the main musical instruments. These days the harmonium is also used. The dance goes on for long hours of the night. At times the dance becomes quite vulgar, which is why ghatu sessions are usually held outside populated localities. Generally Muslims form ghatu groups, as well as the audience for the dance. Among the Kishoribhajan, a Vaishnava sub-sect, teenaged girls sing bhajans and dance. It is possible that ghatu songs and dances, based on the story of Radha and Krishna, were influenced by the Kishoribhajan. These days ghatu dances are performed on modern stages at Kishoreganj and netrokona.

Ghazal : In poetry (and as the lyrics in songs), the ghazal is a poetic form consisting of couplets which share a rhyme and a refrain. (The word "ghazal" is of Arabic origins, and is pronounced roughly like the English word "guzzle", but with a different first consonant.) Ghazal in Arabic literally means "speaking with women".

The form is ancient, originating in 10th century Persian verse. It is derived from the Persian qasida, which in turn derived from a pre-Islamic Arabian form. The ghazal spread into India in the 12th century under the influence of the Mughals. Although the ghazal is most prominently a form of Urdu poetry, today, it has influenced the poetry of many languages.

A Ghazal, in short, is a collection of couplets (called sher) which follow the rules of Matla, Maqta, Beher, Qaafiyaa, Radif, Khayaal and Wazan. The traditional complete ghazal has a matla, a maqta, and three other shers in between. The first two shers of a ghazal have the form of a qatha (a specific variation of which is a ruba'ee; most familiar to modern readers from Khayyám's Rubayyat). Te ghazal is a common song form in India and Pakistan today. Strictly speaking, it is not a musical form, but a poetic recitation. Today, however, it is commonly conceived of as an Urdu song, with prime importance given to the lyrics.

Ghaziabad : Ghaziabad is a city, the headquarter of the district by the same name, that lies on the Grand Trunk road about a mile East of the Hindon river at Latitude 28° 40' North and Longitude 77° 25' East, 19 Kilometres East of Delhi and 46 Kilometres South-West of Meerut. It is located in the state of Uttar Pradesh in India. Ghaziabad is an industrial city with manufactures in railway coaches, diesel engines, electroplating, bicycles, tapestries, glassware, pottery, vegetable oil, paint and varnish, heavy chains, typewriter ribbons, etc. It is also the home to Advanced Level Telecommunication Training Centre(ALTTC). The city was the scene of fighting during the Indian Mutiny, 1857–58, revolt that began with Indian soldiers in the Bengal army of the British East India Company but developed into a widespread uprising against British rule in India

Ghaznavid Empire : The Ghaznavid Empire was a state in the region of today's Afghanistan that existed from 963 to 1187. It was created under Turkish Khan Sebuk Tigin with the city Ghazna (Ghazni) as capital, replacing the Samanids. Sebuk Tigin made himself lord of nearly all the present territory of Afghanistan and of the Punjab. In 997, Mahmud, the son of Sebuk Tigin, succeeded his father upon his death, and with him Ghazni and the Ghaznavid dynasty have become perpetually associated. Issuing forth year after year from the capital, Mahmud carried fully seventeen expeditions of devastation through northern India and Gujarat, as well as others to the north and west. From the borders of Kurdistan to Samarkand, from the Caspian Sea to the Yamuna, his authority was acknowledged.

Ghee : Ghee is a type of clarified butter important in Indian cuisine and tradition, as well as in Pakistan and Bangladesh. Ghee is made by simmering unsalted butter in a large pot, until its water has boiled off and its protein has settled to the bottom. The clarified butter is then spooned off, taking care not to disturb the milk solids on the bottom of the pan. This method of preparation gives ghee a somewhat nutty aroma that Western clarified butter does not have.

Gheria Dance : It is performed by members of the shepherd community, while holding a stick in one hand and a peacock feather in the other.

Ghiyasuddin Azam Shah : Ghiyasuddin Azam Shah (1390-1411 AD) the third sultan of the early Iliyas Shahi dynasty of Bengal, who devoted himself more to the task of consolidation than to conquests and annexations. But during the initial period of his reign, Ghiyasuddin Azam Shah led an expedition against kamarupa, conquered it and kept it under his control for some years. Assam Buranjis have on record that he invaded the territory of the Raja of Kamta, which was inconsequential

Ghiyasuddin Azam Shah earned a good name for his ideal character, patronage of learning and for good administration. He had a profound regard for the law. It is on record that the sultan while practising with a bow hit the son of a widow with an arrow and caused his death. Ghiyasuddin Azam Shah, a very interesting personality, was a great sultan of the early Iliyas Shahi dynasty. The events of his life are so variegated that he may be compared to a prince in a fairy tale.

Ghiyasuddin Azam Shah : Ghiyasuddin Azam Shah (1390-1411 CE) the third Sultan of the first Iliyas Shahi dynasty of Bengal and one of the more widely known of medieval Sultans of Bengal. His tomb is situated in Narayanganj of current day Bangladesh.

Ghiyasuddin Azam Shah's Tomb : Ghiyasuddin Azam Shah's Tomb the earliest existing structure of the Sultanate period in Bangladesh. It is a stone sarcophagi-tomb at Shahchilapur of sonargaon and is ascribed to Sultan ghiyasuddin azam shah, the third Iliyas Shahi ruler of Bengal. The tomb stands on the edge of a dried up pond, locally known as Magh Dighi, located about a hundred feet east of the Panch Pir Dargah, and on the southern outskirts of the old city.

Ghiyath al-Din Tughluq : Ghiyath al-Din Tughluq (real name Ghazi Malik; died in 1325), founder and first ruler (1320–25) of the Muslim Tughluq dynasty in India. He has been the founder of the third city of Delhi called Tughluqabad. Ghiyath al-Din rose against rule of Khusraw Khan, who killed Qutb ud din Mubarak Shah, the last ruler of the Khilji dynasty. He was succeeded by his son Muhammad bin Tughluq.

In the historian Isami's book Futuh-us-Salatin it is implied that Ghiyath al-Din Balban poisoned his son-in-law Sultan Nasiruddin Mahmud. This act was possibly linked to the issue of control of Lakhnaurti, the ancient Hindu capital of Bengal, which is now known as Gaur, the ruined city.

Ghizer : Ghizer is a district in northern Pakistan. The capital town of Ghizer is Ghakuch. Ghizer is also a contact point between Gilgit and Chitral. Historically the region has been ruled by indigenous rajas such as those of Yasin and Puniyal and later it was divided between the Mehtar of Chitral and the Maharaja of Kashmir. After 1895 all of Ghizer was annexed by the Kashmiris and was made part of the Gilgit Agency which was directly ruled by the British and not by the Kashmir Durbar.

Ghode Modni : It is a dummy horse presentation, where the dancers, attired gorgeously and armed with swords, recapitulate, through step and movement, the valour and deeds of the Goan warriors of old times.

Ghoust : A ghoust is a type of Pakistani or Indian curry dish made from lamb. Also spelled ghost or gosht and other variants, as this is transliterated from the Urdu script. Some types include the saag or sag ghoust, which includes spinach or the karahi ghoust which is cooked in a traditional cooking pot from which it takes its name.

Ghulam Ali : Ghulam Ali (1940-) is a famous Pakistani ghazal singer. Ghulam Ali was born in the village of Kaleke, Sialkot, Pakistan. He belonged to a musical family, his father was a vocalist and sarangi player who gave him early training. At the age of 15, Ghulam Ali became a disciple of the legendary classical singer Bade Ghulam Ali Khan, who was a master of the Patiala Gharana to which Ghulam Ali also belongs.

Ghulam Ishaq Khan : Ghulam Ishaq Khan (born January 20, 1915) was President of Pakistan from August 17, 1988 until July 18, 1993. Khan was born on January 20, 1915 in Bannu District of North-West Frontier Province. He completed his education in chemistry, and joined the Indian civil service prior to Pakistani independence. Upon independence, he was involved in irrigation projects in West Pakistan, and later went on to join the Finance Ministry, eventually becoming the Finance Minister.

In the 1985 elections, he won a Senate seat, shortly after which he was elected as Chairman of the Senate of Pakistan. Immediately after the death of Muhammad Zia-ul-Haq in 1988, Khan became acting President in accordance with the Constitutional rules of succession, and was formally elected to the position in December of that year. He held the position of President until 1993.

Khan reportedly vetoed the appointment of former Inter-Services Intelligence (ISI) Chief Hamid Gul as Army Chief, appointing the moderately reformist general Asif Nawaz Khan Janjua instead. Khan's presidency was also marked by his use of Eighth Amendment reserve powers to check the government. While the Prime Minister is the Head of Government, Khan was able to dismiss the governments of both Benazir Bhutto and Nawaz Sharif on charges of corruption, mismanagement, and nepotism, thereby triggering new elections, which the incumbent parties lost. The second dismissal of government exacerbated institutional and political opposition to Khan, leading to his resignation in 1993, and later to a constitutional amendment that reduced the Presidency to a figurehead.

Ghulam Muhammad : Malik Ghulam Muhammad served as Governor-General of Pakistan from 1951 until 1955, shortly before his death in 1956. Born in Lahore, Punjab in 1895, he is best known for the dismissal of prime Minister Nazimuddin, the dissolution of the Constituent assembly, and the imposition of the non-unit scheme.

He was primarily responsible for launching East Pakistan on the path of alienation from West Pakistan, for bringing the armed forces into politics, for confirming the country's subservience to Cold War operation, for creating bad blood between Punjab and the other federating units, and for devaluing democratic norms. Taken together his actions created crises that got aggravated year after year and which have dogged Pakistan to this day with enormous costs to the people, his dismissal of the Prime Minister of Pakistan, Khawaja Nazimuddin, set a trend for future politics in Pakistan.

Ghulam Muhammad also attended Aligarh University after which he worked in the accounting field. When Pakistan was formed in 1947, Ghulam Muhammad served as its first finance minister, owing to his previously-demonstrated extensive experience in that sector. Suffering from bad health, Ghulam Muhammad was almost removed by Prime Minister Liaquat Ali Khan, but the death of the latter gave Ghulam Muhammad the chance to increase his power.

Khawaja Nazimuddin became Prime Minister of Pakistan and Ghulam Muhammad was made the Governor-General. From this position Ghulam Muhammad began to take power away from the Prime Minister, and extended his control over Pakistan. Nazimuddin challenged Ghulam Muhammad's actions, but the latter exercised the reserve powers of the Governor-General's office, dismissing Nazimuddin's government and effectively removing him from office. Muhammad Ali Bogra was installed as the new prime minister.

In 1954, the Assembly of Pakistan tried to change the constitution to establish checks on the Governor-General's powers, in order to prevent a repeat of what had happened to Nazimuddin's government. In response, Ghulam Muhammad dismissed the Assembly, an action that was challenged in the Supreme Court. Ghulam Muhammad emerged victorious when the Court upheld the dismissal in a split decision, despite the dissenting opinion written by the renowned Justice A. R. Cornelius, and despite protests from the members of the Assembly.

Although Ghulam Muhammad prevailed against his political opponents, his health deteriorated, and he took a leave of absence in 1955. The acting Governor-General, Iskander Mirza, soon dismissed him, and Ghulam Muhammad died the next year in 1956.

Ghulam Mustafa Jatoi : Ghulam Mustafa Jatoi (born 14 August 1931) is a Pakistani politician, and was Prime Minister of Pakistan.

Jatoi was born in the Province of Sindh. Jatoi was educated at Karachi Grammar School and passed his senior Cambridge. In 1952, he went to England for his bar at law, but had to return home within one year due to his father's serious illness. He was elected to the first Provincial Assembly of West Pakistan in 1958, and was re-elected in 1965.

Jatoi joined Pakistan People's Party in 1969. In 1970, he was elected to the National Assembly on PPP ticket. He held the Portfolios of Political Affairs, Ports and Shipping, Communications, Natural Resources, Railways & Telecommunications in the Federal Government headed by Prime Minister Zulfiqar Ali Bhutto. In 1973, he was elected Chief Minister of the Sindh, and held this office till 1977. After the imposition of Martial Law, Jatoi remained associated with the Movement for Restoration of Democracy (MRD).

Later, he founded the National People's Party. The NPP and the PML along with 7 other political parties, contested the 1988 elections from the platform of the Islami Jamhoori Ittehad. The PPP won the bout, though with a thin majority. In 1989, he was elected to the National Assembly in by-elections from Kot Addu. After joining Islami Jamhoori Ittehad (IJI), Jatoi was elected leader of the combined opposition parties in the National Assembly in 1989.

Mr. Jatoi was appointed Prime Minister after the dismissal of the Benazir government on corruption and incompetence charges by President Ghulam Ishaq Khan. In protest at the autocratic tendancies of the Nawaz Sharif, the then Prime Minister, Mr. Jatoi joined hands with the opposition lead by Benazir Bhutto in launching a movement against the Sharif government, resulting in its dismissal in 1993. The NPP contested the 1993 elections and later joined the Benazir Bhutto government as a coalition partner till the Governments dismissal in 1997 by the PPP President Farooq Leghari. In the 2002 general election, it was the dominant partner in a new group called the National Alliance which was Chaired by him. The National Alliance won 16 seats in the national Assembly, 16 seats in the Sindh Assembly and 3 Senate Seats.

Ghulam Mustafa Khar : Ghulam Mustafa Khar, was a close ally of Zulfikar Ali Bhutto and his chief minister in Punjab, Pakistan during the 1970s. Khar was one of the founders of the Pakistan People's Party, Khar was also jailed by the Zia ul Haq regime after the 1977 coup.

Ghulam Mustafa Khar, is one of the major landowners in Pakistan where property is still the primary source of power and wealth. The Khars rule their Muzaffargarh area of Punjab province as feudal lords.

Mustafa Khar was once dubbed the "Lion of the Punjab" after a massive election victory, and served as the Chief Minister and Governor of the province in the 1970s.

Ghulam Nabi Azad : Ghulam Nabi Azad (born March 7, 1949 in Jammu and Kashmir, India) is an Indian politician from the Indian National Congress.

He was the Parliamentary Affairs Minister of India in the Manmohan Singh government until October 27, when he was appointed as the Chief Minister of the Indian administered state of Jammu and Kashmir. He married Shrimati Shameem Dev Azad in 1980 and has a son and a daughter.

Ghumar : This is basically a community dance for women and performed on auspicious occasions. This is a characteristic dance of the Bhils. Men and women sing alternately and move clockwise and anti-clockwise giving free and intended play to the ample folds of ghagra.

Ghumra Dance : In Orissa, the 'Ghumra'—a kind of drum of the size of a pitcher—produces a deep musical sound. The drummer ties the rope of the ghumra round his neck, makes it hang and plays on it, sings and dances to its tune at social functions like marriages or any religious festival. Sometimes a competition is held between two parties. Each party consists of twenty to twenty-five men and the dance goes on the whole night. Ghumra is prevalent among the 'Sahara' and other Aborigines and Harijans and songs have love as their main theme. The other forms of folk dance like 'Humo', 'Bauli', 'Jhulki', 'Jamudali', 'Mayalajar', 'Gunjikata', 'Rasarkeli' and 'Puchi' are prevalent among the Oriyas and Aborigines of Orissa.

Ghurids : The Ghurids (or Ghoris) was an Afghan Sunni Muslim dynasty from Ghor in what is today Central Afghanistan. The Ghurids ruled over a massive empire including parts of present day Iran, Pakistan, India, Turkistan, Iraq and parts of other Arab countries. Between 1175 and 1192 under the leadership of Muhammad of Ghor, they occupied Uch, Multan, Peshawar, Lahore, and Delhi. In 1206, one of the Ghurid generals, Qutb-ud-din Aybak, the conqueror of Delhi, made himself independent and founded the first of a succession of dynasties collectively known as the Delhi Sultanate (1206-1526). Currently, the area which once was the heart of the Ghurid Civilization has been deserted and infighting between Afghans, Soviet invasions, and other strife has destroyed many archeologically valuable structures and items across Afghanistan.

Giandari : Giandari is a mountain peak, approximately 4100 ft. in height, in the Giandar range of mountains in southwest Punjab and Balochistan provinces of Pakistan. It is about 40 miles west of Indus river, its geographic coordinates being 29.05N, 69.43E. Giandar range is a part of the larger and more extensive Sulaiman range of mountains and hills. Mithankot (28.57N,70.22E) is the closest town near the Indus river.

Giani Zail Singh : Giani Zail Singh, whose ascendancy in the service of the nation can be traced from the humblest of origins, combines rare qualities of head and heart. The Giani's innings in public life have been long and varied - freedom fighter, social reformer, champion of the down-trodden, State Congress Leader, successful Chief Minister and Union Home Minister. Truly, he was a relentless fighter against princedom, feudalism and foreign domination in the pre-independence days, a tireless crusader against communalism, economic disparities and social injustice, a true friend of the down-trodden and the economically weak. Tall, handsome and immaculately dressed Giani Zail Singh was a firm believer in democratic traditions, most unassuming, a God fearing man and true son of the soil. No wonder that he has been able to carve out a distinguished niche for himself in Indian public life.

Giani Zail Singh, was born on May 5, 1916 in village Sandhwan in Faridkot District in a family of artisans, taken to agriculture. His father Sardar Kishan Singh owned about fifty-six acres of land which was inter shared by Giani Zail Singh and his two brothers. He comes from common stock and was born in a mud house in a remote village having no pull or patronage. Stitching clothes, crushing stones, ploughing in fields, laying roads, digging wells and making swords on the part of Gianiji gave him a rare insight into the psyche of the common man - his problems and aspirations. Also as a form of basic education, he has gone through the Quran, Geeta, Ramayana, besides an intensive study of the Sikh Scriptures.

Displaying precocity from his early childhood, Gianiji cultivated literary tastes. By the time most of the boys of his age had passed their matriculation examination, he had completed the study of Sikh Religion, Sikh History and Sikh Scriptures. He grew to be a Giani which means a Scholar. He was very well versed in Hindi and Urdu. Though not well-versed in the nuances of the English language, the valuable example which he furnishes of the power of self help, of patient purpose, resolute working and steadfast integrity illustrate the efficiency of self respect and self reliance in enabling men of even the humblest rank to work out for themselves and honourable competency and a solid reputation.

The martyrdom of Bhagat Singh and his companions, valiant freedom fighters, on March 23, 1931, moved the young Giani who was then only 16. The story of Giani Zail Singh's ordeals started with setting up of the branch of the All India Congress in the State of Faridkot in 1938. Giani Zail Singh was proclaimed and treated as an ordinary criminal. The Maharaja regarded the opening of the Branch of the Congress as a challenge and the man who did it as an arch enemy. So it was that Gianiji having founded the Congress in the State of Faridkot found himself behind prison bars for five years. He was kept in solitary confinement throughout his imprisonment. Even after his release, Gianiji was harassed and he had to spend sometime outside the State. During this period he canvassed support for the freedom movement in his State. During the same period he was influenced by Mahatma Gandhi's message of non-violence.

In 1946, Gianiji was back in his State to resume the freedom struggle on the lines initiated by Mahatma Gandhi - Father of the Nation. The whole State of Faridkot rose to a man on the question of hoisting the National Flag. But a reign of terror was unleashed by the Maharaja. Hearing of this high-handedness from Gianiji and some of colleagues Pandit Jawahar Lal Nehru decided to visit Faridkot to hoist the Tricolour. This brought Gianiji into close contact with Panditji and ever since that day, Panditji kept his benign eye on the young and promising freedom fighter. Setting up a parallel Government in Faridkot was the most perilous adventure of Giani Zail Singh's life. Giani Zail Singh was held guilty of leading the revolt against the Raja's Government and taken into custody. Then occurred the famous Jeep Episode - a tyrannical response to Gianiji's quest to end the princely and feudal tyranny. Gianiji was bound hand and feet to a jeep and was threatened that he would be dragged along the streets unless he relented. But ultimately good sense prevailed and the threat was not carried out.

When Faridkot State was merged into the State of Patiala and East Punjab States Union, Giani Zail Singh made historic contributions in removing socio-economic injustice of farm labourers, small cultivators and tenants in his capacity as a Minister for Revenue and Agriculture. The conferment of proprietary rights on the actual tillers and the abolition of absentee landlordism and the legislative steps ensuring the security of tenancy and the rights of tenants to share the lands declared as "surplus" after land-ceiling, are all to the credit of Gianiji. The protection given in PEPSU against State ejectments by landlords is till today a shining landmark in the post-freedom history of agrarian reforms in India._chapter in the life of the peasants and workers and the common people. In 1956, Giani Zail Singh became a Member of Rajya Sabha and the Senior Vice-President of the Punjab Pradesh Congress Committee. He injected new fervour among the partymen and struggled selflessly to ensure thumping victories for the Congress in Punjab in 1962 General Elections to Punjab Vidhan Sabha and the Lok Sabha. He was taken as a Minister in the Government headed by the late Sardar Pratap Singh Kairon but in 1962, he sacrificed that office when the Chinese aggression brought new challenges in its wake.

During 1962 to 1972, Giani Zail Singh waged an uncompromising battle against the forces of communalism, reaction and exploitation for about ten long years in Punjab. As a President of the Punjab Pradesh Congress Committee, the spirit he was able to infuse in the rank and file of the Congress against heavy odds, triumphed with decisive and overwhelming majority for the Congress in the 1971 Lok Sabha elections and the 1972 Punjab Vidhan Sabha poll.

In March, 1972, he was elected unanimously by the Punjab Congress Legislative Party to be the Chief Minister of Punjab. For an unprecedented spell of stability for five years and three months, Giani Zail Singh accelerated the pace of Green Revolution and industrialization in the State and strengthened the forces of secularism by promoting the unity of the people of all faiths. Under his dynamic stewardship Punjab saw prosperity, stability, vitality, unity and solidarity. Inspired by the Leadership of Shrimati Indira Gandhi, Gianiji worked with dedication to make the Punjabis realize their dream of a better life.

With the advent of the multiparty governments at the Centre and in certain States including Punjab towards the middle of 1977, Giani Zail Singh had to brave a fresh spate of difficulties, hardships and harassment. The trials and tribulations, however, failed to break his spirit or to deprive him of the love of the common masses. He was elected to the Seventh Lok Sabha in January, 1980, from the Hoshiarpur Constituency in Punjab with a thumping lead of over 1,25,000 votes over his nearest rival, and became Home Minister in Government of India in Smt. Indira Gandhi's Cabinet.

As a Union Home Minister, Giani Zail Singh made a notable contribution in maintaining law and order, handling the Assam agitation and dealing firmly with communal riots in the country. He used his vast administrative experience spanning over more than three decades as Minister in PEPSU and Punjab and as the State Chief Minister to his great advantage. In attending to almost all the major problems facing the nation today, he has shown rare qualities of a seasoned statesman. The most striking, however, is his role in the Assam Crisis. He used all his skill in bringing round the agitation leaders to the negotiating table. His personal intervention at the crucial moments during the talks brought him many laurels, and greatly helped create a congenial climate for mutual discussions. As Home Minister he has abundantly shown his keen alertness to the numerous problems facing the nation. He has been able to strengthen the national integration and has shown tenacity in curbing violence of all types. Giani Zail Singh was elected to the highest office of the President of India on July 15, 1982 and took the oath of office on July 25, 1982.

Giani Zail Singh believes in the efficiency of politeness in expression and penetrative understanding of human relations and problems. This has, however, never impaired his firmness on basic principles of approach and the fundamentals of the policy and programmes. A refined sense of humour, backed by his intense love for children and the suffering humans in all parts of the country, is his inbuilt safeguard against tensions and malice in his public conduct.

Giddha : Giddha is the folk-dance par excellence of women in Punjab. It has almost the same intensity as Bhangra. It leaves plenty of margin for the depiction of feminine grace and elasticity. Women perform this dance mainly on festive and social occasions especially marriages. In Malwa, the Giddha performed during marriages is called 'Viyahula Giddha'. Hard worked village women sometimes get together on moonlit nights and dance in tune with nature. It is customary in the Punjab to celebrate Teeyan in the month of Sawan. The festival lasts from the

3rd lunar day in the month to full moon. Fairs are held at many places, swings are put up and girls swing and dance to their heart's content. At such times Giddha is performed under a peepal or banyan tree. The rainy season is also called the season of Giddha because the drops of rain and the dark clouds inspire the girls to dance out their pent-up feelings as nothing else can. Giddha performed during Teeyan is called 'Teeyan Giddha'. For young girls whether married or unmarried it is an occasion to look forward to. The newly-married ones yearn to come to their parental homes during these days.

Giddha is danced in a circle. The girls form a ring. One of them taking up a small drum (dholki) and sitting in the centre. If a dholki is not available an earthen pitcher is substituted. The deserved rhythm is produced by striking it with a pebble. The starting procedure is the same as in Bhangra. One girl comes forward and sings a boli. As she comes to the end of it, the others pick up the refrain and join. As the dance proceeds they sing more and more spiritedly, keeping time by clapping. The girls dance in twos. The dance is stylistically simple, the jingle of the bells the thumping of the feet and the beat of the drum creating an enchanting atmosphere.

Gilgit : Gilgit is a region in the Northern Areas of Pakistan, bordering the Chinese region of Xinjiang. It has an area of 14,680 mi^2 (38,021 km^2). The region is significantly mountainous, lying on the foothills of the Karakoram mountains, and has an average altitude of 1,500 m (5,000 ft). It is drained by the Indus river, which rises in the neighbouring regions of Ladakh and Baltistan.

Gilgit Agency : Gilgit Agency was the name of most of the area of northern Kashmir which formed a de facto dependency of Pakistan from 1947 to 1970. The Agency was administered directly from Islamabad separately from the neighbouring state of Azad Kashmir and the princely states of Hunza and Nagar. The area of the Agency comprised the traditional region of Gilgit and most of the region of Baltistan. The Agency also bordered the Sinkiang region of China to the northeast, the Indian state of Jammu and Kashmir to the south, and the North-West Frontier Province to the west. The chief towns of the Agency were Gilgit and Skardu with the small town of Ghyari also holding significance for Shia Muslims as the site of a mosque built by Sayyid Ali Hamadani, a fourteenth century Persian who brought Islam to the region.

Gilgit-Baltistan : The Northern Areas or Gilgit-Baltistan is the northernmost region of Pakistani-administered Kashmir. The name 'Balawaristan' is given to the area by a regional nationalist party (Balawaristan National Front) centred in Gilgit. The area west of the Indus river was known as the Gilgit Agency until October 1947. India does not recognise the Northern Areas and Azad Kashmir as part of Pakistan and refers to them as "Pakistan Occupied Kashmir (PoK)".

Gingee : Gingee is a town situated in the South Arcot district, in Tamil Nadu state, India. The nearest town with a railway station is Tindivanam, 28 km away. Gingee is famous for its fort, a popular tourist attraction. The Fort in Gingee was built by the Chola Dynasty in 13th Century. In 1638, Gingee came under the control of Bijapur Sultanate from Vijayanagar. In 1677, was under the control of Maratha hero Shivaji. In 1690, it changed to be under Mughal, under whose rule it became the headquarters of Arcot. It changed hands to the French in 1750, and then to the British in 1762. In the 18th century, it was occupied again by the French for 11 years. During this time, many sculptural aspects of Gingee were shifted to Pondicherry by the French.

Gir Forest National Park : The Gir Forest National Park and Wildlife Sanctuary (also known as Sasan-Gir) is best known as being the sole home of the pure Asiatic Lions (Panthera leo persica). Measuring about 258 km^2 for the fully protected area (the National Park) and 1153 km^2 for the Sanctuary, the area is considered to be one of the most important protected areas in Asia due to its supported species. Established in 1965, the total area of 1412 km^2 is located about 65 km to the south-east of Junagadh city of the Junagadh district in the kathiawar peninsula of Gujarat state, India.

Today, the sustaining ecosystem of Gir, with its diverse flora and fauna, is a result of the efforts of the Government forest department, wildlife activists and NGOs. The forest area of Gir and its lions were declared as "protected" in the early 1900's by the then Nawab of the princely state of Junagadh. This initiative resulted in the conservation of the lions whose population had plummeted to only 15 through slaughter for trophy hunting. The April 2005 census saw the highest lion-count in Gir at 359, an increase of 32 compared to 2001. The lion breeding programme covering the park and surrounding area has bred about 180 lions in captivity since its inception.

Gird : Gird is a region of Madhya Pradesh state in central India. It includes the districts of Bhind, Gwalior, Morena, Sheopur, and Shivpuri. Gwalior is the largest city in the region, and its historic center. The Chambal and Yamuna rivers form the northwestern and northern boundaries of the region. Hadoti region of Rajasthan lies to the southwest, Malwa region of Madhya Pradesh lies to the south, and Bundelkhand region of Madhya Pradesh and Uttar Pradesh lies to the east. Gird is sometimes considered part of Bundelkhand.

The region is one of the Agro-climatic zones of India, characterized by alluvial, loamy soils, rainfall of 800 to 1000 mm/year, and winter temperatures that sometimes drop below zero degrees Celsius. Major crops in the region include Mandarin and sweet oranges and limes under assured irrigation, and guava, ber, aonla, and custardapple without irrigation, as well as coriander, chillies, garlic, and seasonal vegetables.

Giridih : Giridih, is one of the districts of Jharkhand state, India, and Giridih town is the district headquarters. The literal meaning of Giridih is the land of hills & hillocks—giri, a Hindi word, means hills and dih, another word of the local dialect, indicates upland. Giridih district was earlier a part of Hazaribagh district. This town bustled with economic activity in the period from 60s to 80's when the mineral mica processing and export community reaped tremendous gains through exports to the USSR. Since the decline of the USSR however and its split into twelve CIS countries the industry has slowly declined and is currently ailing.

Girish Karnad : Girish Karnad (born: May 19, 1938), is a contemporary Indian playwright in the Kannada language, in addition to being a movie actor and director. Karnad is most famous as a playwright; his plays, written in Kannada, have been widely translated into English and all major Indian languages. His plays mainly draw from historical and mythological sources. Educated at Lincoln and Magdalen colleges in Oxford, as a Rhodes Scholar, Karnad was Visiting Professor and Fulbright Scholar in Residence at the University of Chicago (1987-88). His plays were staged in India and abroad to wide acclaim, and Karnad himself began working in the field of theater. He was awarded the Padma Shri in 1974 and the Padma Bhushan in 1992.

Girna River : The Girna river originates in the Satmala mountains, and flows to the Jalgaon district of India. It has four stages in its flow when it changes direction.In the first path it flows south east. In second stage it flows eastwards. In third sage where it enters Jalgaon district it flows toward north east and in the last stage it flows towards north west in a very winding path.Its initial path and the end path are almost opposite in direction. Thus it follows a semicircular path and empties in tapti river in Jalgaon district. It is a major tributory of the Tapti.

Girnar : Girnar (also known as "Girnar Hill") is a collection of mountains in the Junagadh District of Gujarat, India. The tallest of these rises to 945 meters (3100 feet), the highest peak in Gujarat. The five peaks of Girnar are topped by 866 intricately carved stone temples. A sturdy stone path - a pilgrimage route for both Hindus and Jains — climbs from peak to peak. It is claimed that there are exactly 9,999 steps from the trailhead to the last temple on the highest peak, but the actual number is roughly 8,000. Every year, a race is held, running from the base of the mountain to the peak and back. The locals in nearby Junagadh insist that the fastest-ever time was 45 minutes, which strikes those who have taken 5-8 hours to climb the mountain as distinctly improbable. In the Hindu religion, the legend is that climbing Girnar barefooted earns one a place in Heaven.

Gita Govinda : The Gita Govinda (Sanskrit) or the Song of the Cowherd is a work composed in the 12th century by Jayadeva Goswami. It describes the relationship between Krishna and the gopis (cowgirls) of Vrindavana, and in particular one gopi named Radha. This work has been of great importance in the development of the bhakti traditions of Hinduism.

GMG Airlines : GMG Airlines is an airline based in Dhaka, Bangladesh. It is Bangladesh's leading private domestic airline operating domestic services, with an extension to India. Its main base is Zia International Airport, Dhaka.

Goa : Goa is India's smallest state in terms of area and the fourth smallest in terms of population after Sikkim, Mizoram and Arunachal Pradesh. It is located on the west coast of India, in the region known as the Konkan, and is bounded by the state of Maharashtra to the north, and Karnataka to the east and south. The Arabian Sea makes up the state's west coast. Panaji is the state's capital, and Vasco-da-Gama (Vasco) its largest town. Portuguese merchants first landed in Goa in the 16th century but soon after colonised it. The Portuguese colony existed for about 450 years, until it was annexed as part of India in 1961. Internationally renowned for its beaches, Goa is visited by hundreds of thousands of foreign and domestic tourists each year. Besides beaches, Goa is also known for its world heritage architecture including the Bom Jesus Basilica. Goa also has rich flora and fauna, owing to its location on the Western Ghats range, which are classified as a biodiversity hotspot.

Goa Trance : Goa trance (often referred as Goa or by the number 604) is a form of electronic dance music and is often mistakenly thought to be a style of trance music. It originated in the late 1980's and early 1990's in the Indian state of Goa, which is distinctive as most forms of trance music were developed in Europe.

Goa trance is closely related to the emergence of psychedelic trance during the latter half of the 1990s; however, the distinction between the two genres is largely a matter of opinion (and they are considered by some to be synonymous, some say that the psychedelic trance is more "metallic" and the goa is more "organic".) These two are, however, sonically distinct from other forms of trance, largely by the unique sounds they use. In many countries they are generally more underground and less commercial than other forms of trance. The goa sound is more likely to be heard at outdoor parties and festivals than in clubs.

The first compilations or albums where the Goa trance sound could be heard, distinguishable from "normal" trance music, is likely Dragonfly Records "Project II Trance" and its successor "Order Odonata".

Goaldi Mosque : Goaldi Mosque one of the very few surviving medieval monuments in the city of sonargaon. About six km northwest of the little township of Panam, near Sonargaon in Narayanganj district, there are two such precariously surviving old single-domed mosques in the sequestered hamlet of Goaldi, virtually hidden behind thick bamboo brakes and clusters of mango and jackfruit tree groves.

One of the mosques was built in 1116 AH / 1705 AD by a certain Abdul Hamid, during the reign of Mughal Emperor aurangzeb. Of late, it has been extensively renovated and enlarged. This elegant little pre-Mughal mosque—the oldest in the area—was in utter ruins when declared 'protected' by the Department of Archaeology, but subsequently the monument was carefully restored in 1975 AD.

Provided with three arched entrances to the edifice on the east and one each on the north and the south (now bricked up) the base of the dome rests on squinch arches at the four corners which support the dome on pendentives.

Gobbi Dance : This is a popular dance in coastal Andhra during the Samkranti festival. The courtyards of all houses are cleaned and decorated with different kinds of rangavallis. Gobbillu i.e. balls of cow dung are placed in the middle of these designs and worshipped with flowers, kumkum and turmeric. During evenings young girl's gather around these gobbillu to dance and sing. This dance is a derived form of Garba described in dance treatises.

Godaibari Dhap : Excavation at Godaibari Dhap (Godaibadi Dhap), about three km west of mahasthangarh (Bogra district) unveiled the remains of a temple with several rebuilding phases commencing from the Gupta period. Among the antiquities, a stone piece containing a few letters in kharosthi/Devanagari, large number of terracotta plaques, and some ornamental bricks are worthy of note.

Godavari River : The Godavari River is a major waterway in India, next to the Ganges and Indus rivers. The river is about 1,450 km (900 miles) long. It rises at Triambakeshwar, near Nasik and Mumbai (formerly Bombay) in Maharashtra around 380 km distance from the Arabian Sea, flows southeast across south-central India into Andhra Pradesh, and empties into the Bay of Bengal. At Dhavaleswaram, approximately 10 kms downstream of Rajahmundry, 80 km from the coast, the river splits into two arms namely Gautami and Vasista, thus forming a very fertile delta. At Dhavaleswaram the river is nearly four miles wide.

It is a seasonal river, approximately 80% of its discharge into the Bay of Bengal is during the monsoons between July and October. The colour of the river is turbid yellow during the monsoons, while in the rest of the seasons the water is clear and greenish. After Bhadrachalam the river enters a gorge in the Eastern Ghats, a mountain range and becomes very narrow, at places just 200 metres but also about 60 metres deep.

Godavarikhani : Godavarikhani is a small town in Karimnagar district of Andhra Pradesh in the southern part of India. It is basically an industrial area with a high population. It is surrounded by other mining areas like Srirampur, Ramakrishnapur etc. This town is popular for its coal mines ('khani' means mines), controlled mostly by Singareni Colliers Company Limited (SCCL).The main source of income for most of the inhabitants is the wage provided by SCCL. The work in the mines at times, involve pain-staking efforts. The risk involved can be illustrated by the rate of deaths and injuries in these mines. SCCL takes care of its employees by providing accommodation, water, electricity, health facilities, insurance and also by creating awareness on safety.

Godavari-Krishna Mangroves : The Godavari-Krishna mangroves are a Mangrove ecoregion of India's southeastern or Coromandel Coast. The ecoregion covers an area of 7,000 square kilometers (2,700 square miles), in discontinuous enclaves extending from the state of Orissa in the north to Tamil Nadu in the south. The largest mangrove community in the ecoregion lies in the delta of the Godavari and Krishna rivers in Andhra Pradesh; other mangrove communities can be found at Point Calimere in Tamil Nadu, Pulicat Lake in Andhra Pradesh and Tamil Nadu, and the Bhitarkanika Mangroves and Chilika Lake in Orissa.

Godhra : Godhra is a town in Gujarat, India. It is the administrative headquarters of the Panchmahal district. Godhra's twin town Dahod is the birthplace of mughal emperor Aurangzeb. Few miles from Godhra lie the Pavagadh hills. On the peak of pavagadh hills is famous temple of Goddess Kali. It is one of the oldest place of worship.

On the foot hills of pavagadh is ancient fort of Champaner which was the mediveal capital of Gujarat and seat of Chavda Kingdom. Godhra has about equal number of Hindus and Muslims and is a "communally sensitive" town. Godhra is also one of the religious places in the India which has four bethaks (temples) for Vaisnav Sampraday (Vaisnal Community). Two bethaks are of Lord Gokulnathaji, and one each for Lord Gusaiji and Lord Mahaprabhuji. Godhra was the location of the Godhra riots in 2002.

Goecha La : Goecha La is the pass at an altitude of 4940 meters which gives a view of the South-East face of the mountain. This pass is situated in Sikkim, India and belongs to great Himalaya range. The peak in the you see from Goecha La is actually the South peak of Kanchenjunga, which is about 340 ft lower than the main peak.

The trek to Goecha La starts from the town of Yuksum, where the motorable road ends at an altitude of 1770 meters. It takes approximately five and a half days to reach Goecha la and two and half days to return back to Yuksum. The main halting points in the way are Bakkhim, Tshoka, Phedang, Dzongri and Smriti lake. The trek in the initial days is through dense forest cover, followed by Bugyals and finally totally rocky terrain. Porters for the treks, for carrying the extra load and cooking food, can be found at Yuksum only or at Gangtok through many travel agencies.

Gof Gunthan : It is a variation of the Dandiya Raas in which the dancers carry sticks only in one hand and a length of coloured string in the other.

Going National : National programme was introduced in 1982. In the same year colour TVs were introduced in Indian markets with the Live telecast of the Independence day on 15th August, 1982, followed by the Asian Games being held in Delhi. The eighties were era of Doordarshan with soaps like Hum Log (1984), Buniyaad and mythological dramas like Ramayana (1987-88) and Mahabharat (1988-89) glued millions to Doordarshan. Other popular programmes included Hindi film songs based Chitrahaar and Rangoli and crime thrillers like Karamchand (starring Pankaj Kapoor) and Byomkesh Bakshi.

Now more than 90 percent of Indian population can receive Doordarshan (DD1) programmes through a network of nearly 1400 terrestrial transmitters. About 46 Doordarshan Studios are producing TV software. Presently, Doordarshan operates 19 channels – two All India channels, 11 Regional Languages Satellite Channels (RLSC), four State Networks (SN), an International channel, a Sports Channel and two channels (DD-RS & DD-LS) for live broadcast of parliamentary proceedings.

On DD-1 National programmes, Regional programmes and Local Programmes are carried on time-sharing basis. DD-News channel, launched on 3rd November, 2003, which replaced the DD-Metro Entertainment channel, provides 24-Hour news service. The Regional Languages Satellite channels have two components – The Regional service for the particular state relayed by all terrestrial transmitters in the state and additional programmes in the Regional Language in prime time and non-prime time available only through cable operators. Sports Channel is exclusively devoted to the broadcasting of sporting events of national and international importance

Gojal : Located in the Upper Hunza region, Gojal is geographically the largest Tehsil of the Northern Areas of Pakistan and borders the Xinjiang-Uighur region of China. The Karakorum Highway (KKH) crosses Gojal to go through the Khunjerab Pass linking Pakistan to China and other Central Asian countries such as Tajikistan, Kyrgyzstan, and Kazakhstan. The population is about 20,000 and the majority speaks Wakhi language; while Burushaski and Domaski languages are also spoken in some villages. Shimshal, Chiporsun, Sust, Passu, Hussaini, Ghulkin, Morkhon, Shishkat etc are some of the main valleys of Gojal. Gulmit is the main town and seat of government while Sust is the border check-post and gateway for Pakistan-China overland trade. The people belong to the Ismaili sect of Shia Islam.

Gojra : Gojra is a Pakistani city located near Faisalabad. It is located at almost 50 Km from Fasialabad. It has a population of more than 100,000 and is known for its hockey players. It has contibuted players like Manzoor-ul-hasan Rasheed-ul-hasan Tahir Zaman. The people of Gojra are very famous for their hospitality, but at the same time long life fights between the people of different castes settled in Gojra are also known to the people.

Gokarna : Gokarna meaning "Cow's Ear" is a small town situated in North Kannada district coastal Karnataka, India. Gokarna is about 453 km from Bangalore, 110 km north of Mangalore and about 55 km from Karwar. Sandwiched between the Gangavali and Agnashini river mouth it is named for the ear-shaped confluence of two rivers. The town is known more as a pilgrimage centre than a tourist destination. Locals believe that Gokarna derives its name from the legend in which Lord Shiva emerged from the ear of a cow. Gokarna, with its coconut palms, its blue seas and clean sands, is perfect for an idyllic vacation by the sea.

Situated along the Karwar coast by the Arabian Sea, in northern Karnataka, Gokarna is beach-utopia if you're looking for minimal luxury but maximum privacy, with only the sun, the surf and the sea gulls for company. It is a favourite destination for visitors in search of sun, sea and sand. A charming little town with two principal streets and clusters of traditional tile roofed brick houses and petty shops. Gokarna is also an important centre of Sanskrit learning.

Gokul Medh : Gokul Medh an excavated mound in the village of Gokul under Bogra Sadar Upazila, about two km southwest of mahasthan citadel. It is popularly known as Laksindarer Medh or Behula-Laksindarer Basar-ghar, or the nuptial room of the traditional heroine and hero of a popular ballad, Behula and Laksindar. It is also associated with the angry snake godess manasa.

Excavations in 1934-36 by NG Majumdar revealed a gigantic shrine or stupa plinth built in the terraced cellular style of construction. The plinth was built of 172 blind rectangular cells packed solidly with earth and arranged in gradually rising tiers to support a towering polygonal shrine. This kind of cellular style of terraced construction, in which many buttress-walls were erected side by side to support a central structure on top is a very significant feature in the architecture of ancient Bangladesh.

Golam Azam : Golam Azam (born 1922), is a Bangladeshi political leader. He is also widely known as a war criminal who collaborated with the Pakistan Army during the Bangladesh Liberation War of 1971. Recently released unclassified documents (fortnightly report on East Pakistan.) of Pakistan government reiterates his roles as war criminal. However, Azam justifies his stance, without admitting any of those alleged war crimes (namely killing, rape etc) by the fact that Pakistan, which was created as a result of historical animosity between the Hindus and Muslims of former India, must not be severed.

Entering politics as a student leader at Dhaka University, Azam became the secretary of the fundamentalist Jamaat-e-Islami Bangladesh in 1957. Later, he became the Ameer (president) of East Pakistan in 1969. He was also a participant in the formation of the Pakistan Democratic Alliance in 1967. During the Bangladesh Liberation War of 1971, he was accused of collaboration with the Pakistan Army, and was also accused of war crimes. After the war, the government sought to remove the influence of the fundamentalists and collaborators, and Azam's citizenship was cancelled. He was forced to live in exile in Pakistan and England until 1978, when President Ziaur Rahman allowed him to return to Bangladesh. He became the unofficial Ameer of the party and his citizenship was restored in 1994 by a decision of the Supreme Court of Bangladesh.

It has been alleged that during his time in exile, he travelled to a number of middle Eastern nations, seeking funds to help topple the Bangladeshi government and his party, the Jamaat-e-Islami, is responsible for thousands of human rights violations. Jamaat-e-Islami has also been known as patron of recently (2002-2006) rising militancy and behind a number of terrorist bombings.

Golam Mustafa : Golam Mustafa (1935-2003) is a performing artist mainly in the branches of theatre, cinema and poetry recitation. Born on 2 March 1935 in Khulna district in Bangladesh. Golam Mustafa began his performing career at an early age. He first acted in a play Pallimangal staged at the Aswini Kumar Town Hall, Barisal in 1945. In the same year he drew attention of the audience by reciting of Kazi Nazrul Islam's poem 'Oi Nam' at the Barisal Zilla School on the occasion of 'Fatiha-i-Yazdaham'. Golam Mustafa had been performing mainly in theatre until early 1960s and he extended his performing career to cinemas. He made immense reputation as an actor in both cinema and theatre. One specialty about him as an actor was that he could perform equally successfully in all sorts of roles, be it a hero or a villain. He made his mark even as a side actor.

Golam Mustafa was an accomplished cultural activist and a prominent person in the literary society. He wrote features on social and political issues for the periodicals. He also wrote on modern films. He translated the Fair Wind to Virginia by Colonel Maigs. It was published by the United States Information Service, Dhaka, under the title Natun Juger Bhore. Many of his translation works were published in different weekly magazines. In recognition of his contribution to film Golam Mustafa was honoured with the Ekushey Padak in 2001. He also received the National Film Award and the Bangladesh Film Journalist Association Award.

Golden Bridge : The Golden Bridge that connects Ankleshwar to Bharuch was built in 1881 by the British, who needed a bridge across the Narmada River to create better access to trade and administration officials in Bombay. The Golden Bridge has seen many floods and natural disasters like earthquakes, but it has stood for nearly 125 years, providing daily transportation to the people of Ankleshwar and Bharuch. A railway track was operational adajacent to the bridge but with the construction of a new bridge in the 1970s, the tracks were placed on the new bridge. According to legend, it is known as the "Golden" bridge because the iron used in its construction is very sturdy, resistant to rust and rare hence it is much much more expensive than modern steel.

Golden Temple : The Golden Temple or 'Hari Mandir', situated in the holy city of Amritsar, Punjab, is the most sacred temple of the Sikhs. It is a symbol of the magnificence and strength of the Sikh people all over the world. The temple, a two storied marble structure with a golden dome, stands in the middle of the sacred pool Amrit Sarowar (tank of Nectar) reached through a bridge-Guru's bridge. This temple is a spiritual center and the main pilgrimage place for the Sikhs.

The site of the temple and the tank was sacred to the Sikhs since the time of the 4th guru, Ram Das. Many popular myths and legends are connected with the origin of the Amrit Sarowar. It is said that Guru Amar Das found on the banks of the pool the desired herb for the skin ailment of Guru Angad (the second Guru of the Sikhs). The waters in the pond is believed to have medicinal properties. Guru Ram Das at that time, on a visit to a nearby area came to the place to investigate the above episode and was so much impressed with the beauty of the surroundings that he decided to make it a pilgrim center.

All Sikh people try to make a visit to the temple and take bath in the holy tank of the temple. The devotees believe that a bath in the tank will cleanse the soul. Hari Mandir, a two storied marble shrine in the middle of the tank was built by the 5th Guru Arjan Dev. Within the sanctuary, on a jewel-studded platform, 'Granth Sahib' (The Holy Book of Sikhs) was installed in 1604 three years after the temple was completed. It is kept as the focus of devotion and teaching and the hyms are chanted continuously to the accompaniment of drums, flute etc. The Jubi tree (around 450 years old) in the centre at the east end of the tank is popularly associated with healing power. Many people continue to bring ill relatives to this tree, hoping for a cure.

The great Sikh secular leader, Maharaja Ranjit Singh, donated 100 kgs of gold to the temple in 1830 and thus gold was applied to the copper sheets on the roof and the exterior of the building. The temple compound is entered through a Clock Tower. There is a Sikh museum on top of the clock tower comprising a gallery of paintings telling the story of the Sikhs and their martyrs. The tank is surrounded by an 8m wide white marble pavement, banded with black and brown Jaipur marble. The temple has a Dining Hall, Assembly Hall and Guesthouses. The main complex has numerous plaques commemorating Sikhs who became martyrs. There is a community kitchen which serve free meals to thousands of people everyday. Here, anyone from any religion can have food together. Volunteers from the temple help with the kitchen jobs and other works. The atmosphere in the golden temple is exceptionally peaceful and beautiful. The visitors to the temple are not allowed to carry umbrellas and walking sticks. They are not to wear the shoes and socks. These items can be kept at the cloakroom, in front of the temple, free of charges. Before entering the temple they have to keep their heads covered.

Golghar : This huge and impressive granary of Bihar is situated between Maidan and the Ganga river. Captain John Garstin of the Bengal Engineers build it in 1786 to store grains for the British army following a terrible famine.

This building has an extra ordinary 29 meter high ovoid dome and has a base of 125 meters and 3.6 meters thick walls. It was intended to hold 137000 tons of grains. However, it was never completed. It gives an excellent view of the city and the Ganga river from its top which can be reached by the winding stairway around it.

Golkonda : Golkonda is a ruined city and fortress 11 km west of the city of Hyderabad, Andhra Pradesh state, India. The city and fortress are built on a granite hill that is 120 meters high and is surrounded by massive crenellated ramparts. The beginnings of the fort date to the 1143, when the Hindu Kakatiya dynasty ruled the area. The Kakatiyas were followed by the state of Warangal, which was later conquered by the Muslim Bahmani Sultanate.

According to one story, the fort derives its name from Golla Konda, which is the Telugu word for Shepherd's Hill. It is said that a shepherd boy came across an idol on the hill. This led to the construction of a mud fort by the then Kakatiya ruler of the kingdom around the site. Subsequently the fort was administered by Recherla Vellamas who ruled over Golkonda, Rajaconda and Devarconda. Their capital was Rajaconda. Following the defeat of the Recherla Velamma kingdom, the three forts fell to the Bahamani Kings (1364). Following the collapse of the Bahamani Kingdom, Golkonda rose to prominence as the seat of the Qutb Shahi dynasty around 1507.

Over a period of 62 years the mud fort was expanded by the first three Qutb Shahi kings into a massive fort of granite, extending around 5 km in circumference. It remained the capital of the Qutb Shahi dynasty until 1590 when the capital was shifted to Hyderabad. The Qutb Shahis expanded the fort, whose 10 km outer wall enclosed the city. The Qutb Shahi sultanate lasted until its conquest by Mughal emperor Aurangzeb in 1687. The fortress held out against Aurangzeb for eight months, falling to the Mughals through treachery.

Gomal Pass : Gomal Pass or Gumal Pass is a pass on the border of Afganistan and the southeastern portion of the Northwest Frontier Province of Pakistan. It takes its name from the Gomal River. It is midway between the Khyber Pass and the Bolan Pass.

Gomal River : Gomal River is a river in Afghanistan and Pakistan, with its headwaters in the south-east of Ghazni. Its chief tributary is the Zhob River. Within Pakistan, Gomal river surrounds South Waziristan agency, forms the boundary between the North-West Frontier Province and Balochistan, and more or less between the Pakhtun and Baloch.

Gomti River : The Gomti River, also known as the Gumti or Gomati, is a tributary of the river Ganga. The Gomti originates in the Himalaya Range of Nepal. It extends 805 km through Nepal and Uttar Pradesh state of India. The Indian cities of Lucknow and Jaunpur are located on the banks of the Gomti. The river is polluted owing to the large factories and tanneries in the state of Uttar Pradesh, which has affected fish populations. Hindus believe that the river is daughter of Sage Vashistha, and bathing in the waters of the Gomati can remove sin.

Gondal : The former rulers of Gondal were members of the Jadeja Rajput clan, descendants of Lord Krishna and the moon God, who ruled the princely states of Kutch, Jamnagar (Nawanagar), Rajkot (Sardhar), Morbi and Gondal for more than 300 years. But it was the late 19th and early 20th century under Maharajah Bhagwat Sinhji that saw Gondal grow in to one of the most progressive princely states in the region with an efficient system of a taxless economy, good roads, railways, schools, hospitals, highways, sanitary drainage, irrigation and free compulsory education.

Gondi : Gondi refers to a people and their language in central India. The Gondi, or Gond people are spread over the states of Madhya Pradesh, eastern Maharashtra, Chhattisgarh, northern Andhra Pradesh, and western Orissa. With over four million people, they are the largest tribe in Central India. The Gondi language is related to Telugu and other Dravidian languages. About half of Gonds speak Gondi languages, while the rest speak Indo-Aryan languages including Hindi. The Gonds are traditionally agriculturalists; some practice shifting cultivation, while others raise cereals or herd cattle. Gond society is highly stratified and does not conform to the usual image of egalitarianism among tribals. The Gonds belong to a category of very large tribes (also including Santals and Bhils) that have traditionally dominated the regions in which they have lived. However, like other Adivasis, the Gonds have suffered from increasing landlessness since the 1960s.

Traditional Gond religion involves a distinct pantheon of gods and spirits, which many Gonds practice along with Hinduism. Gondwana or "land of the Gonds", is a loosely-defined area of southeastern Madhya Pradesh, eastern Maharashtra, and parts of Chhattisgarh, Orissa, and northern Andhra Pradesh. The region was home to several

Gond kingdoms from the 15th century to the mid-18th century, when the Marathas expanded into the region from the west. The region gave its name to Gondwanaland, the ancient southern supercontinent which comprised present-day Africa, South America, Australia, India and Antarctica.

The Gonds of Andhra Pradesh effectively lost their only advantage in trying to protect their lands when the Banjaras, a group of nomadic cattle herders that had been settling in Gond territory, were classified as a Scheduled Tribe in 1977. Their newly acquired tribal status made the Banjaras eligible to acquire Gond land 'legally' and to compete with Gonds for reserved political seats, places in education institutions, and other benefits. Because the Banjaras are not scheduled in neighboring Maharashtra, there has been an influx of Banjara emigrants from that state into Andhra Pradesh in search of better opportunities.

Gondwana : Gondwana, sometimes called Gondaranya, is a region of central India, and is named after the Gondi people who live there. The name of the ancient continent of Gondwanaland was derived from Gondwana, because some of the earliest rock formations of this continent were first investigated in part of the region, in modern Orissa. As Gonds are spread widely across central India, and are a minority almost everywhere, there is no unambiguous boundary to the region. However, the core region can be considered to be the eastern part of the Vidarbha region of Maharashtra, the parts of Madhya Pradesh immediately to the north of it, and parts of the west of Chhattisgarh. The wider region extends beyond these, also including parts of northern Andhra Pradesh, and western Orissa.

The region is part of the northern Deccan plateau, with an average height of about 600–700 metres. Much of it is rugged and hilly. Geologically it is mostly Pre-Cambrian rock, with some areas dated to Permian and Triassic periods. Part of it is overlaid with alluvium, and in the west it is overlaid with the igneous rocks of the Deccan Traps. Gondwana has a relatively high proportion of peoples of the "scheduled tribes" of India, which include the Gonds. The scheduled tribes are recognised as economically and socially disadvantaged. They form a majority of the population in many districts. A number of old kingdoms were established by, or together with, ruling families of the Gonds and other scheduled tribes in this region. The region is however, like most of India now, dominated economically by "caste Hindus".

Gopal Krishna Gokhale : Gopal Krishna Gokhale was born on May 9, 1866, in Ratnagiri, Maharashtra. He went on to become one of the most learned men in India, a leader of social and political reformists and one of the earliest, founding leaders of the Indian Independence Movement. Gokhale was a senior leader of the Indian National Congress and the Servants of India Society. The latter was committed to only social reform, but the Congress Party in Gokhale's time was the main vehicle for Indian political representation.

Gokhale was a great, early Indian champion for public education. Being one of the first generations of Indians to receive college education, Gokhale was respected widely in the nascent Indian intellecutal community and acoss India, whose people looked up to him as the least elitist of educated Indians. Coming from a background of poverty, Gokhale was a real man of the people, a hero to young Indians discovering the new age and the prospects of the coming 20th century; he worked amongst common Indians to encourage education, sanitation and public development. He actively spoke against ignorance, casteism and untouchability in Indian society. Gokhale was also reputed for working for trust and friendship between Hindu and Muslim communities. It should be remembered that Gokhale was a pioneer in this work, never done before in Indian history by Indians.

Along with distinguished colleagues like Bal Gangadhar Tilak, Dadabhai Naoroji, Bipin Chandra Pal, Lala Lajpat Rai and Annie Besant, Gokhale fought for decades to obtain greater political representation and power over public affairs for common Indians. He was moderate in his views and attitudes, and sought to petition the British authorities, cultivate a process of dialogue and discussion which would yield greater British respect for Indian rights. In 1906, he and Tilak were the respective leaders of the moderates and extremists in the Congress. Tilak advocated civil agitation and direct revolution to overthrow the British Empire, and the Congress Party split into two wings. The two sides would patch up in 1916.

Gokhale did not support explicit Indian independence, for such an idea was not even understood or expressed until after the World War I. Gopal Krishna Gokhale's biggest contribution to India was as a teacher, nurturer of a whole new generation of leaders conscious to their responsibilities to a wider nation. Gokhale was famously a mentor to a young barrister who had been blooded in the work of revolution in South Africa a few years earlier. Mohandas Gandhi received great warmth and hospitality from Gokhale, including personal guidance, knowledge and understanding of India, the issues of common Indians and Indian politics. By 1920, Mohandas Gandhi would become known as Mahatma Gandhi, and as the undisputed leader of 300 million Indians and the largest non-violent revolution in the history of the world. Sadly, Gokhale himself died in 1915. In his autobiography, Gandhi calls Gokhale his mentor and guide, while Mohammed Ali Jinnah, the future founder of Pakistan, in 1912 wanted to become the "Muslim Gokhale," "Ambassador of Hindu-Muslim Unity."

Gopalganj Twin Temple : Gopalganj Twin Temple situated at a distance of about six km to the north of Dinajpur district head quarter in the village of Gopalganj. One of the two is a twenty-five ratna twelve-sided structure, while the other is a five ratna quadrangular temple. David J McCutchin mentioned 1743 as the date for one, and 1754 for the other, but he has not mentioned his source. A stone inscription, preserved in the Dinajpur Meseum, is believed to have been removed from one of the two temples. It records that the temple was constructed by Raja Ramnath (1722-1752) in 1676 Shaka era (1754 AD). Though it is not certain which of the two temples it refers to, but it seems clear from the character of the letters of the inscription that the temples were contemporaneous with the famous kantanagar temple.

Archaeologically important for their characteristic features, these two temples are in a highly dilapidated condition. The habitation that has grown in the grounds around the temples has utilised the spoils of the temples in building their houses, thereby causing serious damage to the structures.

Gopeshwar : Gopeshwar is the administrative headquarters of the Chamoli district of Uttaranchal in India, on an international border. Located 1550 meters above sea level, it is famous for its weather (often pleasant most of the year, but very cold in December and January) and its temples. Gopeshwar is surrounded by four famous temples: Tungnath, Anusuya devi, Rudranath, and Badrinath. The holy town of Kedarnath is also nearby. A famous temple of Lord Shiva, now known as Gopinath Mandir, is situated here. A story tells of a king named Sagar (for whom a nearby village is named) who was there in ancient times. His cow always came to this place and gave his milk to a Shivling; one day Sagar saw it and he constructed a temple there.

Gopinath Bordoloi : Gopinath Bordoloi (1890-1950) was the state of Assam's first Chief Minister, and also leading Indian freedom-fighter from Assam. After rising through Congress ranks in the 1930s, Bordoloi's biggest battle came as Bengal's Muslim majority wanted to include the overwhelmingly Hindu Assam in a Muslim-majority Pakistan. Organizing protests and engaging the colonial government on the highest level prevented mass communal riots in Assam and allowed for it to preserve its territorial integrity within India.

After India's Independence, he worked closely with Sardar Vallabhbhai Patel to secure Assam against Communist China and East Pakistan, and also organize the return of millions of refugees who fled East Pakistan due to widespread violence and intimidation during partition. His work gave a base of communal harmony, democracy and stability which kept Assam secure and progressive right up till the 1971 war over East Pakistan's independence. He was awarded the Bharat Ratna posthumously in 1999.

Gorai-Madhumati River : Gorai-Madhumati river is a principal distributary of the ganges. The same river has been named as the Gorai in the upper course and Madhumati in the lower course. Once the main flow of the Ganges used to be discharged by this river, although previously Hugli-Bhagirathi was the original course of the Ganges. The Gorai takes off from the Ganges at Talbaria, north of Kushtia town and 19 km downstream from Hardinge Bridge. South of Kushtia its first offshoot, the Kaliganga branches off to join the Kumar near Shailkupa. This river has been dammed by one of the primary canals of the Ganges-kobadak Irrigation Project (G-K Project) and the lower half of the course is now almost a dry bed. The main river bifurcates and rejoins several times as it flows southeast to Mohammadpur upazila in Magura district.

From here it changes its name to Madhumati. The Kumar, the Nabaganga and the Chitra join it through several channels south of Mollahat upazila. There it changes its name to Baleshwar, which in turn changes to Haringhata from the Bogi forest outpost of the Sundarbans. The Gorai-Madhumati has a flood discharge of nearly 7,000 cumec but in winter its flow goes down to five cumec.

Gorakhpur : Gorakhpur is a city in the eastern part of the state of Uttar Pradesh in India. It is the administrative headquarters of Gorakhpur District and Gorakhpur Division It shares a border with Nepal. It is famous for Geeta Press which publishes Hindu religious texts. It is also seat of Nath sect (Gorakhnath Temple). Many historic Buddhist sites (Kushinagar) are nearby. It is also the headquarters of the North Eastern Railways.

In ancient times the geographical area of Gorakhpur included the modern districts of Basti, Deoria, Azamgarh and parts of Nepal. The entire region had been an important centre of Aryan culture and civilization. In ancient times Gorakhpur was a part of the famous kingdom of Koshal, one of sixteen Mahajanapadas (states) existing in India in 6th century BCE. As per Vedic history, the earliest known monarch ruling over this region with his capital at Ayodhya was Iksvaku. He founded a solar dynasty of rulers. The solar dynasty produced a number of illustrous kings. Rama was probably the greatest ruler of this dynasty. In more recent ancient history, Gorakhpur remained an integral part of the erstwhile empires of Maurya, Shunga, Kushana, Gupta and Harsha dynasties. In the 10th century, the Tharu king Mausen of Madan Singh ruled over Gorakhpur city and the adjoining area.

In the medieval period, when the entire northern India lay prostrate before the Muslim ruler, Muhammad Ghori, the Gorakhpur region was not left out. For a longer period it remained under the sway of the muslim rulers, from

Qutb-ud-din Aybak to Bahadur Shah. Tradition has it that Ala ud din Khilji (1296-1316) ordered the conversion of old shrine of Goraksha (a popular deity) of Gorakhpur into a mosque. However, on Akbar's reorganisation of the empire, Gorakhpur gave its name to one of the five Sirkars comprising the province of Awadh.

Gorakhpur District : Gorakhpur District is a District of Uttar Pradesh state in India. Gorakhpur is the administrative headquarters of the district. The district covers an area of 3483.8 km^2. It is bounded by Maharajganj District to the north, Kushinagar and Deoria districts in the east, Ambedkar Nagar, Azamgarh, and Mau districts to the south, and Sant Kabir Nagar District to the west. The district is part of Gorakhpur Division.

The district was ceded by the Nawab of Awadh to the British East India Company in 1801. With this cession, Gorakhpur was raised to the status of a district. The first district collector was Mr. Routledge. In 1829, Gorakhpur was made the headquarters of Gorakhpur Division, comprising the districts of Gorakhpur, Ghazipur and Azamgarh. Mr. R.M. Biad was first appointed Commissioner.

In 1865 Basti District was carved out from Gorakhpur. The latter was further split up in 1946 to form Deoria District. The third division of Gorakhpur led to the creation of Maharajganj District in 1989.

Gorakshanath : Gorakshanath (also known as Gorakhnath) was an 11th century to 12th century Nath yogi who was originally a Vajrayana Buddhist and who became connected to Shaivism as one of the two most important disciples of Matsyendranath, the other being Caurangi. There are varying records of the spiritual descent of Gorakshanath. All name Adinath and Matsyendranath as two teachers preceding him in the succession. Though one account lists five gurus preceding Adinath and another lists six teachers between Matsyendranath and Gorakshanath, current tradition has Adinath identifed with Lord Shiva as the direct teacher of Matsyendranath, who was himself the direct teacher of Gorakshanath.

The Nath tradition underwent its greatest expansion during the time of Gorakshanath. He produced a number of writings and even today is considered the greatest of the Naths. It was Gorakshanath who wrote the first books on Laya Yoga. In India there are many caves, many with temples built over them, where it is said that Gorakshanath spent time in meditation. According to Bhagawan Nityananda, the samadhi shrine (tomb) of Gorakshanath resides at Nath Mandir near the Vajreshwari temple about a kilometer from Ganeshpuri, Maharashtra, India.

Goravayyalu : Gorava or Kuruba or Kuruma is a sub caste of shepherds in Andhra Pradesh, who tend sheep and weave wool blankets. The priests among Kurubas are known as Goravas. They dedicate one male member to the god Srisaila Mallikarjuna when he grows up he is initiated into the Moilara cult by a Ganachari and trained in the lore ritualistic music and dance by a senior Gorava. During the festivals and Kalyanotsavas of their family deities Goravayyalu present their ritualistic dance with great fanfare. During the other days they move from one place to another singing the ballads of Mallanna and other Saiva panegyrics, beg alms and bless the devotees.

They put on a long black coat made out of sheep wool with white strips, a big triangular jar cap made out of bear's skin. One upper cloth hanging from both shoulders, another cloth serving as a waist band. A bag made of deer skin containing the sacred turmeric called Bandaru to be offered to the devotees, a brass cup tied to the waist for drinking milk or Pancamritam. They wear strings of cowries around their necks, tie jingling bells to their ankles. They hold a Damaru in the right hand and a flute in the left hand.

They play these instruments when they dance. While dancing they move in circles and jump forward and backward like fighting rams. They bark at each other like fighting dogs. They call themselves faithful dogs of god. Mallari or Mailaru. They drink milk or Pancamritam contained in the brass cups placed on the ground like dogs kneeling on the ground without holding the cups with their hands. The remnants are shared by devotees as prasadam when they perform this ritual dance in the temple precincts they pierce their cheeks, calf wrist with iron pikes and blued as offering to the deity and beat themselves with big hunters called Veratallu. This dance is purely ritualistic performed during religious occasions.

Gorumara National Park : Gorumara National Park is located in the Dooars (rolling hill slopes) region of Jalpaiguri district in West Bengal. This small forest area famous for its natural population of the Great Indian one horned Rhinoceros was declared a wildlife sanctuary in the year 1949. Later in the year 1992, it was established as a National Park, comprising 80 km of diverse forests.

Gorur Ramaswamy Iyengar : Gorur Ramaswamy Iyengar (1904—1991), affectionately known as Gorur was an eminent Kannada writer; well known for his humor and satire. He was one of the two iconic Iyengar writers of Kannada literature alongwith the great Masti Venkatesh Iyengar. Gorur's most well known book is the humorous travelogue "Amerikadalli Goruru", 1979; which is based on the experience of the traditional Iyengar in the techno-cultural world of the United States. The book had several memorable chapters like "Empire State Bhavana" (Empire State Building) and "Niagarada Manjukanye" (Maid of the Mist). Gorur also wrote several folk and fiction works like

"Rasaphala", "Namma Oorina Rasikaru", "Puttamallige", "Bhoothayyana Maga Ayyu", "Hemavathi", "Garudagambada Dasaiah".

Goti Pua : Towards the end of the 16th century, the tradition of Goti Pua, or boy dancers gained popularity in Orissa. The goti puas are boy dancers who dress up as girls. They are the students of the akhadas, or gymnasia, established by Ramachandradeva in Puri, in the periphery of the temple. As they were offshoots of the akhada system, goti puas also came to be known as akhada pilas - boys attached to akhadas. The goti puas always dance in pairs. Goti puas are now part of professional teams, known as dals, each headed by a guru. A goti pua presentation is ably supported by a set of three musicians, who play the pakhawaj, the gini or cymbals and the harmonium. The boys do the singing themselves, though at times the group has an additional singer. The goti pua performance may include items like Panchadevta Puja, Bhumi Pranam and Battu. A goti pua performance usually commences with Bhumi Pranam (salutation to Mother Earth), and wraps up with Bidahi Sangeet, a farewell song and dance item. The whole performance lasts around three hours.

Gottuvadhyam : The gottuvadhyam (also known as gottuvadyam, chitravina, chitra vina, or mahanataka vina) is a Carnatic music string instrument played mainly in South India. It is usually used as a solo instrument in Carnatic music.

The gottuvadhyam resembles the saraswati veena in its general form. It is a complicated ancient instrument with twenty-one strings. Unlike the traditional veena or sitar, it is fretless. The fretless nature of the instrument makes it the closest instrument to vocal standards. There are six main strings used for melody that pass over the top of the instrument, three drone strings, and about twelve sympathetic strings running parallel and below the main strings.

The approach to tuning is in some ways similar to the sitar; in other ways it is similar to the saraswati veena, but in many ways it is unique. It is played with a slide in a manner somewhat like a lap steel guitar. The fingers on the right hand are usually used with plectra to pluck the metal melody strings while a cylindrical block made out of hardwood (often ebony), water buffalo horn, glass, steel, or teflon held by the left hand is used to slide along the strings to vary the pitch. Appropriately, the name gottuvadhyam literally means "block instrument."

Govardhan Hill : Govardhan hill, literal meaning the increasing cattle, was the name of a mythical hill near Vrindavan. The legend states that Vedic god, Indra was losing his hold over the human beings, and became jealous of Krishna, an incarnation (avatar) of Vishnu. Indra invoked clouds and schemed to flood the region with rains lasting for seven days and seven nights. Krishan lifted the Govardhan hill, and under which all animals and people of the region took shelter, and were saved from the fury of Indra. Ultimately, Indra accepted defeat, and after praying to Krishna, left for his heavenly abode, the Svarga.

Govardhana Matha : The Govardhana Matha is located in the city of Puri in Orissa state (India), and is associated with the Jagannath temple. It is one of those four cardinal mathas said to have been founded by Adi Shankara, and is the eastern matha. As per the tradition initiated by Adi Shankara, it is in charge of the Rig Veda. Its current head or Shankaracharya is Niscalananda Sarasvati.

Government College University Lahore : Government College University Lahore is a co-educational public university located in Lahore, the second largest city of Pakistan. Although the college was granted the status of university by the Pakistan Government in 2002, the word college is still retained in the name for historical reasons and also because of the wide recogonition of the name Government College in Pakistan. The University offers bachelor's, Master's, and Ph.D. degrees in a variety of disciplines. The university currently has more than 6000 students and 323 faculty members. Alumni of Government College are called Ravians after the nearby Ravi River.

Government of India (GOI) : The Government of India, officially referred to as the Union Government, and commonly as Central Government, was established by the Constitution of India, and is the governing authority of a federal union of 28 states and 7 union territories, collectively called Republic of India. The basic civil and criminal laws governing the citizens of India are set down in major parliamentary legislation, such as the India Code. The federal (union) and individual state governments consist of executive, legislative and judicial branches. The legal system as applicable to the federal and individual state governments is based on the English Common and Statutory Law. India accepts compulsory International Court of Justice jurisdiction with several reservations.

Government of Pakistan : The Constitution of Pakistan provides for a Federal Parliamentary System of government, with a President as the Head of State and a popularly elected Prime Minister as the chief executive.

The President of Pakistan is the Head of State and Commander in Chief of the Armed Forces, and is elected for a five-year term by the Electoral College of Pakistan - comprised of the Senate, the National Assembly, and the four Provincial Assemblies. The President's appointment and term are constitutionally independent of the Prime Minister's term.

The Prime Minister of Pakistan is usually the leader of the largest party in the National Assembly and is assisted by a cabinet of ministers drawn from both chambers of the federal legislature.

The bicameral federal legislature comprises the 100 member Senate (with seats equally distributed among the provinces and the FATA and the capital) and the 342 member National Assembly. Both the Senate and the National Assembly have seats reserved for women and religious minorities. Senators are elected for six-year terms, with staggered elections every three years, whilst members of the National Assembly are elected for five-year terms. The Constitution provides for the President to address the federal legislature together at the start of the first session after any general elections.

The last National Assembly elections were held in October 2002, and Senate elections in February 2003. One notable outcome was the election of 91 women to Parliament - the largest number and percentage of women in the parliament of any Muslim-majority country.

Each province has a similar government setup with a Provincial Assembly elected for a five-year term through multi-party elections, which in turn elects a Chief Minister - the executive head of the province. The Chief Minister nominates a candidate for the office of Provincial Governor and the Provincial Assembly ratifies the nominee for a five-year term.

Government of Sindh : Government of Sindh is based in Karachi, Sindh, Pakistan is one of the four provinces of Pakistan and is home to the Sindhis and various other groups. Neighbouring regions are Balochistan to the west and north, Punjab in the north and India to the east. To the south is the Arabian Sea. The main languages are Sindhi and Urdu. Known by various names in the past, the name Sindh comes from the Indo-Aryans whose legends claimed that the Indus River flowed from the mouth of a lion or Sinh-ka-bab. In Sanskrit the province was dubbed Sindhu meaning an ocean. The Assyrians knew the region as Sinda, the Persians Abisind, the Greeks Sinthus, the Romans Sindus, the Chinese Sintow, while the Arabs dubbed it simply Sind, which is what the province is now known as.

Government of Tibet in Exile : The Government of Tibet in Exile, officially named the Central Tibetan Administration (CTA) of His Holiness the Dalai Lama, is a theocratic government-like entity headed by Tenzin Gyatso, the 14th Dalai Lama that describes itself as the rightful and legitimate government of Tibet.

Tibet is currently under the control of the People's Republic of China, a situation that the Government in exile considers an illegitimate military occupation. The Government of Tibet in Exile is headquartered in Dharamsala, India. The Dalai Lama fled Tibet in 1959 after a failed uprising against Chinese rule. Its territorial claims include the entirety of Tibet Autonomous Region and Qinghai province, as well as parts of the neighboring provinces of Gansu, Sichuan and Yunnan — all of which is termed "Historic Tibet" by the PRC government. The Government of Tibet in Exile is not recognized as a government by any major sovereign state, but it has received a large amount of sympathy in the West and India, largely through the efforts of the Dalai Lama. In 2001, for the first time in the history of Tibet, the Government in Exile directly elected their Kalon Tripa, or Prime Minister

Governor-General of Pakistan : The Governor-General of Pakistan was the resident representative of the King George VI in Pakistan from 1947 to 1952 and then Queen Elizabeth II from 1952 until 1956 when Pakistan was proclaimed a republic. When Pakistan became an independent, self-governing nation in 1947, it, like post-partition India, provisionally continued to use the Government of India Act, 1935, as its written constitution until a post-independence constitution could be drafted; by default this contemplated the continuation of the constitutional monarchy as a Commonwealth realm dominion.

The monarch appointed a Governor-General, upon the advice of the Prime Minister of Pakistan to serve as de facto Head of State. Mohammed Ali Jinnah, considered Quaid-e-Azam ("Father of the Nation"), intimated to Lord Mountbatten: "when I am Governor-General the Prime Minister will do what I tell him to" — Mr Jinnah is a rare example of executive governorship by a Governor-General, although in fact Mr Jinnah's rapidly declining health made the issue moot. Mr Jinnah's successors, like most other Commonwealth Governors-General, served as figureheads and but did exercise their virtually unlimited political powers when they deemed fit, which was mostly related to dissolving the parliament. The office of Governor-General was abolished and replaced by a President of Pakistan when Pakistan became a republic in 1956. Governor-General Iskander Mirza became Pakistan's first president.

Govind Ballabh Pant : He (September 10, 1887—March 7, 1961) was a major figure in the Indian Independence Movement.

He was called on to succeed Sardar Patel as Home Minister after Patel's death in 1950; in that position, his chief achievement was the establishment of Hindi as an official language. In 1957, he was awarded the Bharat Ratna.

Govind Pashu Vihar : The park is spread over an area of 192sq.km. in Uttarkashi District. Nearest town from the park is Dharkadhi 17km from the park. The nearest airport is Dehra dun at a distance of 190 km. The rail head is also Dehra Dun. The forest of the park consists of Chirpine, scrub tropical Euphorbia scrub and oak species.

The wild life species found in the park are panther leopard, snow leopard, leopard cat, the brown and the black Himalayan bear, fishing cat, musk deer, serow, thar, bharal, goral, sambar, wild boar, etc. The birds found are monal, snow pigeon, green pigeon. The best period for visiting the best park is from May to October. Rest house accommodation is available.

Govind Vinayak Karandikar : Govind Vinayak Karandikar (born August 23, 1918), better known as Vinda Karandikar is a famous Marathi poet. He is the winner of the 39th Jnanpith Award, India's highest literary award. Karandikar is said to be the most experimental and the most comprehensive of all modern Marathi poets. He has also contributed to Marathi literature as an essayist, critic and translator (he translated Aristotle's poetry into Marathi). He has translated his own poems into English and also written poetry in English (Vinda poems of 1975). He has also modernised old literature like Dnyaneshwari and Amrutanubhav.

Govindan Aravindan : Govindan Aravindan (born January 21, 1935 in Kottayam — died March 16, 1991 in Trivandrum) was a film director from Kerala, India. He was often credited as G. Aravindan. Aravindan directed films in Malayalam language. He won the National Film Award (Golden Lotus Award) for Best Direction in 1978, 1979 and 1987. His 1986 movie Chidambaram won the Award for Best Film.

Govinddev Ji ka Mandir : The presiding deity of Jaipur is Govindeoji, Lord Krishna. The temple is located between the Chandra Mahal and the Badal Mahal in the city palace complex, so that the rulers of the state could view the temple from their residences. The temple attracts large number of devotes specially on the 'Janmashtmi', the day of Lord Krishna's birth.

Gowri Hunnive : This festival observe on the Full moon day of Kartik is participated more by ladies in Karnataka. They worship images of Gowri and small groups of young girls move round the streets singing some songs in honour of the goddess.

Gram Panchayats : Gram Panchayats are local government bodies in India. According to T R Raghunandan, Secretary of Rural Development and Panchayat in the Raj Department, Government of Karnataka, as of 2002 there were 265000 Gram Panchayats in India.

Grameen Bank : The Grameen Bank is a microfinance organization started in Bangladesh that makes small loans (known as microcredit) to the impoverished without requiring collateral. The system is based on the idea that the poor have skills that are underutilized. The bank also accepts deposits, provides other services, and runs several development-oriented businesses including fabric, telephone and energy companies. Muhammad Yunus, the bank's founder, earned a doctorate in economics from Vanderbilt University. He was inspired during the terrible Bangladesh famine of 1974 to make a small loan to a group of families so that they could create small items for sale. Yunus believed that making such loans available to a wide population could ameliorate the rampant rural poverty in Bangladesh.

The Grameen Bank (literally, Bank of the villages, in Bangla) is the outgrowth of Muhammad Yunus' ideas. The bank began as a research project by Yunus and the Rural Economics Project at the University of Chittagong, Bangladesh to test his method for providing credit and banking services to the rural poor. In 1976, the village of Jobra and other villages surrounding the University of Chittagong became the first areas eligible for service from Grameen Bank.

The Bank was immensely successful and the project, with government support, was introduced in 1979 to the Tangail District (to the north of the capital, Dhaka). The bank's success continued and it soon spread to various other districts of Bangladesh and in 1983, it was transformed into an independent bank by the legislature of Bangladesh. The bank's stellar repayment rate was broken in 1995 by a religious fundamentalist boycott by certain sections of society who objected to the bank's focus on improving the status of women. The boycott soon folded, but the bank's repayment rate was again hit following the 1998 flood of Bangladesh before recovering again in recent years. The Bank today continues to expand across the nation and still provides small loans to the rural poor. As of mid-2005, Grameen Bank branches number over 1,500. Its success has inspired similar projects around the world.

Grameen Phone : Grameen Phone is a GSM-based mobile phone company in Bangladesh. It started operations there on March 26, 1997. It is partly owned by Telenor Norway Telecom (62 percent) and Grameen Telecom (38 percent). Grameen Telecom facilitates a 'Village Phone' program, providing a mobile phone to villages without access to fixed land lines. This mobile phone is then cared for by a woman in the village, who charges for the use of the phone and pays a proportion back to Grameen Phone. According to the company, women have been chosen because they have turned out to be more reliable than the men. As of April 2006, Grameen Phone is the largest mobile phone company in Bangladesh, with 6.4 million subscribers.

Grand Trunk Road : The Grand Trunk Road (GT Road) is the Indian Subcontinent's first, largest and oldest major road, linking Sonargaon in Bengal (now in Narayanganj, Bangladesh) with Kabul in Afghanistan via the Khyber Pass. The Grand Trunk Road spans a distance of over 2,500 km, and connects up the important cities of Kolkata, Varanasi, Allahabad, Kanpur, Delhi, Amritsar, and to the Pakistani cites of Lahore and Peshawar. It is also known as the National Highway 1 or (NH)-1(from Delhi onwards and NH-2 from Delhi to Kolkata.

The Grand Trunk Road was built in the 16th century by Sher Shah Suri, the then Pathan Emperor of India, with the intention of linking together the remote provinces of his vast empire for administrative and military reasons. Originally known as the Sadak-e-Azam ('The road of the Emperor'), the Grand Trunk Road was the traditional route for invasions of the subcontinent by Afghan and Persian invaders, as well as one of the most important trade routes in the region. This also helped establish one of the first postal services in the region. There were well-maintained sarais or Inns at regular intervals. Trees were planted on both sides of the road to give shade to the passers-by. Later renamed and improved by the British rulers of colonial India, the Grand Trunk Road was sometimes referred to as the "Long Walk".

Great Andaman : It is the main archipelago of the Andaman Islands of India. It comprises five major islands. From north to south, these are North Andaman, Middle Andaman, South Andaman, Baratang and Rutland Island. The three northern islands are the largest of the entire island group, and the islands' capital, Port Blair, also lies in the archipelago.

Great Himalayan National Park : The park officially known as the Jawaharlal Nehru Great Himalayan National Park, was established in1984 in Kulu district. Bounded by the towering peaks of the Himalayas on three sides with an entrance from the west, the park covers an area of 620sq.km.of the previously-established Tirthan Sanctuary. The park which lies in the Seraj Forest Division in the upper catchments of the rivers Thirthan, Jiwa and Sainj has an altitude varying from 1500 to around 6000 meters with snowy mountains, glaciers, river valleys, cliffs and dense forest

Great Indian Bustard : The Great Indian Bustard (Ardeotis nigriceps) is a bustard found in India and possibly Pakistan. It is a large, brown-and-white bird, the male 122 cm in length and the female 92 cm. It lives in arid and semi-arid grasslands.

The current population is estimated at less than 1,000. The main threat to its existence is habitat loss. The bird is found in Rajasthan and Madhya Pradesh states of India. Ghatigaon and Karera santuaries in Madhya Pradesh had sizeable population earlier but now there is no Great Indian Bustard seen in Karera sanctuary in Shivpuri district.

Great Indian Hornbills : The largest and arguably most impressive members of the hornbill family are Great Indian Hornbills or Buceros bicornis. They have long aroused the interest of their human neighbours playing large parts in tribal rituals. They are long-lived with life spans commonly approaching 50 years in captivity. Unfortunately today their existence is threatened both in the wild and captivity.

Great Indian Hornbills live in the forests of India, Indonesia, Sumatra, and the Malay Peninsula. Deforestation threatens their native habitat and while not currently endangered their status is vulnerable. Local tribes further threaten the Great Indian Hornbill with their desire for its various parts. Chick's blood is said to have a soothing affect on departed souls, before marriage tribesmen need their feathers for headdresses, and their skulls are often worn as decoration. Programs in the west reduce this affect on the local population by sending feathers that fall off captive hornbills and ceramic casques of hornbill skulls to native tribes.

In the wild hornbills eat primarily fruit, but also small mammals, lizards, snakes and insects. In captivity hornbills eat the same things and pretty much anything else you care to feed them. A healthy diet will always be made up, in most part, by fruit and some source of protein. Indian hornbills form monogamous pair bonds and live out their lives in groups of 2-40 individuals. Group courtship displays involving up to 20 birds have been observed. In captivity a few have been "tamed" and hornbill behavior is described as "high-strung", however, there are several examples of extremely tame hornbills.

Great Nicobar : Great Nicobar (known to its indigenous inhabitants as Tokieong Long) is the largest of the Nicobar Islands of India, north of Sumatra. Indira Point, its southernmost tip, is also the southernmost point of India. The island covers 1045 km^2 but is sparsely inhabited, largely being covered by rainforest and known for its diverse wildlife.

Greater India : Greater India is another term sometimes used to describe the region between Central Asia in the North and tropical Indonesia in the South, and from the borderlands of Persia to Tibet and western China, which has had a significant Indian influence on its culture and civilizaton, including religious thought, language, art and literature. The term is difficult to define exactly, and has been largely replaced by the name South Asia, although this is usually used as a term for the political entities of the South Asia rather than for the geographical region itself.

Greater Kushtia : Historically, Kushtia was a larger district consisting of three subdivisions, each of which has now become a district. However, the people of these three districts, Chuadanga, Meherpur and Kushtia, share more than just a common past. Most notably, the dwellers of these districts, as the past inhabitants of an undivided Nadia district, are speak a dialect remarkably close to what is now considered "standard" Bangla in both West Bengal and Bangladesh. Because of the great commonality between the three districts, they are often referred to as the Greater Kushtia District. Several organisations, such as the "Greater Kushtia Association" and "Greater Kushtia Society", are concerned with the welfare of the entire region.

Greco-Buddhist Period : Greco-Buddhism is the cultural syncretism between the culture of Classical Greece and Buddhism, which developed over a period of close to 800 years in the area corresponding to modern-day Afghanistan and Pakistan, between the 4th century BC and the 5th century AD. Greco-Buddhism especially influenced the artistic development of Mahayana Buddhism, before it was adopted by Central and Northeastern Asia from the 1st century AD, ultimately spreading to China, Korea and Japan. It was mainly centered around the area of Gandhara, or modern Afghanistan, the area of the subcontinent that had most been influenced by Persian and Greek contact. Gandhara was roughly contemporary to the other Mahajanapada kingdoms elsewhere in India.

Grida Dance : When rabi crops sway in the fields in full bloom, the parties from different villages of MP, join together and perform the Grida dance. It continues from morning till evening. The host village returns the visit next year by going to the village of their guests of the preceding year. The dance has three distinct phases: (1) Sela—The feet movements are slow and comparatively rigid. (2) Selalarki—The feet movements become brisker and faster. (3) Selabhadoni—With the acceleration of the tempo, every limb of the body begins to sway in mood of exaltation.

Griddhakuta or Vulture's Peak : Griddhakuta in Bihar was the place where the Lord Buddha set in motion his second wheel of Law and for three months every year during the rainy season, preached many inspiring sermons to his disciples. The Buddha Sangha of Japan have constructed a massive modern stupa, the Shanti Stupa (Peace Pagoda), at the top of the hill in commemoration. A bridle path leads up to the hill but it is much more fun to take the Aerial Chairlift which operates every day except Thursday. One way ride takes 7.5 minutes and the view is splendid over the hills of Rajgir.

Guddu Barrage : Guddu Barrage is a barrage across river Indus, near Sukkur in Pakistan. President Iskander Mirza laid foundation-stone of the Guddu Barrage on February 2, 1957. The barrage was completed in 1962. At the time of its construction it has maximum design discharge of 1.2 million cusecs. It is a gate-controlled weir type barrage with a navigation lock. The barrage has 64 bays, each 60 feet wide. The maximum flood level height of Guddu barrage is 26 feet. It controls irrigation supplies to 2.9 million acres of agricultural lands in the Jacobabad, Larkana and Sukkur districts of Sindh and the Nasirabad district of Balochistan. The cost of the project was 474.8 million rupees. It feeds Ghotki Feeder, Begari Feeder, Desert and Pat Feeder canals.

Gudi Padwa : Gudi Padwa is a holiday celebrated in India. Also known as Ugadi, it is celebrated on the first day of the Hindu month of Chaitra, which according to the Gregorian calendar would fall sometime at the end of March and the beginning of April. This festival is supposed to mark the beginning of Vasant or spring. According to the Brahma Purana, this is the day on which Brahma created the world after the deluge and time began to tick from this day forth.

Gudivada : Gudivada' is a small town with more than 100,000 inhabitants, lying as junction of Vijayawada-Machilipatnam-Bhimavaram-Nuzvid in the Krishna district of Andhra Pradesh of India. Gudi means temple and vada means town in Telugu. Gudivada might be derived from existence of number of temples in the past. Gudivada was known as Vidarbhapuri in past. Gudivada was a culture centre during the period of Vijayanagar Empire. The excavations discovered certain archaeological remains such as Buddhist and Jain relics. There are also about 99 low mounds with the ruins of Buddhist stupas. The notable one among the old Buddhist Stupas is an elevated mound in a cylindrical form with a semi-spherical top

Gugga Naumi : Gugga Naumi, which is a festival in honour of Gugga Pir, also falls in Bhadon. The Pir's devotees paint his image on the wall in turmeric, as also paint a snake in black, right in front of it and then perform the ritual of worship. People also pour butter milk into the holes of snakes. Sweet Sevian is the special dish of the festival. The Halbagis, who are devout followers of Gugga Pir, also known as Zahir Pir, erect a long pole covered with flags, coloured cloth, coconuts etc and render worship to it as to a god. The devotees carry the Pir's stand from house and beg. The disciple who carries the standard is known as the Pir's house. To propitiate Gugga Pir women sing songs in his admiration.

Guggapir : Guggapir is celebrated on the next day of Janamashtami in Haryana. Gugga Pir is worshipped by both Hindus and Muslims. A dance procession is taken out in which Panch Pirs are the main dancers. They sing songs in praise of Gugga.

Gugumal National Park : This park is spread over an area of 361sq.km in the district of Amaravati. The nearest airport is Sonegaon (Nagpur) about 200km from the park. The railhead is Badnera at a distance of 124km. The nearest bus-station is Paratwada, 60km from the park The vegetation of the park is of dry deciduous type. The mammals found in the park are leopard, panther, tiger, sloth bear, fishing cat four horned antelope, sambar, barking deer, wild beer, cheetah etc. Python is also found. The bird life is plentiful.

Guindy National Park : This park spread over an area of 27.6 sq. km. is situated in Madras district. The nearest rail head, airport and town is Madras, at a distance of 5km. The park was set up in 1976. The fauna of the park are chital and black buck. There is also a snake park.

Gujar : Gujar is a member of a South Asian ethnic group mainly located in eastern Pakistan, Kashmir, Gujarat and northwestern India. Gurjars traditionally belonged to the Kshatriya caste, and formerly ruled the Gurjara-Pratihara Kingdom, which included much of northern India during the 8th and 9th centuries.

Gujjars are possibly the partial descendents of any number of Eurasian peoples, including the Scythians, Georgians, and Khazars of the Caspian Sea, who took part in the Scythian invasions of South Asia from the 5th century BCE to the 1st century CE or some other Turko-Iranian tribes that merged with local Indo-Aryan-speaking groups, mainly settling in the Gujarat, Punjab and Kashmir regions. These sun-worshipping and Buddhist tribes ruled kingdoms covering much of present-day Afghanistan, Punjab, NWFP, Jammu and Kashmir, Gujarat, Rajasthan, Uttar Pradesh, Haryana,Madhya Pradesh, Maharastra, Karnataka, Andra Pradesh and Orissa.

The Gujjars of today are mainly a combination of local South Asian peoples who have absorbed Central Asian elements over time. Many Gujjars are well represented in agriculture, the urban professions, civil service and officer class. They are now settled on large tracts of lands in India and Pakistan. They are known as very good farmers.

Gujarat : Gujarat contained many of the former Princely states of India, and is the second-most industrialized state in the Republic of India after Maharashtra. Gujarat borders the states of Rajasthan to the north-east, Madhya Pradesh to the east, Maharashtra and the Union territory of Dadra and Nagar Haveli to the south. The international border with Pakistan is to the north-west. The Arabian Sea makes up the state's western coast. Its capital is Gandhinagar, a planned city which is close to Ahmedabad, the former state capital and the current commercial center of Gujarat.

After India's independence in 1947, 217 princely states of Kathiawar and Saurashtra, including the former kingdom of Junagadh, were grouped together to form the province of Saurashtra, with its capitol at Rajkot. On November 1, 1956, Saurashtra was merged into Bombay State. The modern state of Gujarat was created on May 1, 1960, out of the northern, predominantly Gujarati-speaking portion of Bombay State. The southern, predominantly Marathi-speaking portion became the state of Maharashtra.

Gujarat has become one of the fastest-growing states in the country; with an average recorded per-capita income of Rs. 15,800 in 2004, compared to the national average of Rs. 6,400. Though mostly noted for their entrepreneurial spirit, people from Gujarat, also refered to as Gujarati (pl. Gujaratis), have also been leaders in the arts and the sciences. Three of India's most prominent leaders in the independence movement were from Gujarat: Mahatma Gandhi, Sardar Vallabhbhai Patel, and Morarji Desai. Mohammed Ali Jinnah, the first Governor General of

Pakistan, spoke Gujarati as his mother tongue and his father hailed from what became the Indian state of Gujarat. Vikram Sarabhai was the father of India's space program. Gujarat is the only state in India where there is a prohibition on liquor.

Gujarat Earthquake (2001) : The 2001 Gujarat earthquake took place on January 26, 2001 at 8:46 in the morning in Bhuj in Gujarat, India. This 6.9 magnitude quake, was the most devastating earthquake in India in recent history. The earthquake is considered an intraplate earthquake because it occurred a great distance from any plate boundary, where the theory of plate tectonics says most earthquakes of this size happen. Because of this, this area was not completely prepared for an earthquake of such size, causing much of the devastation. As many as 15,000 -20,000 people were initially reported dead but within a few days after the earthquake, the death toll kept on rising. As of 3 February 2001, the official toll had climbed to more than 30,000. However, the final death toll may never be known with certainty. At least 30,000 more people were reported as injured. This too may be an underestimate.

Gujarati : Gujarati is one of the 22 official language and 14 regional languages spoken in India. It is a language native to the state of Gujarat in western India. There are about 46 million speakers of Gujarati worldwide, making it the 23rd most spoken language in the world. Of these, roughly 45.5 million reside in India, 150,000 in Uganda, 250,000 in Tanzania, 50,000 in Kenya and roughly 100,000 in Pakistan. Gujarati is the chief language of India's Gujarat state, as well as the adjacent union territories of Daman and Diu and Dadra and Nagar Haveli. A considerable population of Gujarati speakers exists in North America and the United Kingdom as well. In the United Kingdom, Leicester (Midlands) and Wembley (North London) are two areas popular with Gujaratis. And in America, states such as New Jersey, New York, California, and Texas are quite popular with Gujaratis. Gujarati was the mother-tongue of both Mohandas K. Gandhi, the "father of India" and Quaid-e Azam Mohammed Ali Jinnah, the "father of Pakistan".

Gujranwala : Gujranwala is a city in Punjab, Pakistan with a population of 3.5 million. It is located at 32.16° North, 74.18° East and is 700 feet above sea-level. The district of Gujranwala, with a population of about 11 million has an area of 3198 sq. miles. Gujranwala is the 5th largest city in Pakistan. Punjabi is the local language, however English and Urdu are also common, as in Pakistan they are the only languages allowed in schools and places of government business. It's home to the international cricket stadium called Jinnah Stadium and has many hospital and several colleges affiliated with the University of the Punjab. The city is renowned all over Pakistan for its food, especially meat dishes. Gujranwala has been always been famous for its pehlwans (wrestlers) which is why it is also called The City of Wrestlers.

The rural areas around Gujranwala produce a large variety of agricultural goods, the main crops grown here are wheat, cotton, rice, barley and millet. Today, Gujranwala is playing a major role in supporting the economy of Pakistan. It is a large industrial city with numerous textile mills, and large agricultural processing plants. Gujranwala's major exports are rice, textiles, carpets, transformers, clothing, glass goods, electric fans, surgical equipment, hosiery, leather products, metal utensils, auto parts and sanitation equipment. Gujranwala's hydro-electric project provides power from the Chenab River.

The city of Gujranwala is about 500 years old. The first name of the settlement, according to the compilers of the first edition of the district Gazette, was Khanpur Shansi after an individual of the Jat caste called Khan Shansi who founded 11 villages in the region. Later, the Jat tribe "Gujar" occupied the land. They reached such dominance that the town came to be known as Gujranwala, which means "Land of the Gujars". In present day too, the Gujars form the majority population of the city. It seems likely that the district once contained the capital of the Punjab at an epoch when Lahore had not begun to exist. Later, the Sikh Empire made the city its capital. The famous Sikh leader Maharaja Ranjit Singh was also born in this city. The manor in which he was born still stands today in the center of the city. After the partition of India in August 1947, Gujranwala became the capital of the district 1951.

Gujrat District : Gujrat is a district in Pakistan located in Punjab Province. It is an ancient district of undivided India located in between two famous rivers, the Jhelum and Chenab. Because of its proximity with the rivers the land is good for cultivation with rice and sugar cane as main crops. It is bounded on the northeast by Jammu and Kashmir, on the northwest by the River Jhelum which separates it from Jhelum District, on the east and southeast by the Chenab River, separating it from the districts of Gujranwala and Sialkot, and on the West by Mandi Bahauddin district. District Gujrat is spread over an area of 3,192 square kilometres, and is divided into three tehsils, Gujrat, Kharian, and Sarai Alamgir. The founding stones of Gujrat were laid by Daswandi Khan. There are many historic villages in the district such as Chakdina.

Gul Lasht Zom : Gul Lasht Zom is a snowy pinnacle easily visible once you climb up on Tirich Glacier from the Shagroom side. It offers easy climbing and was first climbed by Kurt Dimberger of Austria.

Gulab Jamun : Gulab Jamun is a popular Indian sweet dish comprised of fried milk balls in a sweet syrup flavoured with cardamom seeds and rosewater or saffron.

Mixes and finished products are often available in supermarkets, though it is still popular to be made from scratch.

Gulab Jamun is one of the few Indian desserts that is generally appreciated by Westerners, perhaps because of its resemblance to other syrup-covered pastries (e.g., pancakes). Because of that, Gulab Jamun appears to be increasing in popularity, and is probably the most common sweet served in Indian restaurants in the West.

Gulbarga : Gulbarga is a town in the Indian state of Karnataka. It is the administrative headquarters of Gulbarga District, and of Gulbarga Division. Gulbarga is 613 km north of Bangalore and well connected by road to Bijapur, Hyderabad and Bidar. A railway line connecting the southern part of India to Mumbai and Delhi passes through Gulbarga.

Gulbarga was earlier known as Kaliburgi (stony land in Kannada). Recorded history of this district dates back to the 6th century when the Rashtrakutas gained control over the area, but the Chalukyas regained their domain and reigned for over two hundred years. The Kalachuris who succeeded them ruled till the 12th century. Around the close of the 12th century the Yadavas of Devagiri and the Hoysalas of Dwarasamadra took control of the district. About the same period the Kakatiya kings of Warangal came into prominence. The present Gulbarga and Raichur districts formed part of their domain.

The Kakatiya power was subdued in 1321, and the northern Deccan, including the district of Gulbarga, passed under the control of the Muslim Sultanate of Delhi. The revolt of the Muslim officers appointed from Delhi resulted in founding of the Bahmani Sultanate in 1347 by Hassan Gangu, who chose Gulbarga to be his capital. When the Bahmani dynasty came to an end, the kingdom broke up into the five independent Deccan sultanates, Bijapur, Bidar, Berar, Ahmednagar and Golconda. The present Gulbarga district came partly under Bidar and partly under Bijapur. With the conquest of the Deccan by Aurangezeb in the 17th Century, control of Gulbarga passed to the Mughal Empire. In the early part of the 18th Century, when Mughal Empire was declining, Asaf Jah I, a general of Aurangzeb, became independent and formed state of Hyderabad in which a major part of Gulbarga area was also included.

In 1948 Hyderabad state was annexed to the newly-independent Indian Union, and in 1956 the Indian state of Hyderabad was partitoned among neighboring states along linguistic lines. Most of Gulbarga district became part of Mysore state, later renamed Karnataka, excluding two taluks which were annexed to Andhra Pradesh.

Gulf of Khambhat : The Gulf of Khambhat (formerly known as the Gulf of Cambay) is an inlet of the Arabian Sea along the west coast of India, in the state of Gujarat. It is about 80 miles in length, and divides the Kathiawar peninsula to the west from the eastern part of Gujarat state on the east. The Narmada and Tapti rivers empty into the Gulf. The Gulf is shallow and abounds in shoals and sandbanks. The Gulf is known for its extreme tides, which vary greatly in height and run into it with amazing speed. At low tide the bottom is left nearly dry for some distance below the town of Khambhat.

The Gulf of Khambhat has been an important center of trade since ancient times; its ports connect central India to the maritime trade routes of the Indian Ocean. Bharuch (Broach), Surat, Khambhat, Bhavnagar, and Daman are historically important seaports. Bharuch has been important since ancient times; Khambhat was the gulf's chief port in the Middle Ages, but after the silting of its harbor, Surat rose to prominence as the most important harbor of the

Mughal empire. Traces of a neolithic culture have been found submerged in the Gulf in 2002. A piece of carbonized wood recovered from the area has been radiocarbon dated to a calibrated age of some 9,500 years. The finds pre-date the Harappan civilization by at least 4,000 years.

Gulf of Kutch : The Gulf of Kutch is an inlet of the Arabian Sea along the west coast of India, in the state of Gujarat. It is about 99 miles in length, and divides Kutch and the Kathiawar peninsula regions of Gujarat.

Gulshan Town : Gulshan Town is one of the towns in Karachi, Sindh, Pakistan. This town was named in honor of Pakistan's national poet Allama Muhammad Iqbal. Gulshan-e-Iqbal literally translates to 'Garden of Iqbal'. The town is bordered by Gadap Town to the north, the Faisal and Malir Cantonments to the east, Jamshed Town to the southwest, and Gulberg and Liaquatabad to the west.

The population of Gulshan Town was estimated to be about 650,000 at the 1998 census, of which 99% are Muslim. There are several ethnic groups in Gulshan Town including: Urdu speakers, Punjabis, Sindhis, Kashmiris, Seraikis, Pakhtuns, Balochs, Memons, Bohras and Ismailis.

Gulzar : Gulzar (born Sampooran Singh on August 18, 1936) is an Indian poet, lyricist, film-maker, director, and playwright from India. He works in Hindi and Urdu languages.

Gulzar was born in Dina, located in the current-day Pakistan. He is best known for penning some of Bollywood's popular songs composed by Rahul Dev Burman. He is a widely acclaimed song-writer in Bollywood movies. He has worked exhaustively in the Indian film industry for over thirty five years. Gulzaar saab, as he is affectionately known has written in Hindi, Punjabi, and dialects of Hindi like Marwari (Rajasthani) and

Bhojpuri. He is best known in India as a lyricist for songs that form an integral part of Indian cinema. Gulzar began his career under two other artists—Bimal Roy and Hrishikesh Mukherjee. His book Ravi Paar has a narrative of Bimal Roy and the agony of creation.

Gulzari Lal Nanda : Born on July 4, 1898, in Sialkot (Punjab), Shri Gulzarilal Nanda was educated at Lahore, Agra and Allahabad. He worked as a research scholar on labour problems at the University of Allahabad (1920-1921) and became Professor of Economics at the National College (Bombay) in 1921. He joined the Non-Cooperation Movement the same year. In 1922, he become Secretary of the Ahmedabad Textile Labour Association in which he worked until 1946. He was imprisoned for Satyagraha in 1932, and again from 1942 to 44.

Shri Nanda was elected to the Bombay Legislative Assembly in 1937 and was Parliamentary Secretary to the Government of Bombay from 1937 to 1939. Later, as Labour Minister of the Bombay Government (1946-50), he successfully piloted the Labour Disputes Bill in the State Assembly. He served as Trustee, Kasturba Memorial Trust; Secretary, Hindustan Mazdoor Sevak Sangh; and Chairman, Bombay Housing Board. He was also a Member of the National Planning Committee. He was largely instrumental in organising the Indian National Trade Union Congress and later became its President.

In 1947, he went to Geneva as a Government delegate to the International Labour Conference. He worked on the 'The Freedom of Association Committee' appointed by the Conference and visited Sweden, France, Switzerland, Belgium and England to study labour and housing conditions in those countries.

In March 1950, he joined the Planning Commission as its Vice-Chairman. In September the following year, he was appointed Planning Minister in the Union Government. In addition, he was also given charge of the portfolios of Irrigation and Power. He was elected to the House of the People from Bombay in the general elections of 1952 and was re-appointed Minister for Planning Irrigation and Power. He led the Indian Delegation to the Plan Consultative Committee held at Singapore in 1955, and the International Labour Conference held at Geneva in 1959.

Shri Nanda was elected to the Lok Sabha in the 1957 general elections, and was appointed Union Minister for Labour and Employment and Planning and, later, as Deputy Chairman of the Planning Commission. He visited the Federal Republic of Germany Yugoslavia and Austria in 1959.

He was re-elected to the Lok Sabha in the 1962 general elections from Sabarkantha Constituency in Gujarat. He initiated the Congress Forum for Socialist Action in 1962. He was Union Minister for Labour and Employment in 1962 and 1963 and Minister for Home Affairs from 1963 to 1966. Following the death of Pt. Nehru, he was a sworn in as Prime Minister of India on May 27, 1964. Again on January 11, 1966, he was sworn in as Prime Minister following the death of Shri Lal Bahadur Shastri at Tashkent.

Gulzaribagh : It is about 8 kms east of the Golghar near Kumrahar in Bihar. This is an old opium godown (warehouse) of former East India Company. This warehouse, hall and ballroom are open to visitors.

Gumti River : Gumti river is originates from Dumur in the northeastern hilly region of Tripura state of India. From its source it flows about 150 km along a meandering course through the hills, turns west and enters Bangladesh near Katak Bazar (Comilla Sadar). Then it takes a meandering course again and passes through the northern side of Comilla town and east of Mainamati. Keeping Burichang upazila on the north, it cuts through Debidwar upazila and reaches Companiganj Bazar. The distance from Mainamati to Companiganj Bazar is about 60 km. From Companiganj it turns west and finally falls into the Meghna at Shapta in Daudkandi upazila. The segment between Companiganj and Daudkandi is about 50 km long. The Gumti is about 135 km long within Bangladesh. The Dakatia is one of the important tributaries of the Gumti and the Buri river is its distributary.

Gundla Brahmeswara Sanctuary : Gundla Brahmeswaram Sanctuary lies between Kurnool and Prakasam districts in Andhra pradesh, spread over 1194 sq.km at a distance of 30 Km. from Nandyal. This sanctuary has mixed deciduous forests of Teak, Prerocarpus etc.

Guntur : Guntur is a city located in the south-eastern part of India in the state of Andhra Pradesh. The city has a population of 514,707 (2001 census), making it the fourth-largest city in the state, and is the Administrative center and Capital of Guntur District. It is the Home of the famous Amaravati and Ancient Sitanagaram, Also the home of Acharya Nagarjuna University one of the largest universities of India.

The earliest reference to Guntur, a variant of Guntur, comes from the Idern plates of Ammaraja I (922-929), the Vengi Chalukyan King. Guntur also appears in another two inscriptions dated 1147 and 1158. The original Sanskrit name (ageless vedic culture/tradition) for Guntur is Garthapuri. The place of Sitanagaram and Guthikonda can be traced (through Vedic Puranas) back to the last Treta Yuga and Dwapara yuga (1.7 to 0.5 million years ago). The region also has been historically known for Buddhism.

Gupta Empire : The Gupta Empire was an Indian empire ruled by the Gupta dynasty in ancient India from around 320 to 550 CE. The origins of the Guptas are shrouded in obscurity. The Chinese traveller I-tsing provides the first evidence of the Gupta kingdom in Magadha. He came to India in 672 CE and heard of 'Maharaja Sri-Gupta' who built a temple for Chinese pilgrims near Mrigasikhavana. I-tsing gives the date for this event merely as '500 years before'. This does not match with other sources and hence we can assume that I-tsing's computation was a mere guess.

The most likely date for the reign of Sri-Gupta is c. 240-280 CE His successor Ghatotkacha ruled probably from c. 280-319 CE In contrast to his successor, he is also referred to in inscriptions as 'Maharaja'. At the beginning of the 4th century the Guptas established and ruled a few small Hindu kingdoms in Magadha and around modern-day Uttar Pradesh. The Gupta dynasty ruled India north of the Vindhya Range during the 4th and 5th centuries. Though not as vast as Mauryan empire, The Gupta era left a deep and wide cultural impact not only in the subcontinent but on the adjacent Asian countries as well. We get plenty of information about this illustrious dynasty through coins, inscriptions, monuments and Sanskrit classics.

The Gupta rulers were great conquerors and good administrators. They checked the infiltration of foreign tribes like Sakas and Hunas and established political stability. Economic prosperity followed and led to cultural expansion. Sanskrit language and literature were reached its peak during the Gupta era.

Poets Kalidasa, Dandi, Visakhadatta, Shudraka, and Bharavi all belong to this period. Many puranas and shastras were composed and famous commentaries on sacred works appeared. Buddhist and Jain literature, which was produced earlier in Pali, Ardhamagadhi and other Prakrit languages, began to appear in Sanskrit. The practice of dedicating temples to different deities came into vogue followed by fine artistic temple architecture and sculpture. Of the twenty-eight Ajanta caves, most of them were constructed during this period. Gupta inscriptions, some of them on "victory pillars" provide first hand information not only about royalty but society in general.

Gurdaspur District : Gurdaspur District is a district in the state of Punjab, situated in the northwest part of India. Gurdaspur is the district headquarters. It borders Pakistan, Jammu and Kashmir, the Punjab districts of Amritsar and Hoshiarpur, and the state of Himachal Pradesh. Two main rivers Beas and Ravi passes through the district. Akbar is said to have been enthroned in a garden near Kalanaur, a historically important town in the district.

Gurdwara : A Gurdwara, meaning "the doorway to God", is the Sikh place of worship and may be referred to as a Sikh temple. In the early days of the Sikh Gurus, before the first gurdwara, followers of Guru Nanak formed a congregation whose venue was known as a dharamsala (place or seat of religion). A Gurdwara always houses the Sikh holy book, the Guru Granth Sahib and displays a triangular orange flag called the Nishan Sahib.

Gurdwara Baba Atal : Many of the millions of pilgrims that visit the Harimandir Sahib every year do not realise that one of [[Amritsar[['s finest architectural marvels and one of the Sikh religions most poignant places of worship is just a short walk from the famous Golden Temple.

Built some two centuries ago, the Baba Atal Gurdwara is a touching commemoration of the young life of Baba Atal Rai, the son of Guru Hargobind. Its nine storeys echo his nine years of life before his death in 1628. Today, unfortunatly, it is being steadily defaced, distorted and vulgarised just yards from the marble walkway of the Golden Temple complex.

Gurdwara Bangla Sahib : Gurdwara Bangla Sahib is the most prominent Sikh gurdwara, or Sikh house of worship, in Delhi. It is instantly recognisable by the stunning golden dome and tall flagpole. Gurdwara Bangla Sahib was originally a bungalow belonging to Raja Jai Singh, an Indian ruler in the seventeenth century. The eighth Sikh Guru, Guru Har Krishan resided here during his stay in Delhi. During that time, there was a smallpox and cholera epidemic, and Guru Har Krishan helped the suffering by giving aid and fresh water from the well at this house. The water is now revered as having healing properties, and is taken by Sikhs throughout the world back to their homes. The Gurdwara is now a place of pilgrimage for both Sikhs and Hindus.

The grounds include the temple, a kitchen, a large pond, a school and an art gallery. As with all Sikh Gurdwaras, the concept of langar is practiced, and all people, regardless of race or religion may eat in the Gurdwara kitchen. In a very busy city such as Delhi, a stroll around the tranquil pond is very relaxing. Visitors are reminded to cover their hair, and not to wear shoes inside the compound. As you enter the compound, you can find some helpful people in the information office. Scarves and a shoe minding service can be found there free of charge.

Gurdwara Sri Nanak Mata Sahib : Gurdwara Sri Nanak Mata Sahib (Village Nanakmata) is situated between Khatema and Sitarganj on the Khatema–Panipat Road, 18 km from Khatema and 12 km from Sitarganj, in district Udham Singh Nagar.

Gurdwara Sri Nanak Mata Sahib is associated with the first Guru, Guru Nanak Dev ji. However, the sixth Guru, Guru Hargobind Sahib ji also came to this place. Guru Nanak Devji came here during his Third Udasi in 1514 A.D

Gurgaon : Gurgaon is a city in the northern Indian state of Haryana, and is a suburb of the Delhi metropolitan area. It is also a part of the National Capital Region of Delhi. It is located in Gurgaon District. The origins of the city's name are steeped in Hindu mythology. Legend has it that Gurgaon is the ancestral village of Guru Dronacharya, the teacher of the Pandavas and Kauravas in the Indian epic Mahabharata. Gurgaon comes from Guru (from Guru Dronacharya) and Gaon (meaning village). The village was gifted by the Pandavas and Kauravas to their Guru (Dronacharya), and was known as Guru ka Gaon (Village of the Guru), and later Gurgaon.

Gurkha : Gurkha are people from Nepal who take their name from the eighth century Hindu warrior-saint Guru Gorakhnath. His disciple Bappa Rawal, born Prince Kalbhoj, founded the house of Mewar. Later descendants of Bappa Rawal moved further east to found the house of Gorkha, which in turn founded the Kingdom of Nepal. Gurkhas are best known for their history of service as foreign soldiers in the British Army and the Indian Army.

Gurmukhi : The Gurmukhi script, derived from the Later Sharada script and standardised by Guru Angad Dev in the 16th century, was designed to write the Punjabi language. The whole of the Guru Granth Sahib's 1430 pages are written in this script. The word Gurmukhi is commonly translated as "from the Mouth of the Guru". Gurmukhi is a form of writing system called an abugida, as each consonant has an inherent vowel (a), that can be changed using vowel signs.

Modern Gurmukhi has forty-one consonants (Vianjans), nine vowel symbols (Laga Matra), two symbols for nasal sounds (Bindi and Tippi) and one symbol which duplicates the sound of any consonant (Addak). In addition, four conjuncts are used: three subjoined forms of the consonants Rara, Haha and Vava, and one half-form of Yayya. Use of the conjunct forms of Vava and Yayya is increasingly scarce in modern contexts

Gurramkonda : Gurramkonda is Big Hostorical place.Which was ruled by Great waariors of India like Tippu sultan and othere Nawab's. Gurram + Konda (Whcih actually mean's "HORSE + HILL). The name was given to this place because guy's of kingdom use to go to the palece which is there on the top of the hill on horses.

It is a good historic place as Hyderabd. The main places to visit there are Ranginmahal whcih is King's Palece, And Maqbira there place where u can find the Uncle's tumb of the Great south inidan king Tippu Sultan.Which will almost resumbles like the one which is there in Hyderabd and know as the tumb of Kuliktub sha. Who built Charminar. And this place is Mandal Head qurater's and lies in between Cuddapah and Bangalore highway.And the main econamy builder's are farmer's.There main crops are Paddy, Tamota, Groundnet. It is a must place to visit if you are around Bangalore or Tirupati or Cudappah.

Guru Amar Das : Guru Amar Das (5 April 1479 – 1 September 1574) was the third of the Ten Gurus of Sikhism and became Guru on 26 March 1552 following in the footsteps of Guru Angad Dev, who died 29 March 1552. Before Guru Amar Das died, he nominated Guru Ram Das as the fourth Guru of the Sikhs.

Amar Das, on whom the choice of successorship fell, was the most faithful follower of Guru Angad. He was born at Vasarki, a village in the Amritsar district, in 1509. On the death of Angad, Amar Das established himself at Gowindwal. He was a successful teacher, and his zeal and passic secured him many converts to the new faith. He composed many beautiful verses, which have been incorporated in the Granth. He disapproved of satti, a practice of burning widows, and encouraged the re-marriage of Hindu widows. Amar Das was also a big proponent of the langar, or community kitchen, in the Sikh temples. Amar Das sent 22 of his chosen disciples to visit various parts of the country to spread the religion of Nanak. Amar Das died in Gowindwal, on May 14th, 1574, having reigned as Guru for a period of 22 years.

Guru Angad Dev : Guru Angad Dev (31 March 1504 – 29 March 1552) was the second of The Ten Gurus of Sikhism. He became Guru on 7 September 1539 following in the footsteps of Guru Nanak, who was the founder of the Sikh religion. Before becoming the second Guru, he was known as Lehna. Because of his proved loyalty and devotion, Angad became the Guru appointed by Nanak. Angad was born in 1504 in the village of Khadur, on the river Bias. The Sikh religion, would, in all probability, have gradually died out and sunk into oblivion, had it not been for the foresight and wisdom of its founder, in establishing an apostolic successorship.

Angad was strongly attached to Nanak, his most fervent server and ally. He was hardly possessed of any merits of his own. He commited to writing much about his great predecessor. He also recorded the results of his own devotional observations which have been incorporated in the Granth, the scriptures of the Sikhs. Angad also created Gurmukhi, the Punjabi script used in the Granth. Guru Angad died in 1552, the 13th year of the reign of Akber. His tomb was erected in his native village.

Guru Arjan Dev : Guru Arjan Dev (15 April 1563—30 May 1606) was the fifth of the Ten Gurus of Sikhism and became Guru on 1 September 1581 following in the footsteps of Guru Ram Das. He was born at Goindval. Before he died, he nominated his son Guru Hargobind as the next Guru of the Sikhs.

Arjan, the 3rd son of Guru Ram Das, became the Guru in 1581 after his death. Arjan established himself in Amritsar, and was the first Guru who dressed himself in a more princely fashion. He created the Harmandar, or Golden Temple, the most sacred temple to the Sikhs. He organized the Sikhs into a community, and devised measures for extending his spiritual authority. With a view to uniting the followers by one common religious tie, he gave a religious code, in which he incorporated the sayings and verses of Nanak, the compositions of his predecessors, and his own. This code he called the Granth, or the holy book. A copy was kept in the Harmandar, or holy temple, and recited each day. Hymns were sung in the praise of the Lord. The Guru organized a system of taxation and created a system of government.

Arjun refused to marry his son, Har Govind, to the daughter of a powerful financial minister in Lahore. The minister, becoming angry, convinced Emperor Jahangir of Lahore to charge the Guru of treason, and eventually the Guru was thrown in prison, where the Emperor wished to extort a large sum of money from him, which the Guru was unable to pay. The Guru was tortured and died of heat apoplexy. Arjun reigned as a Guru for 24 years, and his tomb now stands opposite the fort of Lahore, near the museum of Maharaja Ranjit Singh. Guru Arjan was a prolific writer, composed verses in the Granth and Gian Ratnaoli. The death of Guru Arjan is a great turning point in the history of the Sikh nation, for it inflamed passion of the Sikhs, and it was a time that those seeds of hatred of the Musalman power were in deep root.

Guru Dutt : Guru Dutt Shiv Shankar Padukone, the famous director and actor was born on 9th July 1925 in Mangalore, Karnataka. He received his early education in Calcutta. Guru Dutt learned dancing at Uday Shankar's, India Cultural Centre at Almora for two years. Later he moved to Maharashtra where he began his association with the film world. He learned every aspect of film making by assisting major directors in studios like Prabhat, Famous Pictures, Bombay Talkies etc.

Dutt's earliest assignments in the world of commercial cinema was that of a choreographer in the film 'Hum Ek Hain' and as an actor in the film 'Lakhrani' in 1944. His first big break as a director came with ' Baazi' (1951), produced by Dev Anand's Navketan Studio but it was with 'Aar Paar'(1954), that Guru Dutt entered his most popular phase as a director. He also proved his mettle as an actor by playing the hero in the film with a style of his own. During this time he married the popular playback singer, Geeta Roy who was to sing some of the best songs in his films.

With Aar Paar, Guru Dutt started his own production company. Other films that established Dutt's reputation— as an excellent director, 'Pyaasa'(1957), 'Kaagaz Ke Phool'(1959) ; as an actor and producer, 'Chaudvin Ka Chand'(1960) and 'Sahib Bibi Aur Ghulam'(1962). The story of Kaagaz ke Phool has glimpses of his personal life. Almost all his films had female as central characters. Famous actresses like Meena Kumari and Waheeda Rehman have given powerful performances in his films. He was so different from his fellow directors in the sense that he made good purposeful, films though not hits at the box office. He had a tragic end at the young age of thirty nine.

Guru Gobind Singh : Guru Gobind Singh (Patna, Bihar, India, December 22, 1666 – October 7, 1708, Nanded, Maharashtra,India) was the tenth and last of the Ten Gurus of Sikhism and became Guru on November 11, 1675 following in the footsteps of his father Guru Teg Bahadur. Before he died, he nominated the Guru Granth Sahib as the next perpetual Guru of the Sikhs. This Granth is more than a holy book for the Sikhs. Guru Gobind Singh (also sometimes less accurately transliterated as 'Govind') was the last of 10 Sikh Gurus, the founders of the Sikh religion. Guru Gobind Singh played a monumental part in the development of the Sikh faith.

Guru Granth Sahib : The Guru Granth Sahib — Granth is Punjabi for book; Sahib is Hindi meaning master, from Arabic, meaning companion, friend, owner, or master — is more than a holy book of the Sikhs. The Sikhs treat this Granth (holy book) as a living Guru. The holy text spans 1430 pages and contains the actual words spoken by the founders of the Sikh religion and various other Saints from other religions including Hinduism and Islam.

The Adi Granth is often — incorrectly — used to refer to the Guru Granth Sahib. The Adi Granth only forms the portion of the Granth which Guru Arjan compiled in 1604. This term is often used interchangeably so it is important to note the context within which it is used. The Granth was made a guru by the last of the living Sikh Masters, Guru Gobind Singh in 1708.

When one visits a Sikh Temple or Gurdwara the Granth forms the main part of the Darbar Sahib or Main Hall. The Holy Book is placed on a raised platform and covered in finery. The platform is always covered by an ornate canopy. The original text of the Granth is written in the Gurmukhi script and contains many languages including Punjabi, Sanskrit and Persian. The holy text comprises over 5000 Shabhads or hymns which are poetically constructed; and set to classical form of music rendition Ragas; can be set to predetermined musical Talas (rhythmic beats) and have a definite message for the whole of humanity.

Guru Har Gobind : Guru Har Gobind (19 June 1595—03 March 1644) was the sixth of the Ten Gurus of Sikhism and became Guru on 25 May 1606 following in the footsteps of his father Guru Arjan Dev. Before he died, he nominated Guru Har Rai, his grandson as the next Guru of the Sikhs.

At the death of Guru Har Gobind, his son, Har Gobind, became the Guru. Har Gobind combined the qualities of a warrior, a saint and a sportsman. He was the first Guru who organized a military system, and, arming his followers, made them buckle the sword and prepared to defend. In Amritsar, Har Gobind had revenge taken on the financial minister that had his father tortured. The Guru maintained a large establishment, had fine horses, and built the town of Hargovindpur on the banks of the Bias river, to serve as a retreat. Because Har Gobind failed to pay the balance of a heavy fine imposed on his father, the Emperor imprisoned the Guru in a state of semi-starvation. The faithful continuously flocked the prison the Guru was held, and after 12 years, released the Guru.

After some time, the Sikhs and the Mahomedans quarrelled, which would mark the first time the two sides fought in the Punjab. After some years, the Guru retired to the jungles of Bhatinda, to avoid further encounter with the imperial army. While in the jungles, the Guru converted great crowds to the faith of Nanak, and this behavior inflamed the king with violent anger, which ignited more battles between the Sikhs and the Mahomedan army. Towards the close of his life, Har Govind withdrew to the hills where he died in peace in 1645, after nominating his grandson, Har Rai, as the Guru. He reigned as Guru for 31 years, and his death was considered a national calamity. Har Govind had three wives, by whom he had five sons.

Guru Har Krishan : Guru Har Krishan (7 July 1656—30 March 1664) was the eighth of the Ten Gurus of

Sikhism and became Guru on 7 October 1661 following in the footsteps of his father, Guru Har Rai. Before Har Krishan died, he nominated his granduncle, Baba Bakala, as the next Guru of the Sikhs.

His father made Harkishan as his apostolic successor, although he was only 6 years of age. A violent contest rose among the Sikhs regarding the succession, and the emperor issues a mandate to Harkishan to repair to Delhi without delay. The emperor tested his intelligence and character in multiple ways, and he declared his right to succeed to the office of Guru to be indisputable. The infant Guru was, however, attacked by small-pox, and died on March 14th, 1664, at Delhi. While at his deathbed, the disciples asked who should be their spiritual leader, and the Guru indicated that Tegh Bahadur to be the Guru.

Guru Har Rai : Guru Har Rai (26 February 1630—6 October 1661) was the seventh of the Ten Gurus of Sikhism and became Guru on 8 March 1644 following in the footsteps of his grandfather, Guru Har Gobind. Before he died, he nominated Guru Har Krishan, his other son as the next Guru of the Sikhs.

On succeeding Har Govind, Har Rai established himself at Kartarpur on the banks of the Sutlej river. He was quite and contented man, with no taste for war. Because of the hostility of the empire, Har Rai withdrew from the scene and stayed in Kartarpur. Aurangzeb, the ruler of the Moghals, issued orders demanding the Guru to be present in imperial court of Delhi, but the Guru was able to dodge the demand with a letter to the king sent by his son, Ram Rai. Aurangzeb was satisfied with the letter and kept Ram Rai at his court, as a hostage. After 33 years as the Guru, Har Rai died in tranquillity at Kartarpur, in 1661.

Guru Nanak Dev: The first date in Sikhism is 1469, the year in which Guru Nanak was born. Guru Nanak's father, Kalyan Chand, who belonged to Bedi clan of the Kshatriyas and his mother Tripti, lived in a village of Talwandi Rai Bhoe, (now in Pakistan) and now named as "Nankana Sahib". According to the 'Janamsakhis' (traditional accounts of Guru Nanak's life) "Light flashed across the mud-built room in which the birth took place". The family priest, who came to cast the child's horoscope, told his father that his son would sit under Canopy. He further spoke: "Both Hindus and Turks will pay him reverence. He will worship and acknowledge but one formless Lord and teach others to do so. Every creature he will consider as god's own creation." Those early years of his life are described in 'Janamsakhis' in a variety of legends and miracles. Guru Nanak was the favourite of both Hindus and Muslims in the village, which was agreed by the early biographers.

Seeing that Nanak did not take to any useful calling in life, his father sent him to Sultanpur where his daughter, Nanaki lived with her husband. At Sultanpur, Nanak was put to work in the local Lodi chief's modihhana or stores, but he distributed things free to fakirs. So his father, at the age of 14 got him married to Sulakshna and they had two sons. But at the age of twenty seven, he left Sultanpur to embark on his long preaching odysseys called Udasis in the Sikh tradition.

The first words he uttered, after three days of silent communion were: "There is no Hindu, there is no Musalman". Guru Nanak thus rejected distinctions between man and woman by reason of creed or caste. He showed people the way to look beyond these barriers. His equal attention to Hindu and Muslim identities and use of some of their religious vocabulary have led some to depict him as the reconciler of the two faith and to see Sikhism as "a deliberate mingling of Hindu and Muslim practices". Accompanied by a Muslim follower, called Mardana, Guru

Nanak went to different parts in India and spread the message of love, faith and equality.

Guru Nanak Dev University (GNDU) : Guru Nanak Dev University was established at Amritsar, India on 24th November,1969 to commemorate Guru Nanak Dev's birth quincentenary celebrations. It is a both residential and an affiliating university. In conceiving the future course of the University, the objectives enshrined in the Act 1969, emphasised that the new university would make provision for imparting education and promoting research in the humanities, learned professions, sciences, especially of applied nature and technology. Studies and research on the life and teachings of Guru Nanak, in addition to working towards the promotion of Punjabi language and spreading education among educationally backward classes and communities were the other commitments.

Spread over a stretch of 500 acres towards the west of the Amritsar City, G.N.D.U. presents a picture of modern architecture. Traditional red brick geometrical blocks represent its regard for time-honoured values and commitment to scientific advancement. Making its humble beginning in an annexe of the adjoining Khalsa College, the University today boasts of 37 academic departments, two regional centres, two colleges and a score of support service departments besides several administrative offices.

Guru Nanak Devji Gurudwara : Constructed in the year 1940 this gurudwara in Raipur is the oldest and biggest of all the 500 gurudwaras found in the original state of Madhya Pradesh. This gurudwara welcomes all people, irrespective of religion, cast, creed and wealth.

Guru Ram Das : Guru Ram Das (24 September 1534 – 1 September 1581) was the fourth of the Ten Gurus of Sikhism and became Guru on 30 August 1574 following in the footsteps of Guru Amar Das. Before he died, he nominated Guru Arjan Dev, who was his youngest son, as the next Guru of the Sikhs.

Guru Ram Das was a native of Lahore. His parents moved to Gowindwal, where, in consequence of their poverty, Ram Das had recourse to selling boiled grain to support his parents. He was a man of considerable merit, well worthy of the choice of his master. He gave himself up to literary pursuits, in which he expounded his doctrines, which have been incorporated in the Granth. In Lahore he had a meeting with the tolerant Akhbar, who was highly pleased with his accomplishments, and who granted him a piece of land. Here Ram Das restored an old tank which he called Amritsar, or pool of immortality, and built a temple, which he named Harmandar. At another interview, Ram Das convinced Emperor Akber that because many poor people cannot afford food to remit a year's rent for them. Akhbar granted his request, being impressed with the Guru's sympathy, and such an action made the Guru immensely popular among the Jats and the zemindars. In founding the temple in Amritsar, the Guru laid the foundation of the future greatness of the Sikhs as a nation. Ram Das died in March, 1581, having reigned as a Guru for seven years.

Guru Shikhar : Guru Shikhar, a peak at an altitude of 5,676 feet (1722 meters), is the highest point in Rajasthan. It is located at a distance of 15 km from Mount Abu. It has a commanding view of Abu and its surroundings.

This peak is the home to the temple of Dattatreya, an incarnation of Lord Vishnu. There is a huge brass bell outside the shrine, that overlooks the lush greenery of Mount Abu.

Guru Teg Bahadur : Guru Teg Bahadur (April 1, 1621 - November 11, 1675) was the ninth of the Ten Gurus of Sikhism, and he became Guru on March 20, 1665 following in the footsteps of his grand-nephew, Guru Har Krishan. Before he died, he nominated his son, Gobind Rai – who later was renamed - Guru Gobind Singh, as the next, and as it turned out, the last Guru of the Sikhs – in human form.

Tegh Bahadur had established himself at Bakala, near Govindwal, where there was distention about who was the Guru. Being the cherisher of the poor and supporter of the hungry, numerous followers flocked to his banner, and he became a very popular Guru. Tegh Bahadur was a peaceful faqir and aspired to no political power, and he preferred the life of a recluse. He retired for a time to Bengal, where he founded a college for the Sikhs. He lived with his wife, and they had a son, Govind Singh. He gave his time chiefly to devotion and meditation, and often in places away from human habitations.

After some time, Emperor Aurangzeb, whose efforts were directed to converting the whole world to the Mahomedan faith, urged the Sikh Guru to embrace Mahomedanism. Before leaving for Delhi, he hailed his son Govind Singh, then 15 years of age, as the future Guru of the Sikhs. He told Govind Singh he was going to die, but asked him not to leave his body in Delhi. The emperor already had thrown hundreds of Brahmans into jail in the hope they would embrace Islam and spread it to their followers. The emperor had many religious disputations with the Guru, forced him to show miracles, and forced him to make Hindus embrace Islamism. The Guru refused, and eventually the Sikh was thrown in prison and was subject to bodily tortures. The Guru wrote on a piece of paper and declared the sword would fall harmless on it by the effect of the charm which was written upon it. The executioner was now summmoned to test the miraculous charm. The blow was given, and the head of the Guru was rolled on the floor. The paper was then read and said:

he had given his head, but not his secret. The courtiers, tinged with superstition, were struck with horror and surprise. Tegh Bahadur reigned as a Guru for 13 years.

Gurudongmar Lake : Gurudongmar Lake (also known as Gurudogmar Lake) is one of the highest lakes in the world located at an altiude of 16,890 feet (5,148 m).It lies on the North side of the Khangchengyao Range in a high plateau area contiguous to the Tibetan Plateau. The stream emerging from the lake is one of the source-streams of the Tista River.

The lake is named after Guru Padmasambhava, who is also known as Guru Dongmar. It is located close to the Indo-China Border in the province of North Sikkim, Sikkim, India. The lake remains completely frozen in the winter months from November to Mid-May except for one small part of the lake which is supposed to be touched and blessed by the Guru Padmasambhava.

The lake is highly revered by the Sikkimese and Buddhists and the waters are supposed to have healing properties.In recent times the building of a Sikh Gurdwara on the shore of the lake by an Indian Army unit posted in the area has given rise to Sikkimese resentment. Due to the extremely inhospitable surrounding terrain and the difficulties associated with reaching the place, the lake sees only a handful of visitors each year.

Gurukul : A Gurukul is a type of ancient Hindu school in India that is residential in nature with the shishyas or students and the guru or teacher living in close proximity, many a time within the same house. The Gurukul is the place where the students resided together as equals, irrespective of their social standing. The students learns from the guru and also helps the guru in his day-to-day life, including the carrying out of mundane chores such as washing clothes, cooking, etc.

The guru-shishya parampara is a hallowed tradition in Hinduism, and has also carried over into Sikhism. At the end of a shishya's study, the guru asks for a "guru dakshina," since a guru does not take fees. A guru dakshina is the final offering from a student to the guru before leaving the ashram. The teacher may ask something or nothing at all.

Guru-shishya Tradition : The guru-shishya tradition (also guru-shishya parampara or lineage) is a spiritual relationship found within traditional Hinduism which is centered around the transmission of teachings from a guru to a 'sishya'. The term shishya roughly equates to the western term disciple, and in some parts of India is synonymous with the term chela. In a Hindu context, the term guru signifies one who teaches or imparts knowledge. Such knowledge, whether it be Vedic, Agamic art, architecture, music or spirituality, is imparted through the developing relationship between guru and disciple. The principle of this relationship is that knowledge, especially subtle or advanced knowledge, is best conveyed through a strong human relationship based on ideals of the student's respect, commitment, devotion and obedience, and on personal instruction by which the student eventually masters the knowledge that the guru embodies.

The guru-shishya relationship is a practice which has evolved into a fundamental component of Hinduism, since the beginning of the oral traditions of the Upanishads (c. 2000 BC). The term Upanishad derives from the Sanskrit words upa (near), ni (down) and sad (to sit) — "sitting down near" a spiritual teacher to receive instruction in the guru-shishya tradition. An example of this dynamic can be found embodied in the relationship between Krishna and Arjuna in the Bhagavad Gita portion of the Mahabharata, and between Rama and Hanuman in the Ramayana. In the Upanishads, gurus and shishya appear in a variety of settings (husband answering questions about immortality, a teenage boy being taught by Yama, or Death personified, etc.). Sometimes the sages are women and at times the instructions (or rather inspiration) are sought by kings.

Guruvayoor Shri Krishna Temple : The Guruvayoor Shri Krishna Temple is one of the most important and sacred pilgrim centres of Kerala. Located in the Guruvayoor town of Trissur district in Kerala (south India) it is easily accessible by road and rail. The presiding deity is MahaVishnu, in standing posture with four hands carrying Sankhu, Sudarshana chakram,lotus and mace. He is worshipped as BalaKrishna, the full avatar (Purnaavatara) of Mahavishnu. The idol is made of a rare stone known as patalaanjana. The Guruvayoor temple is thought to be at least 5,000 years old, having been installed after Krishna ascended to Vaikuntha. The idol was installed by Brahaspati and Vayu and blessed by Shiva and Parvati. The temple was built by Vishwakarma the divine architect. Over the past thousands of years, Guruvayoor increased in popularity, especially in the 16th century when it had become the most popular pilgrimage centre in Kerala.

The structure of this historic temple is typically Kerala style with gopurams (gateways), repeated mandapas, sreekovil, subsidiary shrines around a courtyard circumbulatory. Precious materials are everywhere, as in a golden flagstaff and flimsy replicas of the arms, legs, ears and other affected parts of worshippers that are given as offerings. The temple faces east with two gopurams (gateways) one on the east and the other in the west. The Eastern 'gopuram' (Kizhakkenada) of the Sri Krishna temple, also known as Bhooloka Vaikuntam, is the main entrance to the shrine. In the centre of the inner courtyard stands a pillared hall known as the 'Nalambalam' or 'Chutambalam' with scores of oil lambs fixed on its walls. Inside the Chutambalam or outer enclosure is the square two-storeyed Sreekovil (main shrine) with three rooms, the innermost of which is the sacred sanctum sanctorum housing the main deity and can be viewed from the temple entrance. This idol of Vishnu, with four arms carrying the conch, the discus, the mace and the lotus, and adorned with a thulasi garland and pearl necklaces, is made of a particular stone called 'patala anjanam'. The walls of the main shrine are filled with beautiful 17th century paintings depicting the stories from the life of Krishna and the roof and the two doors inside are covered by gold. In the eastern side in front of the Chutambalam stands the tall 33.5 mt high gold plated Dwajasthambam (flag post) and adjacent to it is a 7mt high Dipastambham (pillar of lamps) whose thirteen circular receptacles provide a truly gorgeous spectacle when lit. The western gopuram (Padinjarenada) is flanked by two dipastambhams.

Guruvayoor Ekadesi : The festival of Ekadesi is celebrated here in the month of Vrischiyam in Kerala. Besides the devotees, there are those who come to take part in the annual fair. Merchants erect booths in front and behind the temple and carry on trade in various articles. The celebration with in the temple consists of Pujas and processions.

Gusadi Dance of Gonds: Deepavali is the biggest festival for the Raj Gonds of Adilabad district. As the harvest is over and the season is cool and congenial the Gonds dressed in colourful costumes and decorated with ornaments go to neighbouring villages in troupes, singing and dancing. Such troupes are called Dandari dance troupes. Each troupe consist of twenty to forty members. 'Gusadi' is a part of Dandari and consists of two to five members. This starts on the full moon day and goes on till the fourteenth day of the dark fortnight of Deepavali. Each member puts on a turban of peacock feathers and horns of the deer, artificial beard and moustaches and goatskin to cover the body. Dappu, Tudumu, Pipri and Kalikom are the accompaniments. The Dandari troupe dance accompanied by beats of Gumela reaches its climax with regulated steps and rhythm in a circular form.

The Dandari dance starts with stepping slowly towards the left side and swinging the right foot on to the left foot at every step. Every dancer has two small sticks in his hands. First everyone strikes the two sticks in his own hands, then strike at the sticks of the person on the right side then strike his own sticks and then the sticks of the person on the left side. In this way, with steps and striking together of sticks held in hands they play kolattam and come back to the original position. Then they bend down and touch the ground with their sticks and step on to the four sides. This is paying obeisance to the gods. After this they put into order their circular form and lay down the sticks. Then they sing and clap their hands. They sing a group song in duet, one group singing the first line and the second group singing the second line of the song.

Guwahati : Guwahati is a city in India, often considered to be the gateway to the north-east part of the country. A Guwahati suburb, Dispur, is the capital of the Indian state of Assam. The city is between the southern bank of the Brahmaputra river and the foothills of the Shillong plateau. The name Guwahati is derived from two words: guwa (betel nut) and haat (market place). It was situated midway between two powerful kingdoms: the Ahom and the Koch kingdoms. Later when the Koch regions were overrun by the Mughals, Guwahati would intermittently be the seat of a forward Mughal commander. Neither the Mughals nor the Koch could maintain power at Guwahati, however, and it became better known as the seat of the Borphukan, the civil and military authority of the region appointed by the Ahom king.

Gwadar : Gwadar is a coastal town in Balochistan, Pakistan, 650 km by road from Karachi. The population of the town is almost 100,000. Gwadar is the headquarters of Gwadar District. Gwadar is located on the southwestern coast of Pakistan, close to the important Straits of Hormuz, through which more than 13 million bbd of oil passes. It is strategically located between three increasingly important regions of the world: the oil-rich Middle East, heavily populated South Asia and the economically emerging and recource-rich Central Asia.

The Government of Pakistan has initiated several projects, with majority financial and technical assistance from China, to develop Gwadar's strategic location as a goods transit and trade point. The primary project is the construction of a deep-sea port at Gwadar to enable high-volume cargo movement to and from the landlocked Central Asian states. The new port will also encompass conversion facilities to allow for the movement of natural gas as a part of plans for a termination point for the Turkmenistan-Afghanistan-Pakistan natural gas pipeline. The secondary project is a coastal highway connecting Gwadar to Karachi, whose $200 million cost will be completely financed by the Chinese. Gwadar will serve as a port of entry for oil and gas to be transported by land to the western regions of China. China has been promised sovereign guarantees for use of the ports.

Gwadar Bay : Gwadar Bay is located in near the maritime border of Pakistan and Iran. The name is from Persian, Khalij-e Gavader or 'Gulf of Gwadar' on Arabian Sea. It is an inlet of the Arabian Sea indenting the sandy Makran coast at the Iran–Pakistan border. It is about 20 miles (32 km) long and 10 miles (16 km) wide. The Dashtiari River flows into it from the northwest, and the Dasht River from the northeast. The town of Gwadar, Pakistan, lies on the Arabian Sea coast about 30 miles (48 km) to the east of Gwadar Bay.

Gwadar Port : Gwadar Port Gwadar is located at the entrance of the Persian Gulf on Arabian Sea and about 460 km west of Karachi in Balochistan, Pakistan. Gwadar has had immense geostrategic significance on many accounts. In 1993, Pakistan started technical and financial feasibilities for the development of Gwadar Port. The Gwadar port project started on 22 March 2002. The first phase of the project will be completed in December 2005.

Gwalior : Gwalior is a city in Madhya Pradesh, India. It lies 76 miles (122 km) south of Agra with a population of 690,342. It occupies a strategic location in the Gird region of North India, and the city and its fortress have served as the center of several of North India's historic kingdoms. Gwalior is the administrative headquarters of Gwalior District and Gwalior Division. At the heart of Gwalior is its fortress, one of the most formidable in India. It occupies an isolated rock outcrop, and is surrounded by high walls which enclose buildings from several periods. the old town of Gwalior lies at the eastern base of the fortress. Lashkar, formerly a separate town that originated as a military camp, lies to the south, and Morar, also a formerly separate town, lies to the east. Gwalior, Lashkar and Morar are presently part of Gwalior Municipality. Historically and architecturally, Gwalior is interesting first as a very ancient seat of Jain worship; secondly for its example of palace architecture of the best Hindu period (1486-1516); and thirdly as an historic fortress.

H

Habib Wali Mohammad : Habib Wali Mohammad is a very senior and highly regarded ghazal singer. Habib Wali belongs to the Tabani family, an industrial house with large business holdings in Pakistan, including Aero Asia, an airline. (His brother Ashraf Tabani was governor of the province of Sindh around 1988.)

Born in 1921, he received his MBA from Syracuse University in 1947, and then lived in Bombay for about 10 years before moving to Pakistan. He is practically from the very second group of singers to ever record the art from and is still at his peak today. But probably because of his background and place as a member of a well-established family, Habib Wali has never pursued as aggressive and mainstream a career as a singer as others, though is still very highly regarded.

Habibur Rahman : Habibur Rahman is a former chief justice of Bangladesh supreme court. He was the chief advisor of the 1996 caretaker government which oversaw the Seventh parliamentary elections in Bangladesh.

Habiganj : Habiganj is a district of Sylhet division of Bangladesh. With an area of 2636.58 sq km the district is bounded by Sunamganj district on the north, Tripura State of India on the south, Maulvi Bazar and Sylhet districts on the east, Brahmanbaria and Kishoreganjdistricts on the west. Annual average temperature maximum 33.2 C, minimum 13.6 C. Total rainfall 3334 mm. Noted rivers are Khowai, Sutang, Korangi, Kalni, Kushiyara, Gopala, Ratna, Barak. Habiganj subdivision was established in 1874 under Sylhet district and was turned into a district in 1984. It consists of 4 municipality, 36 wards, 124 mahallas, 8 upazilas, 77 union parishads, 1241 mouzas and 2093 villages. The upazilas are Ajmiriganj, Baniachang, Bahubal, Chunarughat, Habiganj Sadar, Lakhai, Madhabpur and Nabiganj.

Hadiqa Kiyani : Hadiqa is one of the most famous pakistani female pop stars. She holds a Masters degree in Psychology. Hadiqa has held several concerts all over the world.She began her career as a child star in musical program "Angan Angan Taray" and used to be the blue eyed girl of Sohail Rana's Rang Barangi Dunya; a weekly musical. She represented Pakistan in International children festivals in Turkey, Jordan, Bulgaria, and Greece and was bestowed upon with top medals.

Hadoti : Hadoti, also known as Hadauti, Hadaoli, or Hadavati, is a region of Rajasthan state in western India. It includes the districts of Bundi, Baran, Jhalawar and Kota, and is bounded on the west by the Mewar region of Rajasthan and on the south by the Malwa region of Madhya Pradesh state.

The name of the region is derived from the Hada Rajputs, a branch of the great Chauhan Rajput clan. The Hadas moved into the region in the 12th century. Hada Rao Deva conquered Bundi in 1241 and Kota in 1264. Kota became a separate state in 1579, and Jhalawar a separate state in 1838.

Haji Ali Mosque : Situated at the end of a 500m causeway protruding into the Arabian Sea is the whitewashed Haji Ali Mosque, containing the tomb of a Muslim saint Haji Ali who is believed to have meditated on these very shores. It is said that Haji Ali was a wealthy Muslim merchant who renounced all his worldly belongings before embarking on a pilgrimage to Mecca. He died in Mecca and the casket miraculously drifted and came to the spot where the mosque and tomb were built by his devotes in the early 19th century. The Mosque lies opposite to the famous Mahalakshmi temple and can be approached from Lala Rajpatrai Marg.

Haji Ali is a handsome example of Islamic architecture standing on an island. In fact, this holy place is visited by many devotees as well as visitors who are attracted by the beauty of the site. The widespread belief is that whoever prays to the deity here is never disappointed. A number of pilgrims come here for thanksgiving. Haji Ali's sister also followed her brother's footsteps and became his companion in ascetic suffering. There is a mausoleum built for her a little distance away on Worli Bay.

The mosque has a narrow concrete pathway about a kilometer built over water to reach the shrine and can only be reached at low tide. The walkway is lined with pitiful wailing beggars. A short flight of marble steps leads into the dargah where the body of the saint is enclosed in a semi-circled tomb,in an exquisite silver frame engraved with all the ninety-nine names of Allah. The top of the tomb is covered with a zari cloth and flowers and other offerings by devotees lie scattered around the tomb. The devotees pray and touch their heads and lips to the cloth. Ladies, as is the case in all mosques, have a separate room for prayers. All visitors need to remove their shoes before entering the shrine.

Hakim Mohammed Said : Hakim Mohammed Said (1920-1998) was a notable scholar and philanthropist of Pakistan. He established Hamdard Pakistan in 1948. Within few years, the herbal medical products of Hamdard became household names. Hakim Mohammed Said wrote or compiled about 200 books. These include books on Religion, Tibb, Health & Sciences, books on Literary, Social and Scientific topics and Travelogues.

Hal Punhya : In Jharghand, the cultivation year begins with the fall of winter. The first day of Magh month which is known as Akhain Jatra or Hal Punhya, means the beginning of ploughing. The farmers, to symbolize this auspicious morning plough two and half circles of their agricultural land. This day is also considered as the symbol of good fortune.

Hala : Hala is a gotra of Jats found in Punjab, Uttar Pradesh states in India and in Sindh area of Pakistan. According to the Bards of the Hala gotra, King Shalvahan, son of Gaj founded his capital at Sorath in Gujarat, where the descendants of King Krishna, brother of King Shalbahan ruled for several generations.

Halda River : Halda river rises from the Badnatali Hill Ranges in the Chittagong Hill Tracts and enters Chittagong district through Fatikchhari upazila. Then it flows southwest keeping off the higher regions to the north and then due south past Bibirhat, Nazirhat, Sattarghat and other important places of Fatikchhari, Hathazari, Raozan and Kotwali of Chittagong which form its basin. It falls into the Karnafuli at Kalurghat. Its total length is about 81 km, of which 29 km up to Nazirhat are navigable by big boats throughout the year; small country boats can ply further up for 16 to 24 km to Narayanhat. Forest resources like timber, bamboo, sungrass from the southern parts of Ramgarh upazila are floated down the river and the bulk of merchandise from Chittagong town is carried up in big cargo boats.

The Halda has a very turbulent tributary, the Dhurung river which rises in the Pakshmimura ranges in the Hill

Tracts, traverses the whole of Fatikchhari upazila running almost parallel to Halda in the east, and joins it at Purba Dhalai about 48.25 km downstream. During the past century the Dhurung carved out for itself several courses. Several attempts were made to confine its current to its original bed but none proved a success. It now joins the Halda to the southwest of the Fatikchhari upazila headquarters leaving its original course of about 24.14 km to decay. The Halda also has several hill streams flowing down into it from the Chittagong Hill Tracts to its east watering and irrigating the entire Halda basin up to Kalurghat where it falls into the Karnafuli River.

Haldighati : Haldighati is a mountain pass in the Aravalli Range of Rajasthan in western India. It connects Rajsamand and Pali districts, 40 kilometres from Udaipur. The name is believed to have come from the turmeric-coloured soil (Turmeric is haldi in Hindi).

Haldighati : Haldighati is a mountain pass in the Aravalli Range of Rajasthan in western India. It connects Rajsamand and Pali districts, 40 kilometres from Udaipur. The name is believed to have come from the turmeric-coloured soil (Turmeric is haldi in Hindi). The mountain pass is historically significant as the location of the Battle of Haldighati, which took place in 1576 between Rana Pratap Singh of Mewar and the Mughal emperor Akbar. The battle between Rana Pratap and Akbar's army under the leadership of Man Singh has been immortalized by a great classic poem by Shyam Narayan Panday. This poem entitled "Haldighati" is must read for all lovers of Hindi poetry.

Haldwani : Haldwani (in the Nainital district) is one of the most populous towns in the Indian state of Uttaranchal. It is known as the "Gateway to Kumaon". In Kumaoni (the local dialect), the place is called "Halduvani", after the tree named "Haldu" which was found in abundance prior to deforestation for agriculture and settlement. Kathgodam is a satellite town of Haldwani. One of the oldest landmarks in Haldwani is the Kalu Sayyad Temple, established when the area was still under dense forest cover. In 1815, after the British defeated Gorkhas, Gardner was appointed as the Commissioner of Kumaon. Later on Gerorge William Trail took over as Commissioner. In 1834 Trail renamed Halduvani as Haldwani.

Halebid : Halebid, (Halebidu in Kannada), located in Hassan district, Karnataka, India, is home of one of the greatest examples of Hoysala architecture. The Temple complex comprises of two temples. In front of these temples there is a big lake. So it is said that it was called Dhwara samudhra which means entrance from ocean. The two nandi bulls which are in front of the temples are monolithic. It is said that soap stones are used for the construction of these temples. But a number of sculptures in the temple are destructed by the invaders. So the temple is incomplete. It is said that the name Halebid means Destroyed City. Now there is an archeological museum in the Temple complex.

The Hoysaleswara Temple, dating back to the 12th century, is astounding for its wealth of sculptural details. The walls of the temple are covered with an endless variety of gods and goddesses, animals, birds and dancing girls. Yet no two facets of the temple are the same. This magnificent temple—guarded by a Nandi Bull—was never completed, despite 86 years of labour. The Jain basadis nearby are equally rich in sculptural detail. Belur and Halebid are 222 and 216 km from Bangalore, respectively. This temple is now being proposed as UNESCO World Heritage Site.

Haleem : Haleem is a soup-like Indian and Pakistani dish, brought to India from Persia. Made of wheat, meat (usually mutton, but sometimes chicken or minced meat), lentils and spices, this dish is cooked for seven to eight hours before it is ready to be served. As a result of being cooked for so long, the dish is in a form of a paste with the taste of spices and meat blending in the wheat.

Haleem is popular in Pakistan and amongst Indian Muslims throughout the world, especially during Ramadaan. In India, haleem is prepared in Hyderabad, during the Ramzan (Ramadaan) season and exported all over the country.

A vegetarian version, substituting vegetables and dry fruits instead of meat, has been developed by a restaurant in India.

Halva : The word halva is used to describe two distinctly different types of confections. One type of candy called halva is popular in India and neighboring countries, and is made with semolina wheat, sugar or honey, and butter or vegetable oil. Raisins, dates or other dried fruits are often included.

Another type of candy called halva is popular in the greater Middle East, the Balkans, and other areas around the Mediterranean. The primary ingredients in this confection are tahini and sugar or honey. Vanilla is typically included. Other ingredients such as pistachio nuts, orange juice, or chocolate are often added to the basic tahini and sugar base, resulting in a variety of flavors.

Hamdard University : Hamdard University is located in Karachi, Sindh, Pakistan. This private university was founded by Hakim Said of Hamdard Foundation. Hamdard University campus in Karachi comprises of Faculty of Humanities and Social Sciences, Faculty of Eastern Medicine, Faculty of Health Sciences and Medicine including Dentistry, Faculty of Management Sciences,

Faculty of Engineering Sciences and Technology including Information Technology, Faculty of Legal Studies and Faculty of Pharmacy, Institute of Advanced Studies and Research, Hafiz Mohammad Ilyas Institute of Pharmacology and Herbal Sciences and Hydro Chemistry Laboratory. University maintains various institutions in downtown Karachi. These include Hamdard School of Law, Hamdard Education Net, Regional Cisco Networking Academy, Hamdard Institute of Management Sciences, Usman Institute of Technology and Hamdard Institute of Information Technology. Hamdard University's sphere of activity in education science and technology is well extended in major cities of Pakistan. The Islamabad campus offers teaching in pharmaceutical sciences, management sciences and information technology. The Faisalabad campus offers programs in Management Sciences, Information Technology and Engineering.

Hameed Nizami : Hameed Nizami (October 3, 1915 - 1962) was an eminent journalist from Pakistan.

He was the founder for Urdu newspaper Nawa-i-Waqt, and played important part in Pakistan movement.

Hamidur Rahman : Hamidur Rahman, better known as Shaheed Sepoy Hamidur Rahman was a Sepoy in Bangladesh Army during the Liberation War. He was born on February 2, 1953 in Khardo Khalishpur village under Jessore district and joined the Army on February 2, 1971, enroled in the Infantry corps. In an attempt to capture the Pakistani Army's position which finally fell to advancing Mukti Bahini column, Hamidur Rahman was killed on October 28, 1971 at Dhalai. He was posthumously awarded the Bir Sreshtho, the highest recognition of bravery of Bangladesh.

Hamidur Rahman : Hamidur Rahman, better known as Shaheed Sepoy Hamidur Rahman was a Sepoy in

Bangladesh Army during the Liberation War. He was born on February 2, 1953 in Khardo Khalishpur village under Jessore district and joined the Army on February 2, 1971, enroled in the Infantry corps. In an attempt to capture the Pakistani Army's position which finally fell to advancing Mukti Bahini column, Hamidur Rahman was killed on October 28, 1971 at Dhalai. He was posthumously awarded the Bir Sreshtho, the highest recognition of bravery of Bangladesh.

Hamirpur : Hamirpur is one of districts in Himachal Pradesh, India. It is famous for the National Institute Of Technology.Hamirpur is a central Distt. of Himachal Pradesh. This is not only the tourism potential Distt. of Himachal Pradesh but also as historical importance. This history of Hamirpur is closely associated with the Katoch dynasty Hamirpur was the part of old Jallandhar-Trigarta empire. Panin referred to the people of this Kingdom as great warrious and fighters. The Katoch dynast became predominating during the period of Raja Hair Chand who ruled from 1700 A.D. to 1740 A.D. It was Raja Hamir Chand who built the fort at Hamirpur and the present town derived its name from this ruler. Situated at an altitude of 785 meters, Hamirpur is a District Headquarters. It is on a busy highway, therefore, tourist coming from Shimla and Chandigarh to Kangra, Dharamsala, Nurpur, Dalhousie, Khajjiar and Chamba were not find the wayside amenities anywhere in district Hamirpur. Even being the thickly populated town the local residents were also not have any place to eat in a proper restaurant. No conference/multipurpose hall was also available in the area.

Hamoodur Rahman : Hamoodur Rahman (born November 1, 1910) was Chief Justice of the Supreme Court of Pakistan and Vice Chancellor of Dhaka University. Justice Hamoodur Rahman was born in Patna, India. He obtained his graduation from the St. Xavier's College of the University of Calcutta and an LLB from London University, studied in Gray's Inn, London, and was called to the Bar in London in 1937.

Hamoodur Rahman began his career as a lawyer in Calcutta High Court in 1938. He was a councillor of the Calcutta Corporation (1940) and Deputy Mayor of Calcutta (1943). Hamoodur Rahman was a member of the Junior Standing Counsel of the province of Bengal from 1943 to 1947. After the partition of India he opted for East Pakistan and came to Dhaka in 1948. He was appointed Advocate General of East Pakistan in 1953 and held it till 1954 when he was elevated to the bench as a judge of the Dhaka High Court.

Justice Hamoodur Rahman was a judge of the Dhaka High Court from 1954 to 1960 and vice chancellor of Dhaka University from November 1958 to December 1960. Hamoodur Rahman was appointed a judge of the Supreme Court of Pakistan in 1960, and was made Chief Justice of Pakistan in 1968 and retired in 1976.

HAMSAT : HAMSAT is a microsatellite weighing 42.5 kg, providing Amateur Radio services for Indian and international Amateur Radio enthusiasts. This satellite carries the in-orbit designation of VO-52, and is an OSCAR series satellite. It was launched by PSLV-C6 on May 05, 2005. The main payload was an Indian Remote Sensing satellite, CARTOSAT-1 weighing 1560 kg. HAMSAT was placed into a polar sun synchronous orbit. It carries two transponders, one built by William Leijenaar (Call Sign: PE1RAH), a Dutch Radio Amateur and graduate engineering student from the Higher Technical Institute at Venlo and the other by enthusiasts at ISRO (Indian Space Research Organisation). The satellite joins many previous satellites in amateur radio service; mostly launched by AMSAT.

Hamzanama : The Hamzanama is an artistic masterpiece created about 1558–1573 under the Mughal emperor Akbar. It originally comprised 1,400 canvas folios. On one side of most folios is a painting, about 54cm x 69cm in area, done in a fusion of Persian and Indian styles. On the other side of most folios is Arabic text in nastaliq script. The folios are ordered, and the text on the back of one folio accompanies the painting on the subsequent folio.

The Hamzanama was designed to augment a story-telling performance of the adventures of Hamza. This romance originated more than 1,000 years ago, probably in Persia, and subsequently spread throughout the Islamic world in oral and written forms. The adventures of Hamza never became defined by a canonical written text. The Hamzanama supports a broad world of possibilities for story-telling and seems to have been created to better enable diverse subjects to make sense of persons like themselves within the world of the romance.

Hangu : Hangu is a town in the Northwest Frontier Province of Pakistan. It is located in the district of Hangu, which gets its náme after this town. Hangu is situated in the upper Miranzai Valley bordering the Samana Range.

Hanif Sanket : Hanif Sanket is a popular Bangladeshi comedian and entertainer. He first gained prominence in the early 1980s when he performed comic skits on Fazle Lohani's variety show Jodi Kichhu Mone Na Koren (If You Don't Mind). Since then, he has become a household name in Bangladesh, and is arguably the nation's favorite entertainer. Sanket's variety show Ittyadi (Et cetera) is one of the most popular programs on Bangladeshi television, and each new episode is anticipated by millions of viewers.

Sanket has a wide following among the Bangladeshi diaspora, and he frequently travels abroad with cultural troupes to perform for expatriate Bangladeshis. He has also released a number of comedy albums, and has acted in television dramas on several occasions.

Hannan Sarkar : Hannan Sarkar (born December 1, 1982 in Dhaka) is a Test cricketer for the Bangladesh cricket team. He made his Test debut aged only 19 as an opening batsman against Sri Lanka in July 2002, but he has not been selected for Bangladesh since playing against New Zealand in October 2004. Along with Sunil Gavaskar, he holds the dubious distinction of being the only Test cricketer to be dismissed with the first delivery of the Test match on three occasions. His record is unique in that it was West Indian Pedro Collins who claimed his wicket on each occasion, the second and third in consecutive matches at the end of May and beginning of June 2004.

Haora River : The Haora River flows through the city of Agartala, it is the major river which flows in the Sadar subdivision of the Western District of Tripura. It is called as saidra in kokborok by the original inhabitants of the state.

Har Mandir : This is one of the holy sites of Sikhs, located in the Chowk area at old Patna. This shrine was built by Maharaja Ranjit Singh in white marble with kiosks on the terrace in commemoration of Guru Gobind Singh, the 10th guru of the Sikhs who was born in Patna in 1660. It is the second of the four great Takhts or Thrones in the Sikh world. There is a museum which exhibits the photos, holy scriptures and personal possessions of the Guru.

Haramosh Peak : Haramosh Peak (also known as Haramosh or Peak 58) is a mountain located in the Karakoram range of Pakistan. Its height is also often given as 7,409m. Haramosh lies in the south-central region of the Rakaposhi-Haramosh Mountains, a subrange of the

Karakoram range. It rises steeply above the north bank of the Indus River, a little ways upstream of its confluence with the Gilgit River.

Harand : Harand is an old city in Pakistan located in Rajanpur district of Punjab. Its original name was Hari Nand, but now it is called Harand. It is supposed that during the attack of Alexender this city was part of Iranian empire. After conquering this area Alexander reached this city and was married to the daughter of Darius. There is detail of this event in famous Persian book Sikander Nama. It should be pointed out that most historians are skeptical of this "story".

Harappa : Harappa is a city in Punjab, northeast Pakistan, located beside a former course of the Ravi River; about 35km southwest of Sahiwal. The modern town is built beside the remains of an ancient fortifed city, which was part of the Cemetery H and the Indus Valley Civilization. The city existed from about 3300 BC until 1600 BC.

Harballabh Fair : The most notable event in Jalandhar is the annual national Harballabh Fair which is held every year from 26th to 29th of December. Prominent exponents of classical music, both vocal and instrumental, from all over the country gathers to provide a rare feast of music for the connoisseur. The Sangeet Sammelan is held in the premises of Devi Talab 1.5 km from the Railway Station. Even Mahatma Gandhi was attracted to the festival in 1929. Jalandhar has been in the thick of the fight for freedom from the British Raj and has produced many patriots. A Desh-Bhagat Memorial Hall has been constructed here to perpetuate the memory of such martyrs.

Hardeol : Hardeol or 'Temple of God' is a Himalayan peak which has an altitude of 7,151 m. It is situated at the end of Milam valley in the Pithoragarh district of Uttaranchal, India. It is to the south of Trishuli peak and north of Rishi Pahar peak on north-south ridge. The best approach is through eastern side through Ikualari glacier and to the right to Trishuli valley towards Hardeol icefall. The first ascent was made by I.T.B.P. team in 1978, led by S.P.Mulasi through Trishuli ridge. The nearest road to Hardeol is Munsiyari

Hardinge Bridge : Hardinge Bridge a steel railway bridge made up of prefabricated trusses and named after Lord hardinge, the Viceroy of India (1910-1916). The bridge crosses the lower ganges at Sara between Paksey and Bheramara stations on the broad gauge railway from Khulna to Parbatipur. The broad gauge lines are laid side by side with a separate footpath on the downstream side. A high-tension electric line is passed over upstream side of the bridge. The headroom of the bridge is rested by the structural frame up to a height of 6.71m from the floor level. Jamuna Multipurpose Bridge Authority (JMBA) has a plan to renovate the bridge so that light and heavy vehicles can also use it.

Hardoi : Hardoi is a city in Lucknow division, Uttar Pradesh state, India. It is the administrative headquarters of Hardoi District. Hardoi district is contiguous of Shahjahanpur and Lakhimpur Kheri districts on the north, Lucknow and Unnao districts on the south, Kanpur and Farrukhabad districts on the west and Sitapur district on the east. Hardoi is located at 110 km from Lucknow (capital of Uttar Pradesh) and 394 from New Delhi (capital of India). The Ganges and several of its tributaries are crossing the south of Hardoi district.

Hargobind Khorana : Dr. Hargobind Khorana was born on 9th January 1922 at Raipur, Punjab (now in Pakistan). Dr.Khorana was responsible for producing the first man-made gene in his laboratory in the early seventies. This historic invention won him the Nobel Prize for Medicine in 1968 sharing it with M.W. Nuremberg and R.W. Holley for interpreting the genetic code and analyzing its function in protein synthesis. They all independently made contributions to the understanding of the genetic code and how it works in the cell.

Khorana, born into a poor family attended D.A.V. High School in Multan, took his M.Sc from Punjab University at Lahore and in 1945 he went to England on a government scholarship and obtained a PhD from the University of Liverpool (1948). Dr. Khorana spent a year in Zurich in 1948-49 as a post-doctoral fellow at the Swiss Federal Institute of Technology and returned to India for a brief period in 1949. He returned to England in 1950 and spent two years on a fellowship at Cambridge and began research on nucleic acids under Sir Alexander Todd and Kenner. His interest in proteins and nucleic acids took root at that time. In 1952 he went to the University of British Columbia, Vancouver on a job offer and there a group began to work in the field of biologically interesting phosphate esters and nucleic acids with the inspiration from Dr. Gordon M. Shrum and Scientific counsel from Dr. Jack Campbell.

In 1960 he joined the University of Wisconsin as Professor and co-Director of the Institute of Enzyme Research and Professor of Biochemistry (1962-70) and became an US citizen. Khorana continued research on nucleic acid synthesis and prepared the first artificial copy of a yeast gene. Dr. Khorana is also the first to synthesize oligonucleotides, that is, strings of nucleotides. These custom designed pieces of artificial genes are widely used in biology labs for sequencing, cloning and engineering new plants and animals. The oligo nucleotides, thus, have become indispensable tools in biotechnology. In 1970 he became the Alfred Sloan Professor of Biology and

Chemistry at the Massachusetts Institute of Technology, USA. Khorana now settled in America, is married to Esther Elizabeth Sibler from Switzerland and they have three children.

Apart from the Nobel Prize, Khorana has won many awards and honors for his achievement. Distinguished Service Award, Watumull Foundation, Honolulu, Hawaii (1968); American Academy of Achievement Award, Philadelphia, Pennsylvania (1971); Padma Vibushan, Presidential Award, India (1972); J.C.Bose Medal, Bose Institute, Calcutta (1972) and Willard Gibbs medal of the Chicago Section of American Chemical Society (1973-74). He was elected a member of the National Academy of Sciences, Washington as well as a Fellow of the American Association for the Advancement of Science. In 1971 he became a foreign member of USSR Academy of Sciences and in 1974 an Honorary Fellow of the Indian Chemical Society.

Khorana's work, which is an important scientific landmark of the twentieth century, has brought closer the day when synthetic DNA may be introduced into the defective human tissues to bring about their repair or treat mentally retarded people and change them into more intelligent and healthy human beings. His synthesis of RNA, capable of replication in laboratory, is a step towards the creation of life artificially. In fact, the researches has opened up a new branch called Genetic Engineering in Science.

Hari Shivaram Rajguru : Hari Shivaram Rajguru (1908 - March 23, 1931) was an Indian revolutionary. He is best known as an accomplice of Bhagat Singh and Sukhdev in the killing of a British police officer in 1928 in order to take revenge for the death of veteran leader Lala Lajpat Rai due to excessive police beating. All three were convicted of the crime and hanged on March 23, 1931.

Rajguru was hiding in Nagpur. He met Dr. K. B. Hedgewar and was hiding in one of the RSS worker's house. But after some days he went to Pune and later was arrested there.

Haridwar : Haridwar (also known as Hardwar) is a holy city in the Haridwar District in the state of Uttaranchal in northern India. Literally meaning Gateway to God, Haridwar is considered one of the seven holiest places according to Hindus, as the devas are said to have left their footprints there. Here pilgrims float diyas on the Ganges, to commemorate their deceased ancestors. The city also stands as a gateway to three other important pilgrimage destinations: Rishikesh, Badrinath, and Kedarnath. In Haridwar you will see a great statue of Shiva at the fork of the river. If you are there for a short visit, it is definitely worth to visit the temple on top of the mountain, with a wonderful view.

Haridwar has very rich ancient religious and cultural heritage. In the ancient scriptures of India, this place is well known by the name of Mayapur. This city is also well known for many other things apart from the holy river Ganges. Haridwar has privilege of having IIT at Roorkee, formerly known as University of Roorkee, founded in 1847 as a first technical institute of India. The city has one of the "navratna PSUs of India" i.e BHEL (Bharat Heavy Electricals India Ltd.). The tomb Piran Kaliar of Shabir Shahib in Roorkee is a living example of religious harmony in India which is visited by the people of all religious sects from all over the world. There is another University in the city called Gurukul Kangri Vishva Vidyalaya apart from the head quarter of Uttaranchal State Public Service Commission also being established at Haridwar. Besides this, Kumbh fair is organized at the interval of every 12 years in this city in which about 1 crore pilgrims from all over the world participate.

Harikatha Kalakshepam : This is the art of extempore story telling for three to four hours. It is introduced into Tamil Nadu from Maharashtra by the Mahratta rulers of Thanjavur. The exponent of this art commands a stage and audience by his knowledge of many languages, by his scholarships in the epics and by handling of Chappalakkattai (a pair of wooden planks) in one hand controlling the movement and tempo.

The themes are drawn from the epics Meenakshi Kalyanam, Sita Kalyanam and Rukmini Kalyanam are popular subjects. The dialogue is forcefully mono-acted in a modulated voice to give the effect of light and shade. The words and music roll as Krishna's chariot wheels at a terrific speed in a high lilting rhythm to carry Rukmini away. In this act music plays a very important role and unless it is carefully fitted and woven into the very texture of the story the artist cannot produce the desired effect.

Hariparbat Fort : Hariparbat Fort is about 5 Kms. from Srinagar where there are holy shrines of the Hindus and the Muslims. This fort which is siluated on a small hillock was built by the Mughal King Akbar.

Hariprasad Chaurasia : Pandit Hariprasad Chaurasia (b. Allahabad, July 1, 1938) is known internationally as the greatest living master of the bansuri, the North Indian bamboo flute. Chaurasia is among a few but growing classicists who have made a conscious effort to reach out and expand the audience for classical music. He is probably the most accessible Hindustani musician who has done a lot to popularize Bansuri and classical music among the masses.

Hariprasad Chaurasia was born into a non musical family. His father was a wrestler. His mother died when he was very young. Hariprasad had to learn music almost in secret, scared of the father who wanted him to become a wrestler. First he started learning vocal music from Pt. Rajaram at the age of 15. Later, he switched to playing the flute under the tutelage of Pt. Bholanath of Varanasi. Much later, while working for All India Radio, he received guidance from the reclusive Smt. Annapurna Devi (daughter of Baba Allaudin Khan).

Pt. Chaurasia is a rare combination of innovator and traditionalist. He has significantly expanded the expressive possibilities of the bansuri through his masterful blowing technique. Hariprasad Chaurasia is one of the busiest North Indian classical musicians, regularly traveling and performing throughout the world.

Chaurasia is among a few but growing classicists who have made a conscious effort to reach out and expand the audience for Hindustani classical music. He is probably the most accessible Hindustani musician who has done a lot to popularize the bansuri and classical music among the masses. The great Indian master of the North Indian bamboo flute has won a number of prestigious awards including the Sangeet Natak Academy (1984), Padma Bhushan (1992), and Padma Vibhushan (2000).

Harishankar Parsai : Harishankar Parsai (1924 – 1995) was a Hindi writer. He was born in Jamnia village of Hoshangabad district in Madhya Pradesh. He completed his M.A. in English from Nagpur University. After pursuing writing alongwith his service for some time, he quit his job and took writing as a full time career. He settled in Jabalpur (M.P) and started a literature magazine called Vasudha. He had to stop the magazine after the publication suffered economic losses.

Har-Ki-Pauri : Har-ki-Pauri in Uttaranchal—the sacred Ghat—was constructed by King Vikramaditya in memory of his brother Bhartrihari. It is believed that Bhartihari came to Haridwar to meditate by the banks of the holy

Ganga. When he died, his brother constructed the Ghat in his name, which later came to be known as Har-Ki-Pauri. This sacred bathing ghat is also known as Brahmakund. The reflection of the golden hues of floral diyas in the River Ganga is the most enchanting sight in the twilight during the Ganga Arti Ceremony. It is the most important ghat on the River Ganga, where a holy dip is a must for every devotee.

Harmandir Sahib : Harmandir Sahib is the most sacred gurdwara in all of Sikhism, located in Amritsar, Punjab, India. It is widely known as the Golden Temple, but its true name is Harmandir Sahib. The temple is the most important sacred shrine for the Sikhs, who travel from all parts of the world to enjoy the blissful environments and offer their thanks by giving prayers. In addition, the sacred shrine is increasingly becoming a tourist attraction for visitors from all over the world.

During 1574, the site of the temple was surrounded by a small lake, in a thin forest. The lake was enlarged and a small township was established during the leadership of the fourth Sikh Guru (Guru Ram Das, 1574-1581). It was during the leadership of the fifth Guru (Guru Arjan, 1581-1606), that full fledged Temple was built. The land on which it was built was gifted to Guru Ram Das by the Mughal emperor Akbar. A Sufi saint Hazrat Mian Mir of Lahore in December 1588 initiated the construction of the building by laying the foundation stone. It was completed in 1601. The temple was later attacked by the Afghans and had to be substantially rebuilt in the 1760s.

Harmonium : During the mid-19th century missionaries brought French made hand-pumped harmoniums to India. The instrument quickly became popular there: it was portable, reliable and easy to learn. Its popularity has stayed intact to the present day, and the harmonium remains an important instrument in many genres of Indian music. It is commonly found in Indian homes. Though derived from the designs developed in France, the harmonium was developed further in India in unique ways, such as the addition of drone stops and a scale changing mechanism.

The harmonium is essentially an alien instrument to the Indian tradition, as it cannot mimic the voice which is considered the basis of all Indian music. Meend (glissando), an integral part of any classical recitation is not possible on the harmonium, and as such, one cannot faithfully reproduce the subtle nuances of a raga on this instrument. The harmonium is thus despised by many connoisseurs of Indian music, who prefer the more authentic yet more technical sarangi, in accomponying khyal singing.

Hartal : Hartal is an Indian term for strike action, used often during the Indian independence movement. It is a mobilisation of mass protest, a total shutdown of workplaces, offices, shops, courts of law, and so on. In addition to being a general strike, it involves the voluntary closing of schools and places of business. It is a mode of bringing mass pressure on a government to make it change an unpopular or unacceptable decision.

Haryana : Haryana is a state in north India. Neighbouring states are Punjab and Himachal Pradesh to the north, Rajasthan to the west and south. The river Yamuna acts as the eastern boundary between Haryana and the states of Uttaranchal & Uttar Pradesh.

Hasan Azizul Huq : Hasan Azizul Huq is a Bangladeshi writer, notable for his short stories. Huq's use of language and symbolism has earned him critical acclaim. His stories explore the psychological depths of human beings as well as portray the lives of the peasants of Bangladesh.

Hasilpur : Hasilpur is a city of east central Punjab between Satluj River and the Indian border. At world's map its position is 29°27'N 72° 39'E. 96 km far from its district Bahawalpur this city is situated in the east.

Hasilpur is too old as the old is Bahawalpur. A Dawod potra by named Jogi Khan Ghumrani's son Hasil Khan settled the city with his own name in 1752. In 1900 there were about 347 houses. Water was supplied by wells, and a small market was north to west in the town.Hasil Khan builded a mosque in 1768.

Hason Raja : Hason Raja literally Hason the king, was a mystical poet and songwriter in Bengal, now Bangladesh. Born at the end of the 19th century 1854 to a traditional Zamindar or landowner family near Sunamgang, Sylhet, though his anchestral home is in Rampasha, Biswanath, Sylhet. Hason indulged himself in material pursuits in his youth. Later, he came to believe worldly pleasures are meaningless and wrote songs that have been described as some of the most thoughtful songs, touching the deepest emotions of the human mind.

Hason's father, Dewan Ali Raja (Choudhury), was a direct descendant of the Hindu king Raja Birendra Singhdev, (who later converted to Islam and became known as Babu Khan). Hason's mother was Ali Raja's second wife, Huramat Jahan Begum. As befitted Hason's ancestry, he was tall, handsome and charming, with a regal manner and dress sense.

Hason's elder half-brother, Ubeydur Raja, died when Hason was a teenager. The death of Ali Raja, about 40 days later, meant Hason became responsible for overseeing his father's vast property at an early age. Despite his youth when taking on this responsibility, he proved to be a very successful Zamindar, acquiring acres of land and many properties in Sylhet. Yet, despite his financially privileged upbringing, Hason is credited with setting up a number of local schools and religious organisations, and is said to have frequently provided for the poor and needy of his community.

Hason Raja had four sons, Khan Bahadur Dewan Ganiur Raja, Hasinur Raja, Khan Bahadur Dewan Eklimur Raja Chowdhury (Kabbo Bisharod) and Aftabur Raja. Dewan Eklimur Raja followed in his footsteps and also wrote poetry and songs; he was also known as the architect of modern poetry of Sylhet area. Dewan Hason Raja donated one third of his property as Waqf in 1918 for the well being of the people and offsprings of his beloved son Eklimur Raja.

Hason Raja's songs are in the folk tradition of Bengal that seeks the ultimate truth beyond the material world. They include songs such as 'Lokey bole', published in his book of songs, Hason Udas. In recent times, they have been modernised and are very popular in both Bangladesh and West Bengal. Many book has been published so far on great mystic poet Hason Raja. Amongst them, one published by his great grandson Dewan Mohammad Tasawwar Raja,(a military officer) could attract the Hason lovers' as a complete book namely, "Hason Raja's Oeuvre" (Hason Raja Shomogro). Hason Raja died in 1922, years before his contribution to the poetry of Bengal was mentioned in lectures at Oxford University by Nobel poet laureate Rabindranath Tagore.

Hassan Sardar : Hassan Sardar (born October 22, 1957) is a former field hockey player from Pakistan, who won the golden medal with the Men's National Hockey Team at the 1984 Summer Olympics in Los Angeles, California. A Karachi native, Sardar graduated from Habib Public School. Arguably the best centre forward Pakistan has ever produced, he started his international career in the early 1980s and played his first World Hockey Cup in 1982. In the 1982 Asiad tournament in Karachi, he helped crush India with a hat-trick as Pakistan triumphed 4-1. He was instrumental in leading Pakistan to a gold medal at the 1984 Olympics in Los Angeles. He later managed the Pakistani Hockey Team.

Hastinapura : In the Hindu epic Mahabharata, Hastinapura is the capital and the kingdom of the Kauravas, the descendents of Kuru, which include the Pandavas. The throne of this city is the prize over which the great war of the epic is fought.

Hatha Yoga Pradipika : The most fundamental text of Hatha Yoga is the Hatha Yoga Pradipika, a Sanskrit classic written by Swami Swatamarama, a disciple of Swami Goraknath. It is said to be the oldest surviving text on the Hatha Yoga.

The book was written in 15th century CE. The work is derived from older Sanskrit texts and Swami Swatamarama's own yogic experiences. It includes information about asanas, pranayama, chakras, kundalini, bandhas, kriyas, shakti, nadis and mudras among other topics.

Hathni Kund : A short drive from the town of *Yamunanagar* begins the Sal forest reserve of Kalesar. At Paonta Sahib the river *Yamuna* crosses over the last lap of the Himalayan foot hills. It flows into the plains of *Haryana*. And, the waters of the western Yamuna Canal are caught in the barrage at Tajewala. Each of these centers is within 5 km. The tourism center of Haryana Tourism at Hathni Kund forms a link between these attractions. Hathni Kund is a delightful location, Built on a raised plinth, the complex over looks the flowing waters of the Yamuna. In the far distance, stand the foothills of the Himalayas slowly blending into the skyline.

Hathni Kund is not the usual quiet retreat it seems at a glance. The summers bring groups of adventurous river rafters. Launching off on an expedition from Paonta Sahib, the rafts bob on till Hathni Kund. The rapids in this stretch are of medium intensity. Perfect for amateurs. A number of expeditions have been run already. Adding a special appeal to rafting is the facility to camp out in the lawns of this complex. Rafting expedition, camping out at night and trekking in the Kalesar forest reserve are the major attractions.

Gangore is celebrated on Chet Sudi-3 (Mar-Apr). Idols of Ishar and Gangore are taken out in procession and songs in their praise are sung till they are immersed into water. This spring festival is held in honor of Gauri, the goddess of abundance. Girls dress up in their finest clothes and pray for a spouse of their choice, while married ladies do the same for the happiness of their husbands. Girls worship the goddess throughout the preceding fortnight. Colorful images of Gauri, beautifully dressed and bejeweled, are taken out in procession with the town band. Thousands of people take part in the procession of the Gangore image from village to village.

Hauz Khas : Hauz Khas is an area in Delhi, India. It has had an important place in Delhi's history. Today, it is a major tourist and commercial sector. Alauddin Khilji(1296-1316) excavated a large tank here for the use of the inhabitants of Siri. Hauz Khas is the second city of medieval Delhi. It was originally known as Hauz-i-Alai after Khilji. Firuz Shah Tughlaq (1351-88) re-excavated the silted tank and raised several buildings on its southern and eastern banks which are known as Hauz-Khas or royal tank. the enclosure wall is partly modern.

A building of historical importance within this enclosure is the tomb of Firuz Shah Tughlaq, which was repaired during the reign of Sikandar Lodhi in 1507 AD, as is evidenced from an inscription on the entrance. The multi-storeyed wings consisting of series of halls and chambers on the north and west of Firuz Shah's Tomb were built by him in about 1354 AD. to serve as a madrasa or college for theological training. Staircases lead down to the tank from the upper storey of the madrasa. At the northern extremity of the enclosure is a small mosque. One of the old entrances to the enclosure is from the west, now closed. The octagonal and square chhatris standing here were built as tombs over the graves possibly of teachers attached to the madrasa.

Taimur, who invaded Delhi in 1399, was highly impressed by the tank and buildings around it, but wrongly ascribed its construction to Firuz Shah Tughlaq. Now Hauz Khas is one of the elitest South Delhi areas. Although Hauz Khas Village is not always kept in perfect condition, it houses exclusive boutiques and is home to several excellent restaurants, and is an expensive shopping district. It is surrounded by Safdarjung enclave, Green Park, Deer Park and the Indian Institute of Technology, Delhi.

Havaldaar Lalak Jan Shaheed : Hav. Lalak Jan of the Northern Light Infantry (NLI) was one of those many who as a junior leader fought from the forefront to thwart heavy Indian attacks. He volunteered himself to be deployed on the front positions located at the jagged peak in May 1999.

Hav. Lalak driven back many aggressive ventures by the enemy and imposed colossal losses on them. On July 7, Hav. Lalak sustained serious injuries as enemies pounded the area with heavy mortar shelling.

But despite being injured, he retained his position and frustrated the Indian assault. He, however, succumbed to his injuries at the same post he was defending. Hav. Lalak was awarded with the Nishan-i-Haider for his dauntless courage and devotion.

Havelian : Havelian is located at the westmost end of the Karakoram Highway that runs along the Silk Route to China. It is second municipality in the Abbottabad District, in the Hazara region of the North-West Frontier Provice of Pakistan.

Hawa Mahal : This 'Palace of the Wind' (Hawa Mahal) is a part of the city palace. This is the most famous building in Jaipur. It is build for the ladies of the harem by Sawai Pratap Singh. The monument was originally conceived with the aim of enabling ladies of the royal household to watch the everyday life and royal processions of the city.

Hawke's Bay : Hawke's Bay is a beach in Pakistan situated a couple of kilometers away from Sandspit Beach near Karachi. Like Sandspit it is rocky beach with natural beauty. Visitors enjoy swimming and camel riding.

Hawla Tenure : Hawla Tenure an intermediate right developed in the agrarian relations of south and southeast Bengal in the nineteenth century. The rise of Madhyasvatvas or intermediate interests standing between a zamindar and cultivating Raiyats was a direct result of permanent settlement. The greatest challenge to the security of zamindars after the Permanent Settlement was the Revenue Sale Law commonly known as Sunset Law. Under this law, the lands of the defaulting proprietors were made liable to be sold at public auctions for recovery of public revenue. Under the operation of this law, a great number of zamindaris, including the mammoth ones changed hands immediately after the introduction of the Permanent Settlement. In response to the crisis, many Bengal zamindars created intermediate interests between themselves and actual cultivators. The hawla tenure was one of them.

Hayagriba Madhava Temple : The Hayagriba Madhava Temple at Hajo is an important place of pilgrimage both for Hindus and the Buddhists. The image of Vishnu installed at the shrine resembles that of Jagannath at Puri in Orissa. A curious feature of this temple is that it is regarded as a Buddhist shrine by Buddhist Lamas and Butiyas, who profess Buddhism. They believe that the Buddha attained Nirvana at this place. This temple had been destroyed by Kalapahar and was rebuilt in 1543 by the Koch king Raghudev. A smaller temple nearby was built by Ahom king Pramatta Singh where 'Doul' is celebrated on a grand scale every year. There is a large pond here inhabited by a giant turtle.

Hayatabad : Hayatabad is a modern residential area at south-eastern fringe of Peshawar the capital of the North-West Frontier Province, Pakistan. It is close to the Khyber Agency which leads to Khyber Pass, a prominent route through the Hindu Kush mountains to Landi Kotal, the highest point of the pass, and the Afghan border. Hayatabad developed as a residential area in Peshawar in the late 1970s. It is divided into seven phases (or zones) for residential and commercial purposes, and also includes a suitable industrial area. Out of the seven phases, six are fully developed, while the seventh is reserved for future needs. There are several different schools, colleges, a national University, hospital, private clinics, parks, shopping malls, and offices to facilitate the residents.

Hazara Division : Hazara Division is located in NWFP, Pakistan. The capital of Hazara Division is Hazara. The population of Hazara Division is estimated to be over 4.5 million in 2005. The total area of Hazara Division is 18013 km^2, of which District Haripur has an area of 1763 km^2 and 0.7 million population; District Abbottabad has an area of 1802 km^2 and 1 million population; District Mansehra has an area of 5957 km^2 and 1.4 million population; District Batagram has an area of 910 km^2 and 0.5 million population and District Kohistan has an area of 7581 km^2 and 0.6 million population. University of Hazara is provides higher education to people of the region.

Hazarganji Chiltan National Park : Hazarganji Chiltan National Park, is another beautiful national park of Pakistan. The area is mountainous with precipitous slopes divided by ravines. The Chiltan Hills and Hazar Ganji Range lie west and east, respectively, of the north-south Chiltan divide. It can easily be reached from the provincial capital Quetta and attracts many visitors. Facilities include a museum, picnic spots and accommodation in rest houses.

Hazaribagh : Hazaribagh town is the headquarters of Hazaribagh district, Jharkhand state, India. Etymologially, the word Hazaribagh is made of two Hindi words, hazar meaning 'thousand', and bagh meaning 'garden'. Hence the literal meaning of Hazaribagh is 'City of thousand gardens'.

Hazaribagh town is located at a height of 2019 feet above sea level. The town is like a health resort. Hazaribagh Lake offers good water sports and peaceful picnics and outings, whereas Canary Hill, which lies very close to the town, has a well-laid out park and has three small lakes. From the top of the hill, one can have a panoramic view of the scenic beauty around and below.

There is a jail in Hazaribagh which housed many leaders of the Indian freedom movement. The popular leader Jayaprakash Narayan was put under arrest at this jail during the Quit India Movement of 1942. His escape from this high security prison and the support he received from the local people is one of the legends of the Indian freedom movement.

Hazariprasad Dwivedi : 'Acharya' Hazariprasad Dwivedi (1907 – 1979) was a Hindi novelist, literary historian, essayist, critic and scholar. He penned numerous novels, collections of essays and a historical outline of Hindi literature.

Hazrat Baba Fariduddin Masood Ganjshakar : Hazrat Baba Fariduddin Masood Ganjshakar was born in 1188 AD (584 Hijri) at Kothewal village of Multan district. Hazrat Jalaluddin Suleman was his father and Maryam Ji was his mother. He was a disciple of Khawja Qutbuddin Bakhtiar Kaki (Dehliwala). Baba Farid is recognised as the first acclaimed poet of Punjabi language. His verses have been collected in Guru Granth Sahib under the chapter Farid's Sayings by Guru Nanak Dev Ji. Jagat Gur Nanak Dev Ji, while on his way to Sindh, had made a brief stop at Pakpattan to visit the shrine of Baba Farid. The place where he had set his foot is called Tibba Nanak Sar. Baba Farid departed from this world on Tuesday, 7th May 1280 AD (679 T-lijri) and since then his mazar (tomb) is the pride of Pakpattan. Khwwj,a Nizamuddin Aulia constructed his tomb. Mazar has two doors, namely Noori darwaza and Bahishti darwaza. Bahishti darwaza opens once a year and during the fair thousands of people pass through it. It (door) is made of silver and floral designs are laid in gold sheet. Thousands of devotees come to visit the shrine daily from within the country and from abroad. His death anniversary is celebrated every year on the 5th of Muharram.

Hazrat Shah Jalal : Shah Jalal (R) a major Sufi saint of Bengal. His full name is Shaikh Jalaluddin. Shah Jalal (R) commands great respect of Muslims of the subcontinent. He lies buried at Sylhet, Bangladesh.

Shah Jalal's name is associated with the Muslim conquest of Sylhet. Tradition goes that a Hindu king named Gaur Govinda ruled the Sylhet area. Burhanuddin, a Muslim who lived in the territory under his control once sacrificed a cow to celebrate the birth of his son. But a kite snatched a piece of flesh of the slaughtered cow and it fell from its beak on the house of a Brahmin. According to another tradition, the piece of flesh fell on the temple of the king himself, which he took as a great offence. At the order of the king, Burhanuddin's hands were said to have been cut off and his son killed. Burhanuddin went to gaur and submitted a prayer to Sultan shamsuddin firuz shah for justice from him. The sultan accordingly sent an army under the command of his nephew Sikandar Khan Ghazi, who was however, defeated twice by Gaur Govinda. The sultan then ordered his sipahsalar (armed forces chief) Nasiruddin to lead the war. During the same time Shah Jalal (R) with his 360 followers reached Bengal and joined the Muslim army in the Sylhet campaign. This time the Muslim army won, Gaur Govinda fled the country and Sylhet came under Muslim rule. His shrine is a significant place of interest in Sylhet.

Hazur Sahib : Hazur Sahib is located on the bank's of Godavari river at Nanded in Maharashtra State of India. This is where Guru Gobind Singh Ji left this world. One of the five most sacred places in Sikhism. The inner room of the temple is called Angitha Sahib and is built over the place where Guru Gobind Singh Ji was cremated in 1708. Sikh historical records show that Guru Gobind Singh Ji ordered his Sikhs not to create a monument to commemorate his leaving this world. Anyone who defied this order, their offspring would perish as a result. Maharaja Ranjit Singh ordered it's construction. It is indeed interesting that most of Maharaja Ranjit Singh's offspring experienced this fate, either through bad luck or unusual circumstances. The temple was finished in 1839, later that year Maharaja Ranjit Singh died.

Hazuri Bagh : Hazuri Bagh is a garden in Lahore, Pakistan, bounded by the Lahore Fort (east side), Badshahi

Mosque (west side), the Samadhi of Ranjit Singh (north side) and the Roshnai Gate (south side). In the center is stands the Hazuri Bagh Baradari, built by Ranjit Singh. The garden was planned and built under the supervision of Faqir Azizuddin. After its completion, it is said, Maharajah Ranjit Singh, at the suggestion of Jamadar Khushhal Singh, ordered that marble be removed from various mausoleums of Lahore to construct a baradari (pavilion) here. This task was given to Khalifa Nooruddin. Elegant carved marble pillars support the baradari's delicate cusped arches. The central area, where Ranjit Singh held court, has a mirrored ceiling. Both the garden and the baradari, originally a 45-foot, three-storey square with a basement approached by fifteen steps, suffered extensive damage during the fratricidal Sikh wars and was only reclaimed and laid out according to the original plan during the British period. On 19 July 1932, the uppermost story collapsed and was never reconstructed.

H D Deve Gowda : H. D. Deve Gowda, a staunch crusader of socio-economic development and an ardent admirer of the rich cultural heritage of India, was born on May 18, 1933 in Haradanahalli village of Holenarasipura taluk, Hassan District in Karnataka.

A Civil Engineering Diploma holder, Shri Deve Gowda plunged into active politics at the early age of 20 when, after completing his education, he joined the Congress Party in 1953 and remained a member till 1962. Coming from a middle class agrarian background and exposed to the hardships of farmer's life, young Gowda vowed to become a fighter who would take up the cause of poor farmers, under privileged and oppressed sections of society.

Starting from lower strata of the democratic set-up, Shri Gowda ascended the political rungs gradually. He earned himself a niche in the minds of people while serving as the President of Anjaneya Co-operative Society and later as a member of Taluk Development Board, Holenarasipura.

Hoping to set right the inequalities prevailing in society, he always dreamt of an ideal utopian State. When just 28 years old, the youthful Gowda contested as an Independent and was a runaway success from day one when he first became a member of the Karnataka Legislative Assembly in 1962. An effective Speaker on the floor of the Assembly, he was acclaimed by one and all, including his seniors. Holenarasipur constituency sent him to the Assembly for three more consecutive terms i.e., the Fourth (1967-71); the Fifth (1972-77) and the Sixth (1978-83) Assemblies. His service as the Leader of Opposition in the Assembly, from March 1972 to March 1976 and November 1976 to December 1977, won him laurels.

Shri Deve Gowda resigned his membership of the Sixth Assembly on November 22, 1982. As a member of the Seventh and the Eighth Assembly, he served as the Minister of Public Works and Irrigation. His tenure as Irrigation Minister saw the switching on of many irrigation projects. He resigned from the Cabinet in 1987 protesting against insufficient allocation of funds for Irrigation.

A crusader for freedom and equality, he earned the wrath of the powers that be at the Centre in 1975-76, and was imprisoned during the days of emergency. Shri Deve Gowda utilised this period of forced rest to enrich his knowledge through exhaustive reading. This, and the interaction between him and other stalwarts of Indian politics who were also jailed during that period, helped him mould his personality and perspective. He was a much more seasoned and determined person when he emerged out of his confinement.

Elected to Parliament from Hassan Lok Sabha constituency in 1991, he was instrumental in bringing the problems of the State—especially of farmers—to the forefront. He earned respect for his forthright espousal of the plight of farmers, in Parliament. He also earned a name for practising and upholding the prestige and dignity and Parliament and its institutions.

Shri Deve Gowda became the President of Janta party twice at State level and President of State Janata Dal in 1994. He was the driving force behind the Janata Dal's rise to power in the State in 1994. He was elected as the leader of the Janata Dal Legislative Party and on December 11, 1994 he assumed office as the 14th Chief Minister of Karnataka. He then contested as a candidate from Ramanagar Assembly constituency and won by a thumping majority.

His prolonged experience in active politics and his strong base at the grassroots level enabled him to plunge straightway into the task of tackling many problems faced by the State. His political acumen was tested again when he brought the Idgah Maidan issue at Hubli to the forefront. It was a ground that belonged to the minority community and was the butt of political controversy. Shri Gowda successfully brought about a peaceful solution to the issue.

In January 1995, Shri Gowda toured Switzerland and attended the Forum of International Economists. His tours to European and Middle Eastern countries were a testimony to his achievements as a dedicated politician. His tour to Singapore, which brought in the much needed foreign investment to the State, proved his business acumen.

Since the 70s, friends as well as foes have been commenting on his singular pre-occupation with politics and its processes. His politics, says Shri Gowda, is the politics of the people and he is happy when he is surrounded by people and is doing something for them.

Shri Gowda is known for giving patient hearing to all shades of opinions and is equally at home with the elite when they come calling. Affectionately called the 'son of the soil' (dharti ke lal), he has proved to be one of the most ardent supporters of liberalisation with a human face.

In 1989, his group of the Janata Party fared poorly in Karnataka winning just 2 of the 222 Assembly seats it contested; Shri Gowda himself tasting defeat for the first time in his career losing in both constituencies he contested. He is therefore, no stranger to the fickleness of political fortunes.

The defeat lent a sharper edge to his pursuit to regain lost honour and power, and spurred him to re-examine his own style of politics. He made friends in Karnataka and Delhi, and put aside his bitter feuds with political rivals. Shri Gowda is a person with a life style that is simple, a profile that is low, but assertive and effective.

Before his political initiation, Shri Gowda had been a contractor taking up minor works. The seven years that he spent as an Independent helped him observe party politics from outside. Ever a workaholic, he was always seen engrossed with books and periodicals in the legislature library. His re-election in 1967 gave him more confidence and in 1969 when the Congress split, he joined the Congress (O) headed by Shri Nijalingappa, which was in power in Karnataka then. But Shri Gowda's big chance came after the rout of Congress (O) in the 1971 Lok Sabha elections. He emerged the leader of a truncated opposition hit by the Indira Gandhi _. Married to Smt. Chennamma, the couple have four sons and two daughters. One of the sons is an MLA in Karnataka and another one was elected to the Lok Sabha. The leadership of the Third Front (a group of regional parties and Non-Congress and Non-BJP combine) leading to Prime Ministership – came to Shri Gowda without him seriously aspiring for it.

Shri Deve Gowda resigned as the Chief Minister of Karnataka on May 30, 1996 to be sworn in as the 11th Prime Minister of India.

HDFC Bank : HDFC Bank, one amongst the firsts of the new generation, tech-savvy commercial bank of India, was set up in January 1995, after the Reserve Bank of India allowed setting up of Banks in the private sector. The Bank was promoted by the Housing Development Finance Corporation Limited, a premier housing finance company (set up in 1977) of India.

Headlines Today : Headlines Today is an English language Indian news and information television channel sponsored by the India Today Group. It is a sister channel of the Hindi Aaj Tak news channel.

Heavy Industries Taxila : Heavy Industries Taxila is backbone of Pakistan's army, being a combination of multiple industries that has grown into a large military complex since 1980. It consists of six major production units and there support facilities. Heavy Industries Taxila is one of the large defence facilities in Pakistan with a manpower of over 6,500 highly skilled personnel and engineers trained in the field of defence production. Out of this 6,500 about 31% are uniformed personnel.

Hega Festival : In Nagaland, the Hega festival is one of the most important festivals among the Zeliang people. It falls in the month of February from 10th to 15th every year. It is a festival invoking the Almighty God to shower his blessings upon his people with richness, luck and courage. It is also a festival of joy, rest and togetherness. The festival lasts for five days.

Heikru Hitongba : Heikru Hitongba, the boat race, is an annual function which takes place on eleventh Langban on the canal in the Bijoy Govinda area in Manipur. It is related to the Govindajee temple as the deities from the temple and palace are made to preside during the function. Offerings of pieces of gold and silver are made before the presiding deities by the Brahmins and the leaders of the two crew parties. The crew-men show a spirited performance. Each party tries its level best to complete with the other or even to overthrow the other boat.

Hemayet Uddin : Hemayet Uddin more widely known by his first name Hemayet, was one of the most fierce freedom fighters in the 1971 Liberation War of Bangladesh. For his valor, he was awarded the honor Bir Bikrom (Powerful Hero), a national award for gallantry. Apart from centrally cordinated Mukti Bahini and Mujib Bahini, a vast numbers of local resistance armies were formed duing the liberation war of Bangladesh against Pakistani occupation. Hemayet Bahini (Hemayet Army), headed by Hemayet was one of the biggest and successful such groups. It operated in the Faridpur region of the country. In influence and impact, it was perhaps only second to Kaderia Bahini of Tangail, created by the legendary Kader Siddique.

Hemis High Altitude National Park : This park was setup in the year 1981at Leh. It has an area of 3550sq.km. The nearest town and airport is Leh,30km from the park. The nearest rail head Jammu is at a distance of 695km.

The elevation of park varies from 3140m to 5854m from the mean sea level. The temperature varies from 20oC to -40oC. The fauna which can survive in these topographic and climatic conditions comprise snow leopard, srapu, bharal, ibex, red fox, rhesus macaque, Hanuman languor, wolf and marmot. The common birds are snow cock, chukor, magpie, Himalayan whistling thrush etc.

Heren : It is a traditional theatre form of Himachal. This dance is performed during Lohri festival by 10-15 members. This style is mostly performed in hilly regions of Jammu.

Hermann Gundert : Rev. Dr. Hermann Gundert (b. February 4, 1814,Stuttgart, Germany – d. April 25, 1893;) was a German missionary, whose greatest achievements include the compilation of the Malayalam grammar book Malayalabhaasha Vyakaranam (1868) and the first Malayalam-English dictionary (1872) and the translation of the bible into the malayalam language. He worked primarily in Malabar coast, South India, in what is today called as Kerala. He was also a close friend of malayalam critic and short story writer, Vengayil Kunhiraman Nayanar. Hermann Gundert obtained a doctoral degree from Tubingen. In Kerala, he took a deep interest in the local culture and the Malayalam language, attempting a systematic grammar of the language for the first time. This was one of the prominent non-Sanskrit-based approaches to Indic grammar. Gundert is held in high regard to this day, among linguistic experts in Kerala, for the high scholastic aptitude exhibited in his work. He published two Malayalam journals, of which Rajya Samacharam is considered to be the first newspaper in Kerala.

Though Gundert came to Kerala as a missionary, he was destined to contribute to Malayalam Language more than any Malayali. People of Kerala still remember him with reverence and affection. In Thalasshery(Tellicherry), people have honored him by a statue in the city. He was the grandfather of Hermann Hesse, German novelist and Nobel Laureate.

Hero Cycles Ltd : Hero cycles ltd. is a Ludhiana based cycle company with the highest market share. The Hero Cycles Factory in Ludhiana is considered to be the largest and the most efficient factory in the world

Hijli Detention Camp : Hijli Detention Camp, located in Hijli, beside Kharagpur, in the district of Midnapore

West, West Bengal, India, was significant in the struggle against the British Raj in the early 20th century. The large numbers of those who participated in the armed struggle or the non-cooperation movement could not be accommodated in ordinary jails. The British Government decided to establish a few detention camps; the first one was located in Buxa Fort followed by the creation of the Hijli Detention Camp in 1930. A significant moment in the struggle against British rule occurred at The Hijli Detention Camp on Sept. 16, 1931 when two unarmed detainees, Santosh Kumar Mitra and Tarakeswar Sengupta, were shot dead by the British Police and Subhas Chandra Bose came to Hijli to collect their bodies. National leaders, including Gurudev Rabindranath Tagore, voiced strong protests against the British Raj over this incident.

The Hijli Detention Camp was closed in 1937 and was reopened again in 1940. In 1942 the camp was again closed and the detainees were transferred elsewhere. In May 1950, the first Indian Institute of Technology was established here. in 1997 the former detention camp buildings were converted to house the Nehru Museum of Science and Technology.

Hikat : Hikat, danced by women, is a modification of a game played by children. Forming pairs, the participants extend their arms to the front gripping each other's wrists and with the body inclined back, go round and round at the same spot.

Himachal Pradesh : Himachal Pradesh, formally the Punjab Hill States, is a mostly mountainous state in northwest India. Neighbouring regions are Tibet to the east, Jammu and Kashmir to the north and northwest, Punjab to the southwest, Haryana and Uttar Pradesh to the south and Uttaranchal to the southeast. It is 55,658 sq km (21,490 sq mi) and the population in 1991 was

5,111,079. The state capital is Shimla (formerly British India's summer capital under the name Simla), other major towns are Dharamsala, Kangra, Mandi, Kullu, Chamba, Dalhousie and Manali. The western Himalaya lies in the north and east and the smaller Shiwalik (or Shivalik) range in the south. The Ghaggar River originates in the Shivalik range. The main rivers are the Sutlej (home of the Bhakra Nangal Dam Project) and the Beas. The bridge on the Sutlej River at Kandraur, Bilaspur District is one of the highest in Asia.

Himalaya : The Himalaya is a mountain range in Asia, separating the Indian subcontinent from the Tibetan Plateau. By extension, it is also the name of the massive mountain system which includes the Himalaya proper, the Karakoram, the Hindu Kush, and a host of minor ranges extending from the Pamir Knot. The name is from Sanskrit himalaya, a tatpurusha compound meaning "the abode of snow".

Together, the Himalaya mountain system is the planet's highest and home to all fourteen of the world's highest peaks. the Eight-thousanders, including Mount Everest. To comprehend the enormous scale of Himalaya peaks, consider that Aconcagua, in the Andes, is at 6,959 m the highest peak outside the Himalaya, while the Himalaya system has over 100 peaks exceeing 7,200 m.

Perspective view of the Himalaya and Mount Everest as seen from space looking south-south-east from over the Tibetan Plateau. The Himalaya stretches across five nations, Bhutan, China, India, Nepal, and Pakistan.

It is the source of three of the world's major river systems, the Indus Basin, the Ganga-Brahmaputra Basin and the Yangtze Basin. An estimated 750 million up people live in the watershed area of the Himalayan rivers, which also includes Bangladesh.

Himalayan Subtropical Pine Forests : The Himalayan subtropical pine forests are a subtropical coniferous forest ecoregion covering portions of Bhutan, India, Nepal, and Pakistan. The ecoregion extends across the lower elevations of the great Himalaya range, from Pakistan's Punjab Province in the west through Azad Kashmir, the Indian states of Jammu and Kashmir, Himachal Pradesh, and Uttaranchal, Nepal, the Indian state of Sikkim, to Bhutan in the east. The predominant tree in the ecoregion is the drought-resistant Chir Pine.

Himu : Himu is a popular fictional character created by the famous Bangladeshi writer Humayun Ahmed in his novels. Himu's real name is Himalaya. When Himu was young, his psychopathic father killed his mother as to prevent her from interfering with the way he intended to bring him up. Himu is actually the shortened form of "Himalaya". His father bestowed this name upon him because the Himalayas symbolized greatness. He could have also been named "Akash" (Sky), but the sky cannot be touched. His father tried to make him a "Mahapurush" (a great man, possibly with supernatural powers) by making him familiar with the evil, greedy, mean and cruel sides of the world.

Himu's characteristics are very strange. He comes from a middle class family. Himu is popular specially for teenagers due to his weird characteristics. The way he responds to situations is very unpredictable. For instance, he can give a 500 taka note to a beggar or a rikshawpuller or he can spend a night in railstation—totally randomly. He attracts people by his great sense of humour. Himu also has a prophetic power, but he denies the fact. Some people think Himu has similarity with the characters created by famous Russian writer Dostoyevsky. Sometimes, his tendency of avoiding girls might give some people the impression that he is impotent or homosexual. However,

Himu has a girlfriend named Rupa whom he hardly contacts.

Himu's appearance is quite different also. He always wears a yellow kurta and carries a bag (Santiniketan Style). His cousin "Badal" is highly influenced by his vagabond like character and Badal tries to behave like Himu all the times. There is a chance readers can get annoyed because of some of his extreme or unexplainable activities. For instance, having cockroach soup. Although it is mentioned in the novels that the name "Himu" is short for Himalaya, Humayun Ahmed admits that he actually got the idea from his own name, Humayun. When asked about if Humayun himself is Himu or not, he says he is half Himu, and half Misir Ali (another popular charecter from his books). In the foreword to one of his books, he mentions that while writing stories about Himu, he feels that he himself is Himu and this feeling isn't there while he is writing any other book.

Hina Jilani : Hina Jilani (born 1953 Lahore) is a well-known lawyer and human-rights activist in Pakistan. She is a law partner and co-founder with her sister Asma Jahangir of Pakistan's first all-female law practice in 1980. She is also the United Nations Special Representative of the Secretary General on Human Rights Defenders. She is one of the founders of the civil society group, the Human Rights Commission of Pakistan. She has recently been appointed on an UN International Fact-Finding Commission on the Darfur.

Hinayana : Hinayana is a term coined by the Mahayana, which appeared publicly around the 1st century CE. There are differing views on the use and meaning of the term, both among scholars and within Buddhism. The meaning of 'vehicle' here is probably best understood as a 'movement', rather than some sort of school or tradition.

Hindi : Hindi an Indo-European language spoken mainly in North, Central, and Western India, is one of the national languages of India. It is part of a dialect continuum of the Indo-Aryan family, bounded on the northwest and west by Panjabi, Sindhi, and Gujarati; on the south by Marathi; on the southeast by Oriya; on the east by Bengali; and on the north by Nepali.

Hindi also refers to a standardized register of Hindustani that was made one of the official languages of India. The grammatical description in this article concerns standard Hindi.

Hindi is often contrasted with Urdu, another standardized form of Hindustani that is the official language of Pakistan and some states in India. The primary differences between the two are that Standard Hindi is written in Devanagari and has supplemented some of its Persian and Arabic vocabulary, with words from Sanskrit; while Urdu is written in a variant of the Persian alphabet and draws heavily on Persian and Arabic vocabulary. The term "Urdu" also includes dialects of Hindustani other than the standardized languages.

Hindko : Hindko is an ancient language spoken in northern Pakistan. The word "Hindko" literally translates to "Indian Mountains." The word "Hind" means Indian referring to Hindustan and "Ko" means mountains. It is spoken in the areas of the North West Frontier Province (including Hazara), Punjab and Kashmir by an estimated 2.2 million people. They are commonly referred to as Punjabi Pathans or simply Pathans.

Hindko Language : Hindko is an ancient language spoken in northern Pakistan. The word "Hindko" literally means (in the hindko language), "Indian Mountains", "Hind" meaning Indian or referring to India (Hindustan) and "Ko" meaning Mountains. It is spoken in the areas of the North West Frontier Province (including Hazara), Punjab and Kashmir by an estimated 2.2 million people. They are commonly referred to as Punjabi Pathans or simply Pathans.

During the pre-Buddhist era in what is today Pakistan, the language of the masses was refined by the ancient grammarian Panini who set the rules of a structurally rigorous language called Sanskrit which was used principally for scriptures. Meanwhile, the vernacular language of the masses, Prakrit developed into many tongues and dialects which spread over the northern parts of South Asia. Hindko is believed to be closely related to Prakrit. Due to the geographic isolation of the regions, it has undergone very little corruption, but has borrowed considerable vocabulary from its neighors, in particular Pashto. It shows close affinity to Punjabi and the Lahnda sub-group of Indo-Aryan tongues and can be sub-divided into a northern and southern dialect.

The main group who speak Hindko are referred to by many academics as Punjabi Pathans as they show substantial intermingling with Pashtuns who comprise the majority in most of the regions inhabited by northern speakers of Hindko. Many claim descent from Pashtun groups of a wide variety and often adhere to Pashtunwali and are almost entirely Sunni Muslim. In more recent times, many Punjabi Pathans have become bilingual in Pashto or Punjabi as well depending upon where they reside.

Hindu Kush : The Hindu Kush, Hindu Kush, Hindoo Koosh or Hindukush is a mountain range in Afghanistan as well as in Balawaristan (Northern Areas of Pakistan). It is the westernmost extension of the Pamir Mountains, the Karakoram Range, and the Himalaya.

The mountains of the Hindu Kush system diminish in height as they stretch westward: toward the middle, near

Kabul, they extend from 4,500 to 6,000 meters; in the west, they attain heights of 3,500 to 4,000 meters. The average altitude of the Hindu Kush is 4,500 meters. The Hindu Kush system stretches about 966 kilometers laterally, and its median north-south measurement is about 240 kilometers. Only about 600 kilometers of the Hindu Kush system is called the Hindu Kush mountains. The rest of the system consists of numerous smaller mountain ranges including the Koh-e Baba, Salang, Koh-e Paghman, Spin Ghar (also called the eastern Safid Koh), Suleiman Range, Siah Koh, Koh-e Khwaja Mohammad and Selseleh-e Band-e Turkestan. The western Safid Koh, the Siah Band and Doshakh are commonly referred to as the Paropamisus by western scholars.

Rivers that flow from the mountain system include the Helmand River, the Hari Rud and the Kabul River. Numerous high passes ("kotal") transect the mountains, forming a strategically important network for the transit of caravans. The most important mountain pass is the Kotal-e Salang (3,878 m); it links Kabul and points south to northern Afghanistan. The completion of a tunnel within this pass in 1964 reduced travel time between Kabul and the north to a few hours. Previously access to the north through the Kotal-e Shibar (3,260 m) took three days. The Salang tunnel at 3,363 m and the extensive network of galleries on the approach roads were constructed with Soviet financial and technological assistance and involved drilling 1.7 miles through the heart of the Hindu Kush.

Hindu Law : Hindu law is a general term for the legal system—including philosophy of law and legal procedure—which existed in traditional India and was therefore coterminous with the institutions of the Hindu religion as they related to law in society. Among the most significant sources of Hindu law is the Manusmriti or 'Institutes of Manu.' Laws governing inheritance were shaped by the 12th century Mitakshara of Vijnaneshwara, which forms the basis of Hindu inheritance law in most of India, and the Dayabhaga of Jimutavahana, from which the inheritance law of West Bengal is derived.

Hindu Nationalism : Hindu nationalism is the political and cultural expression, histriographical and political theories of Indian nationalism distinctive to Hindu society in India, which asserts being Hindu as not merely a religious identity, but a national identity.

Hinduism is the oldest religion in the world, with over 900 million adherents. Ancient Hindu classics have been the foundation of religion, science, society, economy, philosophy and statecraft since ancient times in India. To Hindu nationalists, this exemplifies India as a Hindu Rashtra.

Hindu nationalist thinking takes roots with the days of the Islamic empires in India, the Delhi Sultanate and the Mughal Empire, when Muslim kingdoms governed the wider Hindu populations of India with the aid of small but elite Muslim communities.

The main inspiration of Hindu nationalism arises from the glories of the Mauryan Empire and the Gupta Empire, under whom India was politically and military dominant and prosperous, and Hindu religion and culture at its greatest heights.

The main incitement of Hindu nationalist passions arise from the destruction of Hindu temples such as the Somnath Temple in Gujarat, the descretion of holy Hindu institutions in Ayodhya, Kashi, Mathura, Allahabad and Haridwar and the killings, lootings and rape of an indeterminate but large number of Hindus during a series of Islamic invasions from Afghanistan and Persia, by Muslim kings like Mahmud of Ghazni, Muhammad Ghori, Ahmed Shah Durrani and Nadir Shah.

Hindu monarch-warriors like Shivaji, Maharana Pratap and Prithviraj Chauhan are hailed today as heroes of Hindu society. Hindus draw inspiration and pride from the Hindu empires of the Gupta Dynasty, the Rajput kings of modern Rajasthan, the southern Vijayanagara empire of Karnataka and the Maratha Empire of modern day Maharashtra. The rise of the Sikh Khalsa military order first arose to protect Sikhs and Hindus from the pogroms associated with fanatical Muslim rulers like Aurangzeb. Guru Tegh Bahadur gave up his life in a battle to protect Kashmiri Hindus. This historical relationship with Sikhs has nurtured the pride of Hindu nationalists.

What was perceived as deeply offensive propaganda of Christian missionaries, a Westernization of many educated Hindus, forcible conversion to Islam and Christianity and rising resentment against the practices of untouchability by orthodox Hindus gave rise to the reform and revival of Hinduism by leaders like Dayananda Saraswati and Swami Vivekananda.

The Arya Samaj was founded by Swami Dayananda Saraswati in the middle of the 19th century to revive Hindu society, which was entrenched deeply in the social schasms of untouchability, suttee, as well as poverty, xenophobia and illiteracy. The Samaj prescribed a return to the Vedas, to the basic tenets of Hindu religion with a monotheistic pursuit of One God, instead of minor deities.

Swami Vivekananda is praised by many Hindu nationalists as having defined the Hindu religion as the greatest glory of Indian civilization. Vivekananda hailed India's wealth in religion and philosophy. The Ramakrishna Mission he founded has grown into one of India's most important charities and community organizations. Sri Aurobindo was a militant nationalist who was one of the first to embrace the idea of complete political independence for India, before giving up the struggle to adopt a life devoted to religion and such purposes.

Both Swami Vivekananda and Sri Aurobindo are credited with having found the basis for a vision of freedom and glory for India in the spiritual richness and heritage of Hinduism.

In the Indian Independence Movement, the Indian National Congress was recognized by the vast majority of the people of India as their representative against the British Raj. And most Hindus, being the vast majority of Indian peoples, drove the movement, especially owing to the existence of the Muslim League from 1907 as a specifically Muslim party.

Hindus wanted a free and united nation to result from the end of the war, with Indian heritage and consciousness liberated from foreign cultural and political intrusions. But owing to the separatist politics of the Muslim League, a different expression arose in the era that was specifically Hindu. Hindus desired freedom not only from European colonialism, but to avoid a return to over one thousand years of Muslim rule in India. Many millions of Hindus harbored negative emotions as many great Hindu temples, monuments and communities had been savaged by pogroms conducted by Muslim rulers like Nadir Shah, Muhammad Ghori, Mahmud of Ghazni and Aurangzeb. This freedom would not be achieved if Muslims were accorded special treatment as they demanded.

National leaders like Bal Gangadhar Tilak and Mahatma Gandhi were responsible for inculcating Hinduism's religious values, history, heritage and culture into Indian nationalism and into the political expression during the Indian Independence Movement. Tilak and Gandhi connected with millions of ordinary Indians due to their espousal of Indian cultural values and traditions.

Tilak is credited with having founded the Ganesh Chaturthi festival of immersing Lord Ganesha's statue. The festival allowed millions of Hindus to congregate and celebrate their religion and culture. Gandhi transformed the Indian National Congress from an elitist organization of liberal, educated Indians to an organization committed to the service of the Indian masses, and empowered by the membership and participation of over 10 million ordinary Indians. His adoption of ahimsa, emphasis of Indian languages, Indian clothing and lifestyle, and Hindu religious values before Western influences and English struck a strong chord with India's masses, who were mainly Hindu.

Hindu sentiments firmly rejected Muslim political demands for separate electorates and reservations. They rejected the notion that Muslims deserved a large role in national life despite their numerical minority owing to their rich history in India, anticipating that such an expanded role would come at the expense of the natural Hindu majority.

Such sentiments led to the Congress rejection of the League's offer of coalitions in 1937: the League is said to have asked for its recognition by the Congress as the representative of Muslims. Congress rejected this idea due to its strict and natural adherence to secularism, and also to reject League demands for inflated representations in provinces it had won few seats in.

Though normally remembered simply as leaders of the freedom struggle, Lala Lajpat Rai, Sardar Vallabhbhai Patel, Purushottam Das Tandon, Srinivasa Iyengar, Sarojini Naidu and others were amongst the first to express Hindu nationalistic sentiments and ideas.

Hindu Philosophy : The Hindu philosophy is one of the main divisions of the Indian philosophy and forms an integral part of the Indian culture. Hindu philosophy is difficult to narrow down to a definite doctrine because Hinduism itself, as a religion, resists identification with any well worked out doctrine. However, it is traditionally seen through the prism of six different systems (called Darshanas in Sanskrit) that are listed here and make up the main belief systems of Hinduism.

Hindu Rashtra : Hindu Rashtra, literally Hindu Nation is what Hindu nationalists describe India as—a nation of people whose culture, history is founded in the theology and traditions of Hinduism. In this interpretation, a Hindu is connoted beyond just as an adherent of Hinduism.

Some proponents have argued that even Muslim and Christian Indians are Hindus, as their ancestors were Hindu, and despite their religion, their culture and heritage is the same as that of India's natural Hindu majority.

Many Hindu nationalists also prescribe to a vision of Akhand Bharat (United India), wherein the partition of India is reversed to found a nation based on what they consider as India's natural territorial extent in terms of the bonds of history, culture, economy and people.

Hinduism : Hinduism can be described as the 'museum' of religions. No other religious tradition is so eclectic, so diversified in its theoretical premises as well as its practical expression. Hinduism can be called as Sanatana Dharma or the religion Perenis. As the name implies ananta (without a beginning), it is eternal and ever-lasting (Shashvata). It is the only major religion which has not been traced to a specific founder and the only one which does not have a holy book as the one and only scriptural authority. Sacred texts of Hindu religion consists of Vedas, Upanishads Bhagavad Gita etc. Hinduism always absorbs anything that is good and valuable and at the same time, it shares its wisdom with whomever earnestly seeks it. Its doors are open to all.

Hinduism does not attempt at conversion. It is against any forceful conversion or inflictions on the non-believers. Its faith is that all men are born, children of Sanatana Dharma. Once people become aware of this inheritance and follow its universal principles, there is no need for any further conversion. Even the most uncompromising atheist finds a place in Sanatana Dharma and his philosophy and way of life are duly noticed and his arguments heard with all patience. This arises from the belief that even such a person may one day realise his fundamental values of life and become a follower of Dharma.

Hinduism has not only recognised the different aptitudes and temperaments of people but devised ways of life, catering to such needs. It has also divided individual life into different stages or ashramas. Thus a child is treated as an Anupanita or uninitiated, lives a life of discipline and study and acquires knowledge and virtue (Brahmacharya ashrama). He leads a life of voluntary poverty, subjects himself to strict disciplining of his senses and mind and becomes a well groomed and highly cultured person. Then he marries and leads a family life (Grihastha ashrama) and brings up his children in the right traditions. By learning the Vedas, offering sacrifices to gods and begetting a son, he pays off the three debts — debt to sages, to gods and the manes. As he grows older, he becomes a forest dweller (Vanaprastha Ashrama) with all passions and prejudices removed. There perhaps is no better scheme of life, that harmonises the needs and the development of the individual and society in such a well knit fashion. Thus the Sanatana Dharma emphasises a comprehensive view of life which aims at the realization of both Abhyudaya and Nishreyas—worldly prosperity and spiritual good.

Hinduism is not pessimistic. It has always exhorted men to realize the four Purusharthas or values of Life, namely Dharma (righteousness) Artha (wealth) Kama (desire) and Moksha(liberation). Only it has insisted that wealth and enjoyment should be based on Dharma and aim at Moksha.

One of the aspects of Hinduism that is considered to be not in keeping with the modern democratic tendencies is its "caste-system". The Brahmins (priests, teachers), Kshatriyas (warriors, rulers), Vaisyas (traders, merchants) and Sudras (unskilled workers) were four castes in the society. Originally in the Vedas it was conceived as a system for the proper division of functions in society and it was not rigid and birth-oriented. Later the system deteriorated and the original intention was totally lost.

With the passage of time the caste system became over ridden with dust and filth. Birth became the determinative factor for establishing one's caste and the caste system led to social exploitation in Hindu society. Brahmins and Kshatriyas who were the high castes had certain privileges as compared to other low castes. The impregnable edifice of the caste barrier is crumbling. But caste system has never been a bar against God-realisation. Some of India's greatest saints, who were and are still being venerated even by the highest of Brahmans, have sprung from among the so called untouchables. Sanyasis who are in the height of spiritual evolution, have no caste at all. Even when a Brahman takes Sanyas, he has to give up his caste.

Another important aspect of Hinduism is its free scope for philosophic thought. The six orthodox systems of Indian philosophy, namely, the Nyaya, the Vaiseshika, the Sankhya, the Yoga, the Mimamsa and the Vedanta, as also the heterodox systems like the Charvaka, the Buddha and the Jaina and many a religious movement started by synthesisers have allowed for a wide diversity of thought.

Everything that the Hindu does is God-centered. Hinduism believes in avataras or incarnations of God on earth in human or other form. The doctrine of 'avatara' is a perpetual reminder for a Hindu that he should not stick to outward forms but regard everything as manifestation of divinity and revitalise his life by the new energy from the surroundings.

In Hinduism, the ultimate goal is 'Moksha'; the liberation from the cycle of existence. There are many paths leading to this goal. Until moksha is attained, all human beings are subject to rebirth. The conditions of life in each birth are determined by the cumulative results of the karma (deeds) performed in previous life.

The three gods-Brahma, Vishnu and Siva together form the Hindu Trinity. Brahma creates the world, Vishnu sustains it and Siva destroys it. Hindus are divided into three main groups based on the deity they worship. The worshippers of Siva are known as Saivas, worshippers of Sakti (consort of Siva) as Saktas and worshippers of Vishnu as Vaishnavas. Each of these gods has a consort, and the gods and their consorts have many manifestations. Each god also has a vehicle on which they ride, and a symbol

Hindustan Lever Limited (HLL) : Hindustan Lever Limited (also called HLL) is India's largest consumer products company and is headquartered in Mumbai. Lever Brothers India Limited was formed in 1933 which became Hindustan Lever Limited. It has 41,000 employees. HLL is the market leader in Indian products such as tea, soaps, detergents. As of April 2005, it is headed by Mr M S Banga.

Hindustan Times : The Hindustan Times is a leading newspaper in India. It has its roots in the independence movement of the first half of the twentieth century. It was edited at times by many important people in India, including Devdas Gandhi (the son of Mahatma Gandhi) and Khushwant Singh.

Hindustan Times (established in 1924) is the flagship publication of HT Media Ltd. It is has a nation wide reach in India (barring Southern India), with simultaneous editions from New Delhi, Lucknow, Patna and Kolkata. It is also printed from Bhopal, Chandigarh, Jaipur and Ranchi. HT has also launched India's first youth daily HT Next in 2004. The Mumbai edition was launched on 14th July 2005. Other sister publications of Hindustan Times are Hindustan (Hindi Daily), Nandan (Monthly children's magazine) and Kadambani (Monthly literary magazine). Vir Sanghvi is the editorial director.

Hindustani Music : Hindustani Classical Music is a South Asian classical music tradition that took shape in the North of the Indian subcontinent circa the 13th and 14th centuries AD from existing religious, folk, and theatrical performance practices. The practice of singing based on notes was popular even from the Vedic times where the hymns in Sama Veda, a sacred text, was sung and not chanted. Developing a strong and diverse tradition over several centuries, it has contemporary traditions established primarily in India but also in Pakistan and Bangladesh. In contrast to Carnatic music, the other main Indian classical music tradition originating from the South, Hindustani music was not only influenced by ancient Hindu musical traditions, Vedic philosophy and native Indian sounds but also by the Persian performance practices of the Afghan Mughals. Outside South Asia, Hindustani classical music is often associated with Indian music, as it is arguably the most popular stream of music outside the sub-continent.

Hindustani classical music, like Carnatic music, is organized by Ragas (also called raag) which are characterized, in part, by their specific ascent (Arohana) and descent (Avarohana.) The ascent notes may not be identical to the descent notes. King (Vadi) and Queen (Samvadi) notes and a unique note phrase (Pakad). In addition each raga has its natural register (Ambit) and glisando (Meend) rules, and many other specific features.

Hindustani music was structurally organized into the current That scale by Pt. Vishnu Narayan Bhatkhande (1860-1936) in the early part of the 20th century. Prior to this, Ragas were classified as Male (raag), female (Ragini) and Putra (children) ragas.

When artists, usually performers (as opposed to writers) have reached a distinguished level of achievement, titles of respect are added to their names. Hindus are referred to as Pandits and Muslims as Ustads.

Hindutva : Hindutva ("Hinduness", a word coined by Vinayak Damodar Savarkar in his 1923 pamphlet entitled Hindutva: Who is a Hindu?) is used to describe movements advocating Hindu nationalism. The former ruling party in India, the Bharatiya Janata Party (BJP) is closely associated with a group of organizations that promote Hindutva. They collectively refer to themselves as the "Sangh Parivar" or family of associations, and include the Rashtriya Swayamsevak Sangh, Bajrang Dal and the Vishwa Hindu Parishad.

This right-wing ideology has existed since the early 20th century, but only came to prominence in Indian politics in the late 1980s, when two events attracted a large number of mainstream Hindus to the movement. The first of these events was the Rajiv Gandhi government's use of its large Parliamentary Majority to overturn a Supreme Court verdict that had angered conservative Muslims. The second was the dispute over the 16th century Mughal Babri Mosque in Ayodhya — built by Babar after his first major victory in India, allegedly on the site of an existing temple marking the birthplace of Rama, whom Hindus considered to be an avatar of Vishnu — which came to a head with the mosque's destruction by a Hindu mob in 1992 and subsequent rioting across the country.

Hingol National Park : Hingol National Park covers about 6100.43 km^2 and is the largest of National Parks of Pakistan and lies on the Makran coast in Balochistan and approximately 190 km from Karachi. The area was for the first time declared reserved in 1988. The park area covers parts of the three districts, namely; Lasbela, Gawader and Owaran of Balochistan province containing a variety of topographical features and vegetation, varying from arid sub tropical forest in the north to arid montane in the west. Large tracts of the NP are covered with drift sand and can be classified as coastal semi desert. The National Park includes the estuary of the Hingol river which supports a significant diversity of bird and fish species.

Currently, 20 staff members including 18 game watchers, two deputy rangers are responsible for the management of the Park under the guidance of the park Manager who reports to the Conservator and the Secretary Wildlife, Forest, Livestock, Environment and Tourism.

Hitec City : One of the modern monuments of trade and technology, it embodies the newfound attitude of Hyderabad and today finds a place of pride. Situated on the outskirts of the city, it is the nucleus of Cybera.

Hizbul Mujahideen : The Hizbul Mujahideen (created 1989) is a militant group active in Kashmir. Its headquarters are at Muzaffarabad, Pakistani-administered Kashmir. The current leader of the group is known under the nickname Sayeed Salahudeen, a native from Kashmir. Hizbul Mujahideen is currently the biggest jihadi group operating in Kashmir, and are widely considered by sources on both sides of the Kashmiri conflict to be the most indigenous and widely-supported militany group active in Kashmir. The group has claimed responsibility of carrying out several terrorist attacks against Indian civilians and Indian Army units. They also have alleged ties with the Pakistani and

Kashmiri political party, Jamaat-e-Islami and Pakistan's intelligence organistaion, ISI.

Hmar : Hmar is the name of one of the numerous tribes of India, spread over a large area in the northeast. The Hmars belong to the Chin-Kuki-Mizo group of tribes, and are recognised as Scheduled Tribe under the 6th Scheduled of the Constitution of India.

Hmar live mostly in the hills of south Manipur, Mizoram, Cachar, North Cachar, Meghalaya, Tripura and Chittagong Hill Tracts. Although these areas are within different administrative divisions, they are geographically connected. In Manipur, the Hmars reside in the south, especially in the Churachandpur District and its adjoining areas. These areas, except Tuthaphai (the Khuga Valley/ Churachandpur), are hilly. Tuiruong (Barak), Tuivai and Tuithapui (Khuga) are some of the important rivers flowing through this area. In Mizoram, the Hmar live mostly in the north, especially in the Aizawl District. In Assam, the Hmars live in the Cachar and North Cachar District. In Meghalaya, the Hmars live in the Jaintia Hills District and Shillong in Khasi Hills District. In Tripura, the Hmars mostly live in and around Darchawi, a village on the Mizoram – Tripura border.

The Hmars trace their origin to Sinlung, the location of which is hotly debated. The Hmars are generally short statured, sturdy, dark haired, brown skinned, and known for their bravery. The Hmars still treasure and garner their traditional arts, including folk dance, folk songs, etc., representing scenes of adventure, battle, love, victory, and other experiences throughout history.

The majority of the Hmars are cultivators. The Hmars in South Manipur were introduced to Christianity in the year 1910 by Watkin Roberts, a Welsh Missionary. And with the introduction of Western education, the majority of the Hmar population are educated. Today, the Hmars are one of the highly educated tribes, employed by the Government of India in different fields and department of government services.

Hnathlang : Villagers had certain obligations to do common work for the village and the chief. This was in the form of voluntary labour called hnathlang. Everyone in the village would contribute voluntary labour to build the zawlbuk, clear all jungles in and around the village, clear and fence the source of water supply. A chief could call upon his villagers to contribute for his private work also.

The Lakher villager performed certain common duties which was similar to Lushai hnathlang and was called tlaraihria in lakher. Anyone refusing or failing to do tlaraihria would be fined (leu) to pay rice, fowl, axe or dao or one rupee in cash. If paid in cash or by rice, the chief and the elders would use it to have some beer.

In Lakher villages, there were regular system for contribution by villagers for common entertainment, general feast and other general purposes. By the custom of Sathi a villager was required to kill a pig for a common feast or for entertaining a visiting chief of for some other similar entertainment. By a custom called vohel, a piglet, immediately after its birth would be collected for any purpose chosen by the villagers. Sakhei was a system of subscription of paddy for village entertainment to a distinguished visitor or for a similar other purposes. The Lakhers followed the tradition of hospitality. By duty of tlongang every Lakher was required to be hospitable.

Hogenakal Falls : Hogenakal Falls is a waterfalls in southern India on the Kaveri River. Major cities in the vicinity are Salem, Bangalore & Dharmapuri.

Holi : Holi is a spring festival. It is celebrated in the month of Phalgun, as the lunar month is locally known. The main event of Holi is indeed a carnival of colors. On this day, children, friends and neighbors come out on the streets. And the spree to color-anyone-you-see takes over. Colors of all form and variety. They come in shades of red, orange, blue, green and purple, and the likes. Colored powder, or, gulal was earlier made out of Dried seeds of some tropical flowers like the Palash, and dried silt from the riverbed. This has now given way to dyes, available in the form of pigments. People throw these colored powders in the air as they shout "Holi Hai!", and smear each other with this colored powder. Also they wet each other with colored water from Pitchkaris, a type of water gun. Colored water is prepared by mixing the pigments of dyes. These dyes are available in a range of shades. Also water-filled balloons are used these days to charge the target with a splash of color.

Holi Dance : This exuberant dance is connected with the seasonal festival of spring in Haryana. When the rural community rejoices and relaxes after the completion of their agricultural operations. It is performed in various formations to the accompaniment of drums and pipes. Both men and women participate in this dance. Percussion instruments like dhol, jhajh, chimta, khartal and thalis and anklets on the feet of the dancers produce the rhythm. Abir, gulal and coloured water is sprinkled on each other by the dancers. The dance is accompanied by the Chaupies and Chaumbaulas which sustain performance for hours. Women folk use twisted ropes, Kolars to mock-beat their counterparts. Men in a mood of frivolity wear women's costumes and exhibit their talent in female steps. The men folk not even a guest is spared. The dance is popular in Faridabad, Pulwal and Ballabhgarh. It is also performed in other areas.

Holige : Holige or Puran poli is a traditional sweet prepared in South India and Maharashtra, by stuffing a chapati with a sweet preparation. The chapati is made of wheat or maida flour. The sweet preparation is made of either chana daal, grated coconut and Brown sugar or grated coconut and powdered white sugar. In the latter case, the chapati will be stiffer and crunchier, while in the former, it will softer.

Homi Dady Motivala : Commander Homi Dady Motivala (b.18 June 1958 and sometimes spelt Homi D. Motiwala) is an Indian sportsperson in Yachting. As a distinguished sportsperson, he received the Arjuna award for best performance in Yachting for the year 1993, the Rajiv Gandhi Khel Ratna award jointly with P. K. Garg for overall best performance in sports for the year 1994-95 and the Dronacharya Award for Coaching excellence in Yachting for the year 2002.

He formed a team with P. K. Garg and won the bronze medal in the enterprise class at the 1990 and 1994 Asian Games held at Beijing and Hiroshima respectively. They were also the world champions in the same class in 1993. He is with the Indian Navy and is a recipient of the gallantry award, Shaurya Chakra in 1983.

Homi Jehangir Bhabha : Homi Jehangir Bhabha (October 30, 1909–January 24, 1966) was an Indian nuclear physicist of Parsi-Zoroastrian heritage who had a major role in the development of the Indian atomic energy program. Paul Dirac greatly influenced Bhabha during his study of Mechanical Engineering at Cambridge, to pursue an education in theoretical physics. A research scientist at the Cavendish Laboratories at Cambridge, he was stranded in India as a result of the second World War, and set up the Cosmic Ray Research Unit at the Indian Institute of Science, Bangalore under C. V. Raman in 1939.

With the help of J. R. D. Tata, he established the Tata Institute of Fundamental Research at Mumbai. With the end of the War and Indian Independence, he recived the blessings of Nehru for efforts in India, towards peaceful development of atomic energy. He established the Atomic Energy Commission of India in 1948. He represented India in International Atomic Energy Forums, and as President of the United Nations Conference on the Peaceful Uses of Atomic Energy, in Geneva in 1955.

He died in an air crash near Mount Blanc in 1966. The Bhabha Atomic Research Centre is named in his honour. He was an alumnus of the Cathedral and John Connon School.

Hooghly River : The Hooghly River (alternatively spelled Hoogli or Hugli) is a distributary of the Ganges River in India. It splits from the Ganges near the city of Baharampur, and runs south through the Indian state of West Bengal, past the twin cities of Kolkata and Howrah, to empty into the Bay of Bengal. Two of its well known tributaries are Damodar and Rupnarayan.

It is an essential lifeline for the people of Kolkata. The fish from the river are important to the local economy. The river's presence is one of the reasons chosen by the British to settle there. The French colony at Chandannagar on the Hoogli was once the rival of British Calcutta, but was eclipsed by Calcutta in the colonial wars of the 18th century. The modern container port of Haldia, on the lower Hoogli, now carries much of the region's maritime trade.

Several bridges run over the Hooghly at Kolkata; the Howrah Bridge, the Vidyasagar Setu and the Vivekananda Setu bridges.

The town of Hooghly is located on the river, in the district of the same name. The origins of the name are uncertain, whether the city or the river was named first.

Horse Dance : Horse dancers are popular in Guntur district. Life size horse puppets are prepared with cattle-dung, hay and husk and coloured to look like real horses. These puppets are hollow in the middle, where the dancers -men and women- stand resembling riders on horse back. In Guntur district, real horses are trained to dance according to the rhythm of the drums. Tinkling bells are tied to the fetlocks of the horse. During marriage processions and fairs the horse dance is a popular pass time in this district.

Horsley Hills : Horsley Hills, elevation 1,265 m, is a famous summer hill resort in Andhra Pradesh, about 160 km from Bangalore, India and 144 km from Tirupati. The town of Madanapalle lies nearby. Major tourist attractions include the Mallamma temple and the Rishi valley school. Horsely Hills is the departure point for the Kaundinya wildlife sanctuary at a distance of 87 km.

Many Bollywood films are shot here, and it is also famous for its Banyan tree which is many years old. Horsley Hills is named after a British officer named W.D. Horsley, the Collector of Cuddapah district, who chose this spot for his summer residence.

The narrow road to Horsely Hills is very scenic. It is surrounded throughout its entire length with dense growths of eucalyptus, jacaranda, allamanda, and gulmohar trees.

Horsley Hills, Madanapalle : Horsley Hills is a beautiful hill resort in Andhra Pradesh located at a height of 4,200 ft above sea level. The journey to Horsley Hills is exciting as one tempts to see various species of plants and wild animals.

Hosdurg Fort : Hosdurg Fort is a fort in Kasargod district of Kerala state, south India. Hosdurg fort with its round bastion looks imposing from a distance. Somashekara

Nayak of Ikkeri dynasty built the fort. The place made well known by the Nithyanandasram with 45 caves.

Hoseni Dalan : Hoseni Dalan is a Shia shrine in the old part of the Dhaka, Bangladesh. It was built in the 17th century during the Mughal Period. This commemorates the martyrdom of al-Husain, grandson of Mohammed, during the battle of Karbala on 10 October 680 CE. It is said that one Sayyid Murad built the building during the Subedari (Governorship) of Shah Shuja, son of Mughal emperor Shah Jahan. Shuja belonged to the Sunni sect but he patronized Shia institutions too. Legend has it that Sayyid Murad built the building after a vision of al-Husain. Since then, the building has been enhanced and renovated many times. During the rule of the East India Company, it was repaired in 1807 and 1810. After an earthquake damaged it in 1897 it was further extended and reconstructed.

Although the Sunni sect is a majority in Bangladesh, there is a small number of muslims belonging to the Shia sect in Dhaka. During the first 10 days of Muharram, it becomes a center of mourning and religious celebration in old Dhaka. Both the Sunni and the Shia followers join the mourning, ending in the festival of Ashura when a great procession parades through the streets.

Hoshangabad : Hoshangabad District is one of the districts of Madhya Pradesh state of India, and Hoshangabad town is the district headquarters. The district is bounded by the districts of Raisen to the north, Narsinghpur to the east, Chhindwara to the southeast, Betul to the south, Harda to the west, and Sehore to the northwest. In 1998, the western portion of Hoshangabad District was split off to become Harda District.

The district lies in the Narmada River valley, and the Narmada forms the northern boundary of the district, Hoshangabad District is part of Bhopal division. The Tawa

River is a tributary of the Narmada, rising in the Satpura Range to the south and flowing north to meet the Narmada at the village of Bandra Bhan. The Tawa Reservoir lies in the south-central region of the district.

Hoshangabad District is also home to Pachmarhi, a hill station and popular tourist spot in the Satpura Range in the southern part of the district. Pachmarhi was the summer capital of the British Raj Central Provinces and Berar. The Pachmarhi Sanctuary (461.37 sq km) is part of the larger Pachmarhi Biosphere Preserve, which extends into Betul and Chhindwara districts.

Hoshiarpur : Hoshiarpur District is a district of Punjab state in northern India. The district has an area of 3,365 sq. km and a population of 14,78,045 (2001 census); Hoshiarpur is the district capital. The district is bounded by Kapurthala, Jalandhar and Gurdaspur districts of Punjab state and Kangra and Una districts of Himachal Pradesh state.

It falls into two nearly equal portions of hill and plain country. Its eastern face consists of the westward slope of the Solar Singhi Hills; parallel with that ridge, a line of lower heights belonging to the Siwalik range traverses the district from south to north, while bctween the two chains stretches a valley of uneven width, known as the Jaswan Dun. Its upper portion is crossed by the Sohan torrent, while the Sutlej sweeps into its lower end through a break in the hills, and flows in a southerly direction till it turns the flank of the central range, and debouches westwards upon the plains. This western plain consists of alluvial formation, with a general westerly slope owing to the deposit of silt from the mountain torrents in the sub-montane tract.

The Beas has a fringe of lowland, open to moderate but not excessive inundations, and considered very fertile. A considerable area is covered by government woodlands, under the care of the forest department. Rice is largely grown, in the marshy flats along the banks of the Beas. Several religious fairs are held, at Anandpur, Mukerian and Chintpurni, all of which attract an enormous concourse of people. The district, owing to its proximity to the hills, possesses a comparatively cool and humid climate. Cotton fabrics are manufactured, and sugar, rice and other grains, tobacco and indigo are among the exports. Hoshiarpur is also known as a City of Saints. There are many Deras in this district. The District Govt. College was once a campus for Punjab University.

Hospet : Hospet is a town in Bellary District, in northern Karnataka. The modern name is abbreviated from the original Hosapattana. The town is best known today for its proximity to the ruined city of Vijayanagara. It serves as a transport and accommodation centre for tourists visiting the ruins. Its tourist importance lies in its proximity to Hampi, the site of the medieval Vijayanagar Empire, situated about 12 km away. The Tungabhadra Dam here harnesses the sweet waters of the Tungabhadra River. At the base of the dam is a garden, styled along Japanese lines.

Hossain Mohammad Ershad : Hossain Mohammad Ershad (born 1930) was the military dictator of Bangladesh from 1982 until 1990. After a military coup on March 24, 1982, Ershad became martial law administrator until 1984, abolishing the post of prime minister. In 1983 he became the President, and in 1984 restored the office of prime minister, but did not allow elections. On December 6, 1990, he was forced to resign following massive protests. He was imprisoned until 1995. Even during that time, he was a member of Parliament for his Jatiya Party.

Ershad's personal life has often come to the headlines. During his military rule, he claimed that his wife gave birth to a son, Saad Ershad, though later it was revealed as a publicity ploy, and that Saad was adopted. In the early 2000s, he married a fashion designer, Bidisha, who was 40 years younger than him (he is still married to his first wife, Roushan Ershad). In mid-2005, following allegations that Bidisha Ershad has ties to India, he divorced her, and lodged several cases of theft and fraud against her. Ershad has also been associated with several scandals during his rule, though not all of them were later substantiated.

Hot Springs : Hot Springs in Bihar lies at the foot of the Vaibhava Hill. A staircase leads up to the various temples. Separate bathing places have been organised for men and women and the water comes through spouts from Saptdhara, the seven streams, believed to find their source behind the "Saptaparni Caves", up in the hills. The hottest of the springs is the Brahmakund with a temperature of 450C.

House of Habib : The House of Habib is a prominent family in Pakistan. The Habibs have spread their wealth over a large number of private and public companies and a profile of Rafiq Habib in Economic Review, November 1984 (P 59) said that Habib group had 90 companies it its fold. The history of House of Habib goes back to middle of the last century when Esmail Ali of Jam Nagar, India set up a small utensil factory in Bombay. A son born to him in 1878 was given the name Habib Ismaeel. He later founded the House of Habib. He lost his father at an early age and circumstances forced him to join the business of his uncle Cassum Mohammad, owner of Khoja Mithabai Nathoo, merchant, and manufacturer of copper and brass utensils. It was because of his association with Mithabai Nathoo that Habib Ismaeel came to be known as Seth Habib Mitha.

The House of Habib hold many distinctions in Pakistan's history. Habib Bank was shifted to Pakistan on the personal bidding of Quaid-e-Azam Mohammad Ali Jinnah and came to the help of the nascent state "even before the Govt of Pakistan was ready to issue appropriate govt paper", with a Rs 80 million loan when the Rserve Bank of India failed to deliver Pakistan share of Rs 750 million held by it. It is said that Mohammad Ali Habib had presented a blank cheque on Llyod Bank to Quaid-e-Azam who wrote Rs 80 million in it.

The Habib family is known to have set up offices in Vienna and Geneva as early as 1912 and incorporated Habib and Sons in 1921, which dealt in brass, metal scraps and gold with "Lion of Ali" embossed on it. The Habib Bank still uses this as its insignia. Their companies include Habib Bank AG Zurich, and Indus motors Limited, which is a JV with the Toyota motor corporation.

Howrah : Howrah is an industrial city in West Bengal, India. It is also the name of the Howrah administrative district which includes the city and its surroundings. It is on the west bank of the Hoogli River, and is Kolkata's twin city. It is West Bengal's second largest city. The two cities are linked by the famous Howrah Bridge (Rabindra Setu), as well as the Vidyasagar Setu (the second Howrah Bridge) and the Vivekananda Setu bridges. The city also contains Howrah Station, one of the major train stations serving Kolkata as well as Howrah.

Howrah Bridge : Howrah Bridge, also known as the Rabindra Setu, is a bridge over the Hoogli River in West Bengal, India. It is so named as it links the city of Howrah (at the point of Howrah Station) to its twin city of Calcutta. The bridge was built between 1937 and 1943 to replace a bridge from 1874, and is said to be the busiest bridge in the world. It is 97 metres high and 705 metres long. It is a balanced cantilever truss bridge currently used as a road bridge, but previously carried light rail as well. However, this bridge contains no nuts and bolts—all joins are through studs. The bridge also has sister bridges over the river at different points, namely the Vidyasagar Setu and the Vivekananda Setu.

Howrah Station : Howrah Station is one of the major train stations serving Howrah and Kolkata (India). Kolkata is also served by Sealdah Station. It is situated on the West bank of the Hooghly River. It is reached from Kolkata by crossing the river by Howrah Bridge. The station is said to be one of the biggest (if not the biggest) in India. Trains from this station serve the Kolkata suburbs, the state of West Bengal and most major cities of India. It is the second oldest station and one of the largest railway complexes in India. It has 21 platforms handling over 300 trains each day serving over a million passengers.

Hoysala Empire : The Hoysala Empire, ruled part of southern India from 1000 to 1346 A.D., with Belur, Karnataka as their capital. The Hoysala Empire is remembered today primarily for its architecture. Over a hundred surviving temples are scattered across Karnataka, the finest examples of which are found in the cities of Belur, Halebid and Somnathpura. The Hoysala kings were influenced by Jainism and Hinduism. King Vishnuvardhana and his successors were followers of Vaishnavism.

Hoysalas began their rule as subordinates of the Chalukyas of Kalyani and gradually established their own empire in Karnataka. Hoysalas period is remembered today as one of the brightest periods in the history of Karnataka, next only to the Vijayanagara Empire. Famous kings among the Hoysalas were Vishnuvardhana, Veera Ballala II and Veera Ballala III. Kannada was the native language of the Hoysala Kings. The Hoysalas encouraged both Kannada and Sanskrit literature.

Hriday Kunj : The small house in the Harijan Ashram in Ahmedabad where Mahatma Gandhi carried on his experiments non-violent struggle for the freedom of the country is very aptly called the Hriday Kunj. The ashram was founded by the Mahatma when he left his first Ashram at Kocharb. From 1918 to 1930, when he left the Ashram to launch his famous Salt Satyagraha, the Hriday Kunj was the source of inspiration during the freedom movement. The Ashram has a museum and a prayer ground.

Hrikatha : Harikatha may be defined as a versatile and a composite art in which a single person indulges in the act of dramatization, consisting all the vital components of the theatre craft such as music, dance and dramatic presentation of the themes. Harikatha, is a solo recitation which is a combination of literature and lilting lyrics which reflects rich musical and literary material in its content. Harikatha is known in one form or the other with different names like Katha, Katha Keerthan, Shiva Katha, Katha Kalashepam, Kathaprasangam keertan and Sankeertan etc in the country.

The present form of Harikatha is believed to be 150 years old and existed even during the early sixteenth century. Most of the religious festivals and special occasions are marked by 'Harikatha programmes'. The medium of Harikatha is the cheapest and the simplest mode of communication. It is a theatre craft which does not require a stage, set, scenery, costumes and other paraphernalia.

Hrishikesh : Hrishikesh (from Hrishikesh, another name for Lord Vishnu), in the state of Uttaranchal, is a holy city for Hindus located in the foothills of the Himalaya in northern India. It is 24 kilometers away from another holy city, Haridwar, and is considered an access point for the cities that form the Char Dham—Badrinath, Kedarnath, Gangotri, and Yamunotri.

The sacred river Ganga (anglicized to Ganges) flows through Hrishikesh, adding to its spiritual appeal and natural beauty. In fact, it is here that the river leaves the Himalayas, and flows out into the plains of northern India. Several temples, ancient as well as new, can be found along the banks of the river in Hrishikesh. The city attracts thousands of pilgrims and tourists each year, from within India, as well as from other countries. The city has several Yoga centres that also attract tourists. It is believed that meditation in Hrishikesh brings one closer to attainment of salvation, or moksha, as does a dip in the holy river that flows through it.

The name Hrishikesh is loosely applied to an association of five distinct sections encompassing not only the town but also hamlets and settlements on both sides of the river Ganges. These include Hrishikesh itself, the commercial and communication hub; the sprawling suburban Muni-ki-Reti or the "sands of the sages"; Shivananda Nagar, north of Hrishikesh; the temple section of Lakshman Jhulla, a little further north; and the assorted Ashrams around Swarg Ashram on the East bank.

During the mid-sixties, The Beatles (visited Maharishi Mahesh Yogi's ashram) and several other artists, including The Beach Boys and Donovan, visited the site to contemplate and meditate. More recently also, the place has been of interest to celebrities including Hollywood star Kate Winslet, who stayed in Peasant's Cottage. The word Hrishikesh has been seen to refer to Sri Krishna in the Bhagavad Gita. He refers to Himself as the "Lord of the Senses."

Hub : Hub River is located in Lasbela, Balochistan, Pakistan. It forms the provincial boundary between Sindh and Balochistan, west of Karachi. Hub Dam is a large water storage reservoir constructed in 1981 on the Hub River in the arid plains north of Karachi. The reservoir supplies water for irrigation in the Lasbella district of Balochistan and drinking water for the city of Karachi. It is an important staging and wintering area for an appreciable number of waterbirds and contains a variety of fish species which increase in abundance during periods of high water. The Mahseer (Tor putitora), an indigenous riverine fish found in the Hub River, grows up to 2m in length and provides for excellent angling.

Hub Dam : Hub Dam is a large water storage reservoir constructed in 1981 on the Hub River on the arid plains north of Karachi on provincial border between Balochistan and Sindh, Pakistan. The reservoir supplies water for irrigation in Lasbela District of Balochistan and drinking water for the city of Karachi. It is an important staging and wintering area for an appreciable number of waterbirds and contains a variety of fish species which increase in abundance during periods of high water. The Mahseer (Tor putitora), an indigenous riverine fish found in the Hub River, grows up to 2m in length and provides for excellent angling.

Hubli-Dharwad : Hubli-Dharwad is a twin city in the state of Karnataka in India. It is the administrative headquarters of Dharwad district. The population of the twin cities is 786,000, and is the second-largest conurbation in Karnataka, after Bangalore. Hubli-Dharwad's population increased 22.99% between 1981 and 1991, from 527,108 to 648,298, and by 21.2% between 1991 and 2001. The municipality covers 191 sq. km. Hubli-Dharwad is located 425 km northwest of Bangalore, on the main highway between Bangalore and Pune in Maharashtra.

Hudood Ordinance : The Hudood Ordinance is a law in Pakistan, which enforces punishments mentioned in the quran and sunnah for crimes such as adultry, rape and theft. It was enacted in 1979 as part of then military ruler Zia-ul-Haq's Islamization process. It is based on Muslim law Shari'a.

Humayun : Nasiruddin Humayun (March 6, 1508 – February 22, 1556), second Mughal Emperor, ruled in India from 1530–1540 and 1555–1556. Humayun "The Fortunate" was the eldest son of Babur. He had three younger brothers, Kamran, Askari and Hindal. Born on March 6, 1508, at Kabul, he learnt Turkish, Arabic and Persian at a very young age. He assisted his father in the governance of the country. In 1520, he was appointed the Governor of Badakshan at the age of 12 years. When Babur invaded India in 1526, Humayun joined him with a contingent from Badakshan. Humayun won a maiden victory in this campaign. He also led contingents under his father's rule against various Afghan insurgents, as well as participating in the battle of Kanwaha. After Babur's death in 1530, he was chosen as his successor. Humayun ascended the throne at Agra on December 30, 1530, at the age of 23, four days after his father's death.

Humayun inherited an empire barely held together by force of arms. It lacked a consolidated civil administration. He faced numerous problems right from the start. He faced troubles from the Afghan nobles, the Rajputs, and most of all from his brothers who were mean and disloyal to him. Unable to judge the growing power of Sher Shah, Humayun was defeated in the battle of Kanauj in 1540. He became a fugitive and escaped towards Iran via Sindh.

While in Sindh, he married a young Persian girl, Hamida Bano, who joined him in his wanderings. A year later in Umerkot in upper Sindh, his first son Akbar was born. Legend has it that Humayun had nothing to give to his followers at this happy occasion except some musk. The musk was broken into pieces and passed among his men. He is reported to have said that one day the fame of the prince would spread like the smell of the musk.

For a period of 15 years, the Mughal Empire lay dormant and Sher Shah founded the Suri Dynasty.

However, in 1555 Humayun returned once again, and by his sheer perseverance, was able to recover his kingdom. Although lacking his father's abilities, Humayun was a cultivated gentleman. He was unrivalled in the science of astrology and mathematics. Mild and benevolent in character, he was very kind towards his brothers; and despite their treachery, forgave them again and again. He possessed a very charitable and magnificent personality.

Although Humayun had recovered his kingdom, he was not destined to rule it for long. In January 1556, he met his tragic end by slipping from the famous building known as Din Panah.

Humayun Ahmed : Humayun Ahmed is one of the most popular novelists and dramatists in Bangladesh. His stories and novels involve lives of the middle-class people. He has recently emerged as a successful filmmaker.

Humayun Ahmed had a meteoric rise in Bangla literature. His first novel Nondito Noroke (In blissful hell), written while he was still a student of University of Dhaka, gained immediate popularity and critical acclaim. Ahmed Sharif, a famous critic, predicted the beginning of a great literary career. Equally successful was his second novel, Shankhanil Karagar (The ocean blue prison). Shankhanil Karagar was also made into a successful film by Nasiruddin Yusuf. Ahmed went on to become one of the most prolific writers in Bangla, publishing around a 100 novels to date.

Along with his more traditional novels and short stories, Ahmed is often credited with creating or maturing many a literaray genre in Bangladesh. The coming of age of Bangla science fiction can almost solely be attributed to Ahmed and Muhammed Zafar Iqbal, his brother. Ahmed also created the immensely popular Misir Ali and Himu characters, the first a rational psychologist committed to unravel the myteries around him, another a bohemian whose life goes back and forth between reality and myticism. Humayun Ahmed has said that these two characters, according to him sides of the same coin, are his favorite characters.

His contribution to comic genre also deep. His televised drama Bohubrihi, was one of the most succeessful productions of the national TV, its characters still household names after twenty years. The drama had a subtle combination of comic wit and a social message, as did his successful comic essay collections Elebele. Ahmed later rewrote Bohubrihi as a novel. Though set in the realities of middle class life, Humayun Ahmed's works displays a particular penchant for the mysterious and unexplained. He himself and his literature are often referred to as "moon-struck", and truly the references to the full moon in his prose are numerous.

Humayun Azad : Humayun Azad (Rari Khal, Bangladesh, 28 April 1947—Munich, Germany, 11 August 2004) was a prolific Bangladeshi author and scholar. He wrote more than 70 books including 10 novels, 7 collections of poetry, 7 books of comparative literature and 2 books for children. Azad received the prestigious Bangla Academy Award (1996) and the Shishu Academy Award for his contributions in both adult and children literature.

Dr. Azad got his doctorate degree in linguistics in 1976 at the University of Edinburgh. He later served as a professor of Bangla at the University of Dhaka and in his early career produced pioneering works on Bangla linguistics, notably Bangla syntax. He was regarded as the most important living linguist of the one-thousand-year-old Bangla language.

Later in his career, especially during General Ershad's rule, he became well-known as a liberal socio-political critic as he wrote biting commentaries against the dictatorship in local magazines. His commentaries continued throughout the 1990s and were later published as books as they grew in numbers. A freethinker and an atheist, he fearlessly and openly criticized in his works the extremism in religions, including Islam, the major religion in Bangladesh.

Dr. Azad also published the first comprehensive book in Bangla on the subject of women called Naari (Bangla for "Woman") in 1992. In this monumental tome, Azad painstakingly compiled the feminist ideas of the west that underlie the feminist contributions of the subcontinent's socio-political reformers and exposed the anti-women stance of some legendary Bengali writers including Rabindranath Tagore. The work, critical of the patriarchal and male-chauvinistic attitude of religions towards women, attracted negative reaction from conservative censors and the Bangladeshi Government banned the book in 1995. The ban was eventually lifted in 2000, following a legal battle Azad won in the High Court.

Humayun Saeed : Humayun Saeed is one of the leading actors of Pakistan. Humayun was born into an enlightened family on July 27, 1971, in Karachi. Being the eldest amongst five brothers, his parents expected a lot from him. From 1995 onwards, he associated himself with Pakistani television. First he appeared as an artist in numerous television plays and drama serials. His first play was Yeh Jahan. Later, he started his own production, known as H.S. Production.

From 'H.S. Production', he has produced the serial, Tum he to ho, Pehli Khahish, Adhuray Khawab, Dil wo bay mehar and Undekhi.

Hund Excavations : Hund, the ancient city of Embolima, is believed to be founded by Alexander the Great. Located 80 km away from Peshawar on the western bank of the Indus River, Hund is also famous for being the birthplace of the celebrated Sanskrit grammarian, Panini. In the 7th century A.D., many Chinese pilgrims visited Hund, as it was a revered place for the Buddhists of the period. Later in its history, it was made the capital of Gandhara by Hindu Shahi kings. In the beginning of the 11th century, Sultan Mahmud of Ghazni conquered Hund. One can visit the remnants of this once famous city; floods have washed some of it away. Among the remains numerous coins belonging to the Indo-Scythion and Hindu Shahi Rulers, jewelry and other articles of immense historical value have been found.

Hunza : Hunza is a former princely state in the northernmost part of the Northern Areas of Pakistan, which existed until 1974. The state bordered the Gilgit Agency to the south, the former princely state of Nagar to the east, China to the north and Afghanistan to the northwest. The state capital was the town of Baltit (also known as Karimabad). The area of Hunza now forms the Aliabad tehsil of Gilgit District.

Hunza River : Hunza River is the principal river of Hunza, in a region known as the Northern Areas of Pakistan. It is formed by the junctions of the Kilik and Khunjerab nalas (gorges) which are fed by glaciers. The river cuts through the Karakoram range, flowing from north to south. It is joined by the Gilgit River and the Naltar River before it flows into the Indus River. The Karakoram Highway crosses the Hunza River near Karimabad.

Hurasagar River : Hurasagar river is the joint flow of the Atrai-Baral and the Phuljhar (the Bangali-Karatoya) rivers. The river Gumani meets with the Gur near Chanchkoir to the east of the Chalan Beel and flows as the Gumani. Flowing east of Chatmohar the river again meets with the Baral and flows further as Baral (Atrai-

Baral). The Atrai-Baral receives the Phuljhar as its left bank tributary at 48 km southeast of Chatmohar near Baghabari and the joint flow receiving the name Hurasagar which flows further southeast. Near Bera upazila the Hurasagar receives the Ichamati on its right bank and falls into the Jamuna. Construction of Bera Irrigation Project, a large multi purpose irrigation project on the river is going on at some downstream from Baghabari north-west of Bera Bazar. In the dry season, water will be diverted from the Hurasagar to the command area of the project through the Ichamati river which will be treated as the main supply canal of the irrigation project. Again in monsoon, excess water will be drained from the project area to the Hurasagar through this main canal.

Hurka Baul : This dance is performed during paddy and maize cultivation in the Kumaon region. The name of the dance is derived from hurka, the drum, which constitutes the only musical accompaniment, and baul, the song.

Husari : Husari is a main form of dance of Assam. Husari is carol singing. Batches of boys and young men led by older men go from house to house, sing and dance in the front or back courtyard and collect subscriptions to be spent on repairing the village Namghar (community centre) and on feasting. The dance commences with singing of hymns led by a comparatively elder person. Husari is more religious than festive and gives clear indications of the origin of the Bihu festival in some ancient fertility cult. Bihu songs and dances invariably follow the main item of Husari singing which consists of specially composed songs of religious themes sung by members of the party moving in a circle. These songs have a wide range of folk-tunes and are sung in praise of the great festival with the music of accompanying drums and various bamboo instruments. It is a dance of youth and of the spirit of spring, it expresses an exuberant spirit, like a Bihu song, it tends to express the erotic sentiment more than anything else.

Huseyn Shaheed Suhrawardy : Huseyn Shaheed Suhrawardy (September 8, 1892 - December 5, 1963) was a Pakistani politician of Bengali origin who served as Prime Minister of Pakistan from 1956 until 1957, also known for his controversial role in the Direct Action day, and following riots in Bengal during the last days of India's freedom struggle.

Suhrawardy was born to a prominent Bengali family in the town of Mindapore, West Bengal. He completed his undergraduate studies at St. Xaviares College, and completed a masters degree at Calcutta University. Afterwards, he moved to the United Kingdom to attend Oxford University from where he became a lawyer and was called to bar at Gray's Inn.

He returned to the subcontinent in 1921 where he became involved in politics in Bengal. Suhrawardy served as deputy mayor of Calcutta, Minister of Labor, and Minister of Civil Supplies under Khawaja Nazimuddin among other positions. In 1946, Huseyn Shaheed Suhrawardy established a Muslim League government in Bengal, being the only Muslim League government in India at the time.

The Muslim League Bengal Government declared August 16, 1946 to be a public holiday throughout Bengal, to celebrate the "Direct Action Day". Mobs rioted throughout Bengal resulting in huge loss of life and property.In Noakhali it was estimated that 4,000 hindus had lost their lives. Suhrawardy was directly and widely blamed for not preventing this huge carnage and trying to suppress the news of the same from the media. In 1947 power was transferred from the Muslim League to Congress,and Suhrawardy stepped down from Chief

Ministership. Fearing revenge of Hindus against Muslims in Calcutta, Suhrawardy sought help from Gandhi, who was much respected by the Calcutta population. Gandhi was persuaded to stay and pacify tempers in Calcutta, but he agreed to do so, on one condition—that Shaheed Suhrawardy share the same roof with him so that they could appeal to Muslims and Hindus alike to live in peace in this greatest of all Indian cities. "Adversity makes strange bed-fellows," Gandhi remarked about this strange request in his prayer meeting.

Upon formation of Pakistan, Suhrawardy maintained his work in politics, continuing to focus on Bengal or East Pakistan as it became after independence from the British. In 1949 he formed the East Pakistan Awami Muslim League, which would develop into the Awami League.

In the 1950s, Suhrawardy worked to consolidate political parties in East Pakistan to balance the politics of West Pakistan. Under Muhammad Ali Bogra, Huseyn Shaheed Suhrawardy would serve as Law Minister and later become the head of opposition parties.

In 1956, he was made Prime Minister by President of Pakistan Iskander Mirza after the resignation of Chaudhry Muhammad Ali. Suhrawardy inherited a political schism that was forming in Pakistan between the Muslim League and newer parties, such as the Republican party. The schism was fed by the attempt to consolidate the four provinces of West Pakistan into one province, so as to balance the fact that East Pakistan existed as only one province. Despite this attempt at equality, the plan was opposed in West Pakistan, and the cause was taken up by The Muslim League and religious parties. Suhrawardy supported the plan, but the vast opposition to it stalled its progress.

In order to divert attention from the controversy over the "One Unit" plan as it was called, Suhrawardy tried to ease economic differences between East and West Pakistan. However, despite his intentions, such moves only led to more political friction, and was worsened when Suhrawardy tried to give more money to East Pakistan than West Pakistan from aid received. Such moves led to a threat of dismissal looming over Shurwardy's head, and he resigned in 1957. Huseyn Shaheed Suhrawardy died in 1963 due to complications from heart problems. He is buried at Suhrawardy Udyan in Dhaka.

Husna : Husna was a Pakistani film actress in the late 1950s, 1960s and 1970s. Husna was a very talented and glamorous girl as a child. She was first introduced as a child star in Jan-e-Bahar (1958) and played the role as the daughter of Sudhir and Muzarrat Nazir. Husna never became a top heroine and mainly played the side-heroine or vamp roles in Urdu and Punjabi films during her long career. Then came her big break in the block buster Ajab Khan starring opposite Sudhir. She appeared in Rani Khan amongst other musical films. Her career had lasted 22 years when she retired after her last film which was *Lahu De Rishte.*

Hussain Muhammad Ershad : Hussain Muhammad Ershad was the president of Bangladesh. Born on 1 February 1930 in the district of Rangpur, Hussain Muhammad Ershad had his early education in his home town Rangpur and graduated from Dhaka University in 1950. He was commissioned in the Pakistan army in 1952. During 1960-62, he was an Adjutant in the East Bengal Regimental Centre, Chittagong. He completed the Staff Course from the Staff College in Quetta in 1966. In 1968, he served as Brigade Major of 54 Brigade in Sialkot. After getting promotion as Lieutenant Colonel in 1969 he commanded the 3rd East Bengal Regiment during 1969-70 and the 7th East Bengal Regiment during 1971-72.

After his repatriation from Pakistan, Ershad was appointed Adjutant General of Bangladesh Army in 1973. He was promoted to the rank of Colonel on 12 December 1973 and then to Brigadier in June 1975. He attended the National Defence College at Delhi in 1975. The same year he was promoted to the rank of Major General, and was appointed the Deputy Chief of Army Staff. Ershad was made the Chief of Army Staff in December 1978, and promoted to the rank of Lieutenant General in 1979.

Soon after the assassination of President Ziaur Rahman on 30 May 1981, Ershad's interest in politics became apparent. On 24 March 1982, General Ershad usurped state power by removing the elected government of President Abdus Sattar. General Ershad ruled the country as Chief Martial Law Administrator till December 1983. He then took over the country's Presidency from Justice Afm Ahsanuddin Chowdhury on 11 December 1983. Ershad introduced the upazila system and the first elections to the upazila parishad were held in May 1985.

Ershad was elected to the Presidency for a five-year term in 1986 as a nominee of Jatiya Party, which he established in 1986. All major political parties had boycotted the election. In the general elections of 1986 Ershad's Jatiya Party could manage absolute majority in the Jatiya Sangsad. Although participated by the Awami League, Bangladesh Nationalist Party boycotted the election. The Sangsad was however dissolved by the President on 7 December 1987 in the face of a strong opposition movement. The general elections that followed in 1988 were boycotted by all major opposition political parties. Amidst a relentless combined movement by the opposition, Ershad was forced to step down on 6 December 1990.

General Ershad was subsequently arrested and kept confined. In the Jatiya Sangsad elections of 1991, Ershad contested from jail from five constituencies of Rangpur and won in all the seats. The BNP government instituted a number of graft cases against him on charge of corruption, and in some of those cases he was found guilty and thus convicted. In the 1996 general elections he again secured five seats in the Assembly. After six years of confinement Ershad was released on bail on 9 January 1997. He lost his membership in the Jatiya Sangsad due to his conviction by the court. The Jatiya Party having been divided into three groups in 2000, Ershad still leads one of the factions as chairman.

Hussain Sagar : Hussain Sagar is a lake in Hyderabad, India built by Hazrat Hussain Shah Wali in 1562, during the rule of Ibrahim Quli Qutb Shah Wali. It was built on a tributary of the Musi river to meet the water and irrigation needs of Hyderabad, India. It is now popularly known as Tank Bund, and has become a tourist destination as well as a local attraction. Once the source of drinking water for the twin cities of Hyderabad and Secunderabad, the lake's current condition is far from desirable. Since the 1980s and 1990s the immersion of Ganesh idols during the festival of Ganesh Chaturthi has led to the further pollution of the lake. Currently there are numerous environmentalist groups and government agencies that are trying to improve the condition of the lake.

Hussain Shah Syed : Hussain Shah Syed (born August 14, 1964) is a boxer from Pakistan, who won the bronze medal in the Middleweight division (71-75 kg) at the 1988 Summer Olympics in Seoul. He shared the podium with Kenya's Chris Sande.

Hussain-Doshi's Gufa : Located in the campus of the centre for Environment Planning and Technology in Gujarat, this gallery houses the collaborative efforts of artist M.F. Hussain and architect B.V. Doshi where art and architecture fuse together and complement each other magnificently.

Hyder Ali : Hyder Ali or Haidar 'Ali (c. 1722 - 1782), was the ruler of the Kingdom of Mysore in southern India. Hyder Ali was a Muslim soldier-adventurer, who, followed by his son Tipu Sultan, became the most formidable Asiatic rival the British had ever encountered in India. He was the great-grandson of a fakir or wandering ascetic of Islam, from Gulbarga in the Deccan. His father was a naik or chief constable at Budikota, near Kolar in present-day Karnataka. He was born in 1722, or according to other authorities 1717.

An elder brother, who like himself, was, at an early age, turned out into the world to seek his own fortune, rose to command a brigade in the Mysore army, while Hyder, who never learned to read or write, passed the first years of his life aimlessly in sport and sensuality, sometimes, however, acting as the agent of his brother, and meanwhile acquiring a useful familiarity with the tactics of the French when at the height of their reputation under Joseph François Dupleix. He is said to have induced his brother to employ a Parsi to purchase artillery and small arms from government of Bombay Presidency, and to enroll some thirty sailors of different European nations as gunners, and is thus credited with having been "the first Indian who formed a corps of sepoys armed with firelocks and bayonets, and who had a train of artillery served by Europeans."

At the siege of Devanhalli (1749) Hyder's services attracted the attention of Nanjiraj, the minister of the Raja of Mysore, and he at once received an independent command; within the next twelve years his energy and ability had made him completely master of minister and raja alike, and in everything but in name he was ruler of the kingdom. In 1763 the conquest of Kanara gave him possession of the treasures of Bednor, which he resolved to make the most splendid capital in India, under his own name, thenceforth changed from Hyder Naik into Hyder Ali Khan Bahadur; and in 1765 he retrieved previous defeat at the hands of the Marathas by the destruction of the Nairs or military caste of the Malabar coast, and the conquest of Calicut.

Hyder Ali now began to occupy the serious attention of the Madras Presidency, which in 1766 entered into an agreement with the Nizam of Hyderabad to furnish him with troops to be used against the common foe. But hardly had this alliance been formed when a secret arrangement was come to between the two Indian powers, the result of which was that Colonel Smith's small force was met with a united army of 50,000 men and 100 guns. British dash and sepoy fidelity, however, prevailed, first in the Battle of Chengam (September 3, 1767), and again still more remarkably in that of Tiruvannamalai (Trinornalai).

On the loss of his recently made fleet and forts on the western coast, Hyder Ali now offered overtures for peace; on the rejection of these, bringing all his resources and strategy into play, he forced Colonel Smith to raise the siege of Bangalore, and brought his army within 5 miles of Madras. The result was the treaty of April 1769, providing for the mutual restitution of all conquests, and for mutual aid and alliance in defensive war; it was followed by a commercial treaty in 1770 with the authorities of Bombay. Under these arrangements Hyder Ali, when defeated by the Marathas in 1772, claimed British assistance, but in vain; this breach of faith stung him to fury, and thenceforward he and his son did not cease to thirst for vengeance. His time came when in 1778 the British, on the declaration of war with France, resolved to drive the French out of India. The capture of Mahé on the coast of Malabar in 1779, followed by the annexation of lands belonging to a dependent of his own, gave him the needed pretext for the Second Anglo-Mysore War.

Again master of all that the Marathas had taken from him, and with empire extended to the Krishna River, he descended through the passes of the Western Ghats amid burning villages, reaching Kanchipuram (Conjeevaram), only 45 miles from Madras, unopposed. Not till the smoke was seen from St Thomas' Mount, where Sir Hector Munro commanded some 5200 troops, was any movement made; then, however, the British general sought to effect a junction with a smaller body under Colonel Baillie recalled from Guntur. The incapacity of these officers, notwithstanding the splendid courage of their men, resulted in the total destruction of Baillie's force of 2800 (September 10, 1780). Warren Hastings sent from Bengal Sir Eyre Coote, who, though repulsed at Chidambaram, defeated Hyder thrice successively in the battles of Porto Novo, Pollilur and Sholingarh, while Tipu Sultan was forced to raise the siege of Vandavasi (Wandiwash), and Vellore was provisioned. On the arrival of Lord Macartney as governor of Madras, the British fleet captured Nagapattinam (Negapatam), and forced Hyder Ali to confess that he could never ruin a power which had command of the sea. He had sent his son Tipu to the west coast, to seek the assistance of the French fleet, when his death took place suddenly at Chittoor in December 1782.

Hyderabad : Hyderabad located in Sindh province of Pakistan (formerly known as Neroon Kot). Formerly the capital of Sindh and known as the city of perfumes, it is now a regional headquarter of the district of Hyderabad. Before the creation of Pakistan, it was known as the Paris of India, for its roads used to be washed with perfume every day. The regional and political boundaries stage the city as a district. Hyderabad is a hot and humid city in the south of the nation and has been a staging point for literary campaign and a birthplace of many a poets. Rich with culture and tradition, the city is the largest bangle producer in the world.

I

Iajuddin Ahmed : Prof. Iajuddin Ahmed (born February 1, 1931) is the current President of Bangladesh (since 2002). He was born in Munshiganj District, Bengal (now in Bangladesh). His father was Moulvi Ibrahim. Ahmed received his M.S. and Ph.D. degrees from the University of Wisconsin, and then joined University of Dhaka as an assistant professor in the Department of Soil Science. He moved up in the ranks until he became a full professor in the department. He held the post of chairman of the Soil Science Department of Dhaka University and dean of the Faculty of Biological Science of the same University. He was also provost of Salimullah Muslim Hall. He was responsible for inventing a process of preserving nutrients in the soil and later releasing them according to the needs of the vegetation. Professor Ahmed also worked as visiting professor in Cornell University in 1984 and the German Technical University and Gottingens University of Germany in 1984. Ahmed and his wife, Dr. Anwara Begum, have three children.

Prof. Ahmed was an adviser in the caretaker government in 1991. He was also chairman of the Public Service Commission from 1991 to 1993 and chairman of the University Grants Commission from 1995 to 1999. His election as President of the Republic was seen as an attempt to infuse the Presidency with stability; he was widely seen as a non-partisan choice acceptable to most of the major political parties.

Ibn-e-Insha : Ibn-e-Insha (1927 - 1978) was a famous Urdu poet and a prose writer. He was born in tehsil Phalore, district Jalandhar, in what is modern day Indian side of Punjab.

He migrated to Pakistan after the Partition, and spent much of his time in Karachi. He died very young at an age of just 33 years. He is considered as one of the most versatile poets and writers of his generation. His most famous poem Insha je Utthoo (Get up Insha) is a modern day Classic.

Ibrahim Ismail Chundrigar : He was Prime Minister of Pakistan for approximately 2 months from October 17, 1957 to December 16, 1957.

After merely a year, Huseyn Shaheed Suhrawardy resigned from his Premiership in October 1957. His resignation came as a result of the President's refusal to convene a meeting of the Parliament to seek a vote of confidence. President Iskander Mirza appointed I. I. Chundrigar as the interim Prime Minister. Being a nominated Prime Minister, Chundrigar held a weak position from the very beginning. He headed a coalition government including the Krishak Sramik Party, Nizam-i-Islam Party, the Muslim League and the Republican Party. The Muslim League had agreed to form a coalition government with the Republican Party on the condition that by amending the Electoral Act, the principle of separate electorate would be implemented in the country. After the formation of the Cabinet, Ministers from East Pakistan and the Republican Party started opposing the proposed amendments. The Republican Party opposed the amendment as it wanted to gain advantage over its political opponent, the Muslim League.

Iskander Mirza exploited the differences between the parties and thus made Chundrigar an easy victim as he remained Prime Minister for only two months and therefore could not give any practical shape to his program.

Ibrahim Lodhi : Ibrahim Lodhi (died April 21, 1526) was the last ruler of the Delhi Sultanate. He was an Afghan (specifically of the Ghilzai tribe of Pashtuns) who presided over much of India from 1517-1526, when he was defeated by the Turkic Mughals, who established a new dynasty that would last some three centuries.

Ibrahim attained the throne upon the death of his father, Sikandar Lodhi, but was not blessed with the same ruling capability. He faced a number of rebellions. Rana Sanga extended his empire right up to western UP and threatened to attack Agra. There was rebellion in the east also. He also displeased the nobility when he replaced old and senior commanders by younger ones who were loyal to him. He was feared and loathed by his subjects. His Afghan nobility eventually invited Babur of Kabul to invade India.

Ibrahim died in the Battle of Panipat, where Babur's superior fighters and the desertion of many of Lodhi's soldiers led to his downfall, despite superior troop numbers.

Ichamati River : Ichamati river is an old river, once well-known as the main river on the west of Dhaka. The river originates from the south of Jafarganj opposite to the mouth of the Hurasagar near Nathpur Factory and runs towards Joginighat in Munshiganj. Five pilgrimage ghats (Panchatirtha ghat)-Tirthaghat, Agla, Solepur, Barunighat and Joginighat stand along the river. Joginighat is situated at the confluence of the Brahmaputra and the Ichamati. Ichamati is the name of another channel originating from the ganges at Rayta, northwest of Bheramara in Kushtia. The river first flows west and then follows a southerly direction through Kushtia. The Ichamati is a Trans-boundary rivers and enters India at Darshana. Then it flows south along the Bangladesh-India border and is renamed as the Kalindi at Debhata upazila of Satkhira district. It falls into the Bay of Bengal as the Hariabhanga. Again, there is another river of the name Ichamati in Dinajpur and the map of James Rennel shows that the Ichamati of Dhaka and the Ichamati of Dinajpur are the same river. According to a number of hydrologists, these three Ichamati rivers, in the past were a single channel.

ICICI Bank : ICICI Bank' (Industrial Credit and Investment Corporation of India) is India's largest private bank. ICICI Bank has total assets of about Rs.20.05bn (end-Mar 2005), a network of over 550 branches and offices, and about 1900 ATMs. ICICI Bank offers a wide range of banking products and financial services to corporate and retail customers through a variety of delivery channels and through its specialised subsidiaries and affiliates in the areas of investment banking, life and non-life insurance, venture capital and asset management. ICICI Bank's equity shares are listed in India on stock exchanges at Kolkata and Vadodara, the Stock Exchange, Mumbai and the National Stock Exchange of India Limited and its ADRs are listed on the New York Stock Exchange (NYSE). During the year 2005 ICICI bank was involved as a defendant in cases of alleged criminal practices in it's debt collection operations and alleged fraudulent tactics to sell it's products.

Idakka : Idakka is an hour-glass drum from Kerala, south India. They are very similar to the damaru which is found throughout India. Where the damaru is played by rattling knotted cords against the resonators, the idakka is played with a stick. Like the damaru the idakka's pitch may be bent by squeezing the lacing in the middle.

It is slung over the left shoulder and the right side is beaten with a stick. The left hand is used for tightening and loosening the tape wound round the middle. Varying the tension of the tape produces variations in tones. Simple melodies extending over one octave can be played in this instrument. The Edakka is one of the five instruments that constitute the panchavadhyam of Kerala.

Idli : Idli, also spelled Idly or Iddly, is a food native to southern India, common in the states of Tamil Nadu, Karnataka, Andhra Pradesh and Kerala. It is most often eaten at breakfast or as a snack. The traditional idli is a small, round patty of batter made of rice and lentils (specifically urad dal) and steamed. The 2"-3" diameter idli is usually served in pairs with chutney, sambar, or other condiments such as dry, crushed spice mixtures. The latter, Milagai Podi, may contain ground chilies, spices, seeds and lentils, and is useful if the idlis are to be eaten later away from home. Dipping in oil can prevent more souring of the idlis in the day's heat, and helps the dry seasonings to stick. Plain idlis may have little more than salt as seasoning, but there are many variations in ingredients. Some contemporary versions contain neither rice nor urad dal, but the finished product is still recognizably an idli.

Idu Mishmi Ritual Dance : The Idu Mishmis in Arunachal have a ritual-dance and a fertility-dance. The ritual-dance is performed by the priest or priestess in the ceremonies of Ai-ah, Ai-him, Mesalah and Rren. The fertility-dance is performed on the last day of the Rren ceremony. There is no definite myth about the origin of this dance. According to local tradition, the first priest who officiated in a funeral ceremony was Chineuhu and his brother, Ahihiuh, was the first priest who officiated in the other three ceremonies in which this dance forms a part. This dance is associated with the priestly office.

Besides the priest, there are three or four other dancers who are selected from amongst the spectators. In addition it is the usual dress which consists of a loin-cloth, a short-sleeved coat, and a sword slung on the right side, a leather bag slung on the left side and a few bead-necklaces, the priest wears a few other articles.

Idukki : Idukki is one among the 14 districts of Kerala state, India. The district headquarters is located at Painavu. Other largest towns in Idukki are Thodupuzha, Kattappana and Adimaly.

Idukki is greatly known for the splendid green mountains, streams and spices. It is also a main tourist destination in Kerala with its hill stations and valleys. The famous resort Thekkady (Periyar Tiger Reserve), is in Idukki District. Munnar is another hill resort of the district. Mattupetty is about 11 km away from Munnar. Mattupetty, is the headquarters of the Indo-Swiss Cattle Project.

Idul-Fitr : Idul-Fitr marks the conclusion of a month of fasts (Ramzan) and is comparable in the splendour of celebrations to the Durga Puja of the Hindus. Wearing of New clothes is a must and after the special morning prayer which are joined by every male in front of a mosque or in an open space, there is a general round of embracing. It is a day of feasting and quiet merriment, assembles for religious discourses being a main part of the days observances.

Iftekhar Ahmed Chowdhury : Dr. Iftekhar Ahmed Chowdhury (born 25 October 1946 in what was then British India) is the Permanent Representative (or Ambassador) for Bangladesh to the United Nations.

He presented his credentials to the Secretary-General of the United Nations on 6 November 2001, replacing Anwarul Karim Chowdhury. Iftekhar Ahmed Chowdhury attended Dhaka University, earning a Bachelor of Arts degree in political science in 1967. He then earned his masters and Ph.D in international relations, at the Australian National University in Canberra, Australia. He was appointed Deputy Secretary of the Ministry of Shipping and Aviation in Bangladesh in 1972, and then Deputy Chief of the External Resources Division of the Planning Commission from 1974 to 1976.

Chowdhury first served in the Bangladesh Embassy in Bonn, West Germany as Counsellor, from 1983 to 1986. He was then First Counsellor in the Bangladesh Permanent Mission to the United Nations in New York until 1988, when he was promoted to Deputy Permanent Representative, where he served until 1991.

He was the Bangladeshi Ambassador to Qatar from 1994 to 1996, when he became Bangladesh's Ambassador and Permanent Representative to the United Nations in Geneva, serving in this position until 2001. From 1998 to 2001, he also served as Director-General of Economic Affairs in the Bangladeshi Ministry of Foreign Affairs.

Chowdhury was the Special Adviser to the Secretary-General of the United Nations' Conference on Trade and Development (UNCTAD) from January to September 2001. Iftekar Ahmed Chowdhury sits as a Vice-President on the Executive Board of the United Nations Children's Fund (UNICEF), and was the chairman of the Economic and Financial committee at the 58th General Assembly. He also chairs the Awards committee for the United Nations Population Award.

Iftikhar Ali Khan : Iftikhar Ali Khan (born March 6, 1910, died January 5, 1952) was the Nawab of Pataudi and captain of the Indian cricket team. He was one of few cricketers ever to have played for two countries having also played for the English cricket team. Iftikhar Ali Khan's son Mansoor also later served as captain of the Indian cricket team, a father-son feat without parallel in India.

Iftikhar Ali Khan was born at Pataudi House in Delhi, into the family of the Nawabs of Pataudi, a small non-salute princely state located in the present-day Indian state of Haryana. He was the son of Nawab Muhammad Ibrahim Ali Khan of Pataudi and his wife Shahar Bano Begum, daughter of a Nawab of Loharu.

Educated at Chiefs' College (later renamed to Aitchison College), Lahore, and at Oxford, Iftikhar married Begum Sajida Sultan, second daughter of Hamidullah Khan, last ruling Nawab of Bhopal, in 1939. Hamidullah Khan was to have been succeeded in the titles and privileges associated with the ruling house of Bhopal by his eldest daughter Abida, but that lady emigrated to Pakistan in the aftermath of the partition of India. Sajida therefore succeeded her father and was recognised by the government of India as Begum of Bhopal in 1961. Upon her demise in 1995, Mansoor, son of Iftikhar Ali Khan & Sajida Sultan, succeeded to the estates and titles associated with the Nawabs of Bhopal.

Apart from Mansoor Ali Khan, Iftikhar and Sajida were the parents of three daughters. Iftikhar died at Delhi of a heart-attack, while playing polo, on January 5, 1952, which incidentally was the 11th birthday of his son Mansoor. He was succeeded as Nawab of Pataudi by his son, Mansoor Ali Khan, who was also later to serve as captain of the Indian cricket team. He is also the grandfather of Bollywood actors Saif Ali Khan and Soha Ali Khan.

Iftikhar Muhammad Chaudhry : Justice Iftikhar Muhammad Chaudhry (December 12, 1948-) is the Chief Justice of Pakistan Supreme Court. Chaudhry has a Bachelors in Arts and Bachelors in Law (LLB). He joined the bar in 1974. Later, he was enrolled as Advocate of the High Court in 1976 and as an Advocate of the Supreme Court in 1985.

He was appointed as Chief Justice High Court of Balochistan on April 22, 1999. For his services and seniority he was elevated to Supreme Court on February 4, 2000. He was recently appointed as Chief Justice of Pakistan on June 30, 2005.The appointment of Justice Iftikhar Muhammad Chaudhry as new Chief Justice of Pakistan was ordered by President General Pervez Musharraf. Justice Iftikhar Muhammad Chaudhry is the senior-most judge among the sitting judges of the apex court after the outgoing Chief Justice Nazim Hussain Siddiqui.

Ihsan Danish : Ihsan Danish (or Ahsan Danish; 1914 - 1982), was a prominent Urdu poet from Pakistan. His life marked the struggle of person who didn't have more then a primary level of education, who worked as ordinary laborer for years in odd jobs, and finally became a poet of excellence.

His autobiography Jahan-i-Danish is a classic now and has motivated many.

Ikat : Ikat, the technique by which the warp or weft or both can be tie-dyed in such a way that when woven, the 'programmed' pattern appears in the finished fabric. Of resist-dye techniques, the use of clay or wax-resist has long been known to Indian textile printers and painters, who would stamp or delineate the fabric with resist and then immerse and re-immerse in dye. To reserve areas of the warp or weft or both, before the process of weaving with tied threads, and then to dye the yarn, is a more interesting process that requires greater skill. And this seems to be more closely aligned to processes of tie-resist and warp-resist after weaving, than to the application of impression of a resist to the surface of a fabric.

Up to the beginning of this century, Chirala in Andhra Pradesh was renowned for an exquisite type of cotton sari, lungi, rumal and yardage in a range of Ikat techniques. One of the products of this place is known as telia rumal, a many-purpose cloth used as lungi, loin-cloth, shoulder-cloth and turban cloth which was a popular import item in many Islamic countries. Due to the heavy use of tel (oil), in the process of preparing the yarn for weaving, this variety of textile has deserved the name telia, meaning 'oily'. Chirala, Pochampalli, Puttapaka and Koyyalagudem were given a new lease of life in the middle of this century by the All India Handicrafts Board as a result of which these and other nearby places have become important centres for the production of what is now known as Hyderabadi Ikats. Many new experiments and imitations have been undertaken here ever since. The techniques and designs of telia rumal have been adapted to make saris, spreads, and yardage material.

Ikshvaku : Ikshvaku The Ikshvaku of Andhra are believed to be ancestors of the Rajus of Andhra Pradesh and may have been a distant branch of the main Ikshvaku family of Ayodhya who migrated to the deccan and established their own kingdom in the Krishna River-Guntur region. The Puranas mention them as the Sriparvatiyas (Foresters), Rulers of Sriparvata (Forests) and Andhrabhrityas (Servants of the Andhras). The Satavahanas were also known as Andhras. They were originally feudatories of the Brahmin Satavahanas and bore the title Mahatalavara. They ousted the Satavahanas and from 180-624 AD, they and the Brihatpalayanas, Salankayanas, Vishnukundinas, Vakatakas, Pallavas, Ananda Gotrikas, Kalingas and others ruled over Andhra with their small kingdoms. Though seven kings are said to have ruled for 100 years in all, only a few are known from Inscriptions.

Ilaiyaraaja: Ilaiyaraaja (born June 2, 1943) is an Indian film composer, having composed for over 1000 albums (films) over a career of more than 28 years. He is often called 'Isaingyani' (Musical genius) by his fans and the

Tamil cinema fraternity. Ilaiyaraaja was born in a rural family in Pannaipuram near Madurai, Tamil Nadu, India. Although he did not have any formal education, he completed a course in classical guitar (higher local) with a gold medal at the Trinity College of Music in London.

Ilaiyaraaja is credited with a truly unique orchestration technique, which involves blending of western and Indian instruments. He usually comes up with a tune initially and the lyrics are added later on.

Ilango Adigal : Ilango Adigal was a great tamil poet, who was instrumental in the creation of silappathikaram, one of the five great epics of South India. Prince Ilango Adigal was the brother of the Chera king Cheran Chenguttuvan (in modern day Kerala), in South India.

Ilayaraja : Ilayaraja is an Indian composer, having composed for over 1000 albums (films) over a career of more than 28 years. He is often called as 'Isaingyani' (Musical genius) by his fans and the Tamil cinema fraternity. Ilayaraja is credited with a truly unique orchestration technique, which involves blending of western and Indian instruments. He usually comes up with a tune initially and the lyrics are added later on. Besides scoring music for Tamil, Telugu and other Indian films, Ilayaraja has written two fusion albums, blending western classical with Carnatic ragas.

Iltutmish : Shams-ud-Din Iltutmish, or Altamash, was the third Sultan of Delhi, and the only other significant ruler, besides the founder Qutb ud din Aibak, of the Slave Dynasty. After the establishment of the Delhi Sultanate, Multan became its western frontier. In the beginning it was governed by Nasir-ud-Din Qabacha, then captured by Jaial-al-Din Manakabarni and finally annexed by Shams-ud-Din Iltutmish. Iltutmish was the first king to appoint a woman as his official successor.

He completed the famous Qutub Minar in Delhi, started by the founder of the dynasty, Qutb ud din Aibak.

I M Vijayan : I.M. Vijayan is one of the best football player that Indian football world has ever seen. He was born in Kerala, the beautiful state of India and the land of football as well.

He was the star in Indian Club football and represented all major football clubs in India and the Kerala team in Santhosh Trophy (National Football Tournament). Now he is retired from the football field and is focussing on his business on sports equipments.

Imilchang Dare : A waterfall of immense visual beauty is to be found close to the Tura-Chokpot Road in West Garo Hills district in Meghalaya. The stream on which it is located, flows through a deep, narrow winding bed of crevice rocks till it suddenly emerges on to a broad wide opening and cascades in a thick, wide formation, over a broad chasm, creating an electrifying waterfall of unique beauty. The deep, wide pool at the bottom of the fall with its wide and expansive surroundings make it an exciting swimming pool, full of fish of varied size and colour, besides being an ideal picnic spot.

Imphal : Imphal is the capital of Manipur, India. The Imphal Valley is drained by several small rivers originating from the hills surrounding it. These include the Imphal, Iril, Sekmai, Thoubal, and Khuga rivers. 'Ima Keithel' at Khwairamband Bazar is the only market in the world where, as the name suggests, all the stalls are run by women.

In the heart of the town and surrounded by a moat, are ruins of the old Palace of Kangla. Until 2003, the grounds used to be occupied by the Assam Rifles, a paramilitary force. Another place of historical interest is the Polo Ground which is the oldest existing polo ground in the world. Near the Polo Ground is the Manipur State Museum, which has a good collection of old artifacts and nice pictures depicting the history of Manipur.

Imran Khan : Imran Khan (Imran Ahmad Khan Niazi ; born November 25, 1952) is a Pakistani former cricketer turned politician. Imran played Test cricket for Pakistan between 1971 and 1992, and was captain of the national team when they won the World Cup in 1992.

Currently, Imran is a member of Parliament and chairman of his own political party, the Tehreek-e-Insaf (Movement for Justice).

Inder Kumar Gujral : Shri Inder Kumar Gujral was sworn in as the 12th Prime Minister of India on Monday, the 21st of April, 1997. Son of Late Shri Avtar Narain Gujral and Late Smt. Pushpa Gujral, Shri Gujral is M.A., B.Com. Ph.D. & D.Litt. (Hons. Causa). He was born at Jhelum (in undivided Punjab) on 4th December 1919. He and Smt. Shiela Gujral were married on May 26, 1945.

Shri Gujral belongs to a family of freedom fighters: both his parents participated in the freedom struggle in Punjab. At the young age of eleven, he himself actively participated in the freedom struggle in 1931 and was arrested and severely beaten by the police for organising movement of young children in the Jhelum town. In 1942, he was jailed during the Quit India Movement.

Before assuming the office of the Prime Minister of India, Shri Gujral was the Minister of External Affairs from June 1, 1996 and held additional charge of the Ministry of Water Resources from June 28, 1996. He was the Minister of External Affairs earlier during 1989-1990.

India : The Republic of India is a South Asian country that comprises a major portion of the Indian subcontinent.

It has a coastline of over seven thousand kilometres, borders Pakistan to the west, the People's Republic of China, Nepal, and Bhutan to the northeast, and Bangladesh and Myanmar to the east. On the Indian Ocean, it is adjacent to three island nations — the Maldives to the southwest, Sri Lanka to the south, and Indonesia to the southeast. India also claims a border with Afghanistan to the northwest.

The name India is derived from the Old Persian version of Sindhu, the historic local name for the Indus river. The Constitution of India, and common usage also recognises Bharat as an official name of equal status. This name is derived from the Sanskrit name of an ancient Hindu king whose story can be found in the Mahabharata epic poem. A third name, Hindustan (Persian: Land of the Hindus) has been used since the twelfth century AD, though its contemporary use is unevenly applied due to domestic disputes over its representativeness as a national signifier.

India is the fourth largest economy in the world by purchasing power parity, and the tenth largest by absolute GNP. It is the second most populous country, with a population of over one billion, and the seventh largest by geographical area. It is home to the Indus Valley Civilisation — one of the most ancient civilizations in recorded history — and a centre of important historic trade routes. Four major world religions — Hinduism, Buddhism, Jainism and Sikhism — have Indian origins. India was a part of the British Empire before gaining independence in 1947. In the last twenty years, it has grown significantly, especially in the economic and military spheres.

India Gate : Situated on the Rajpath in New Delhi, India Gate (originally called the All India War Memorial) was built by Edwin Lutyens to commemorate the Indian soldiers who died in the World War I and the Afghan Wars.

The foundation stone was laid on 10 February 1921 by the Duke of Connaught. The names of the soldiers who died in these wars are inscribed on the walls. It was completed in 1931. Burning under it since 1971 is the Amar Jawan Jyoti, the eternal soldier's flame, which marks the Unknown Soldier's Tomb.

Inscribed on top of India Gate in capital letters is the line: To the dead of the Indian armies who fell honoured in France and Flanders Mesopotamia and Persia East Africa Gallipoli and elsewhere in the near and the far-east and in sacred memory also of those whose names are recorded and who fell in India or the north-west frontier and during the Third Afgan War.

The 42 metre tall India Gate is situated such that many important roads spread out from it. Traffic passing around India Gate used to be continuous till the roads were closed to the public due to terrorist threats. The lawns around Rajpath are thronged by people during the night, when the India Gate is lit up.

India Government : India, one of the world's largest democratic countries, is a Union of Twenty Eight states and seven Union Territories. The country is a Sovereign Socialist Secular Democratic Republic with a Parliamentary system of government. The Republic is governed in terms of the Constitution adopted by the Constituent Assembly.

India was a dominion under the British colonial rule for a period of over 500 years till 1947. In August 15, 1947 India became independent after years of struggle, under the leadership of the Non- violent revolutionary advocate Mohandas Karam Chand (Mahatma) Gandhi, popularly referred to as the father of the Nation. The Indian constitution, the world's lengthiest constitution (with 395 articles and 8 schedules) was passed by the Constituent Assembly on 26 November 1949 and came into force on 26th January 1950. The Constitution created a Sovereign Democratic Republic which was officially named 'Bharat' (in National language Hindi, after the legendary king of the Epic Mahabharata) or India, a Union of different states.

India is a federal system, a system of government in which power is divided by constitutional right between national and local units of government in regions. The constitution provides detailed lists dividing up legislative powers between central and state governments. The residual powers of legislation of the Union remain with the central government or the Parliament.

Legislature of the Union (Centre) which is called Parliament consists of the President and two houses, the upper house called Council of States or Rajya Sabha and House of the People or Lok Sabha. The President is the head of executive of the Union and is elected by members of an electoral college consisting of elected members of both Houses of Parliament and Legislative Assemblies of the states for 5 year terms. Supreme command of the Defence forces of the Union also vests in him.

The Prime Minister and a Council of Ministers (The Cabinet) under him, advice and aid the President in exercising his functions and he acts in accordance with such advice. Thus the real executive power of the Union vests in the Council of Ministers with Prime Minister as its head. The Prime Minister is designated by legislators of the political party or coalition commanding a parliamentary majority and is appointed by the President. The President then appoints subordinate ministers on the advice of the Prime Minister. The Vice- President is ex-officio chairman of the Rajya Sabha and acts as President when the latter is unable to discharge his functions due to any reason. He is elected in the same way as the President for a term of five years.

The Rajya Sabha consists of incumbents elected through an electoral college comprising of members of legislative assemblies of the States whereas the Lok Sabha consists of directly elected representatives by the people. The Rajya Sabha shall consist of 250 members out of which the President of India will nominate 12 persons having special knowledge or practical experience in respect of literature, art, science and social service. The remaining 238 seats are to be filled in by the representatives of the States and of the Union territories to be elected by the legislative assemblies of their respective states. One third of its members retire every second year and are re-appointed in staggered re-elections every second year. The Lok Sabha consist of 550 members, i.e., 530 members from the States and 20 members from the Union Territories. Its term, unless dissolved, is five years from the date appointed for its first meeting. The Lok Sabha is Presided over by a Speaker. Each house of the Parliament has to meet within six months of its previous sitting.

The Government of India consists of a number of ministries / departments for its administration, each Ministry assigned to a Minister who runs it with the assistance of a Secretary in charge of the particular Ministry. The Ministries are created and assigned by the President on the advice of the Prime Minister under Article 77 of the Constitution.

The system of Government in the States closely resembles that of the Union. Governor is head of executive of the State, but it is the Council of Ministers with Chief Minister as head in whom the real executive power vests.

India Office : The India Office was the British government department responsible for the government of

British India. It was headed by the Secretary of State for India, who was a member of the Prime Minister's Cabinet. The India Office was established under the provisions of the Government of India Act 1858. This act transferred the powers and functions of the British East India Company to the Crown, which continued to function as the ultimate ruler of India until 1947, when British India was partitioned into the independent states of India and Pakistan. It was unique among the departments of the British government in that it was largely funded out of Indian revenues until the entry into force of Government of India Act 1935. The India Office was intimately involved in the formation of Indian and Imperial policy throughout its existence. It worked behind the scenes forming the nexus between, the British political, bureaucratic and commercial reality and the Government of India.

India Today : India Today is an Indian weekly english newsmagazine, in publication since 1975. India Today is also the name of its sister-publication in Hindi. Aroon Purie is its editor-in-chief from 1975, a position he has held continuously for last three decades. It is part of the India Today group also founded in 1975 and which now includes 13 magazines, 3 radio stations, 2 TV channels, 1 newspaper, a classical music label, book publishing and India's only book club. Until recently, India Today has a weekly circulation of 1.4 million copies and is estimated to be read by 15 million people. With the publication of its 30th Anniversary issue in December 2005, the magazine which had commenced publication in 1975 with a circulation of 5000 copies, is currently have five editions and a circulation of over one million copies with a readership of over 20 million.

India: National Moto-Satyameva Jayate : Satyameva Jayate (Truth Alone Triumphs") is India's national motto. It is inscribed at the base of the national emblem, which is an adaptation of the Buddhist Lion Capital of Asoka at Sarnath, near Varanasi in the north Indian state of Uttar Pradesh. The quote is the 6th Mantra of the 1st Khanda of the 3rd Mudaka from the Mundaka Upanishad.

India's Involvement in Bangladesh Liberation War : On 27 March 1971, Prime Minister of India, Indira Gandhi, expressed full support of her government to the Bangladeshi struggle for freedom. The Bangladesh-India border was opened to allow the tortured and panic-stricken Bengalis safe shelter in India. The governments of West Bengal, Bihar, Assam, Meghalaya and Tripura established refugee camps along the border. Exiled Bangladeshi army officers and voluntary workers from India immediately started using these camps for the recruitment and training of Mukti Bahini guerrillas. As the massacres in East Pakistan escalated, an estimated 10 million refugees fled to India, causing financial hardship and instability in that country. The United States, long a close ally of Pakistan, continued to ship arms and supplies to West Pakistan.

Indira Gandhi launched a diplomatic offensive in the early fall of 1971 touring Europe, and was successful in getting both the United Kingdom and France to break with the United States, and block any pro-Pakistan directives in the United Nations security council. Indira Gandhi's greatest coup was on 9 August when she signed a twenty-year treaty of friendship and co-operation with the Soviet Union, greatly shocking the United States, and providing India with insurance that the People's Republic of China would not be involved in the conflict. China, an ally of Pakistan, had been providing moral support, but little military aid, and did not advance troops to its border with India.

Operation of the Mukti Bahini caused severe casualties to the Pakistani Army, which was in control of all district headquarters. As the flow of refugees swelled to a tide, the economic costs for India began to escalate. India began providing support including weapons and training for the Mukti Bahini, and began shelling military targets in East Pakistan.

India's Official Engagement with Pakistan : By November, war seemed inevitable; a massive buildup of Indian forces on the border with East Pakistan had begun. The Indian military waited for winter, when the drier ground would make for easier operations and Himalayan passes would be closed by snow, preventing any Chinese intervention. On 23 November, Yahya Khan declared a state of emergency in all of Pakistan and told his people to prepare for war.

On the evening of Sunday, 3 December, the Pakistani air force launched sorties on eight airfields in north-western India. This attack was inspired by the Arab-Israeli Six Day War and the success of the Israeli preemptive strike. The Indians had, however, anticipated such a move and the raid was not successful. The Indian Air Force launched a counter-attack and quickly achieving air superiority. On the Eastern front, the Indian Army joined forces with the Mukti Bahini to form the Mitro Bahini (Allied Forces) and the next day the Indian forces responded with a coordinated and massive air, sea, and land assault on East Pakistan. On the western sector Yahya Khan had planned to counter attack India so as to capture some territory which could have been used to bargain for territory that was expected to be lost in the east. The land battle in the West was thus crucial for any hope of a united Pakistan. But the Indian Army quickly responded to the Pakistan Army's moves in the west and made some initial gains, including capturing around 5,500 sq. miles of Pakistan territory and then settled down, keeping the Pakistani Army pinned down. (Gains made by India in Pakistani

Kashmir and Pakistani Punjab sector were later given up voluntarily by India in the Shimla Agreement signed in 1972, as a gesture of goodwill).

Indian Air Force : The Indian Air Force is the air-arm of the Armed Forces of India and has the prime responsibility of conducting air-based warfare and securing Indian airspace. It was established on October 8, 1932 as the Royal Indian Air Force. The prefix Royal was dropped after India became a Republic in 1950. It is the fourth largest air force in the world.

Indian Airlines : Indian is India's state owned primarily domestic airline, under the federal Union Ministry of Civil Aviation and based in New Delhi. Its main bases are Chennai International Airport, Chatrapati Shivaji International Airport, Mumbai, Netaji Subhash Chandra Bose International Airport, Kolkata and Indira Gandhi International Airport, New Delhi.

The company was formerly known as Indian Airlines. On December 7, 2005 The company was rebranded as Indian as a part of a program to revamp the company image in preparation for an IPO. Alliance Air is a fully-owned subsidary of Indian.

Indian Armed Forces : The Indian Armed Forces is India's primary defence organisation. The armed force consists of the Indian Army, Navy (including naval air arm), Air Force, the Border Security Force, Assam Rifles, Rashtriya Rifles, National Security Guards, Indo-Tibetan Border Police, Special Frontier Force, Central Reserve Police Force, National Cadet Corps, Defense Security Corps, and the Strategic Forces Command.

The Military of India has the highest headcount in the world, after the Peoples Liberation Army. Over a million strong, the Indian Paramilitary Forces also form the largest paramilitary force in the world. Combined, the Indian Armed Forces is the largest armed force in the world. The Indian Army maintains the world's 3rd largest active army. The Supreme Commander of the Indian Armed Forces is the President of India, currently Dr. A.P.J Abdul Kalam. Since its formation, the military has fought in both World Wars. Post-independence, it has fought three wars against Pakistan and a war with China. India also fought an extended border skirmish with Pakistan in 1999.

The Indian military possesses nuclear weapons and sufficient means, through a range of missiles and aircraft — to deliver these over considerably long distances. However, India has a nuclear no-first-use policy and maintains a nuclear doctrine based on credible minimum deterrence. India is not a part of the Nuclear Non-proliferation Treaty (NPT), citing concerns that it unfairly favours the established nuclear powers, and provides no provision for complete nuclear disarmament. Indian officials argued that India's refusal to sign the treaty stemmed from the treaty's fundamentally discriminatory character; the treaty places restrictions on the non-nuclear weapons states but does little to curb the modernization and expansion of the nuclear arsenals of the nuclear weapons states. The Indian armed forces is a volunteer only service; the military draft has never been imposed in India.

Indian Army : The Indian Army is the land force of the Armed Forces of India and has the prime responsibility of conducting land-based warfare. The Indian Army maintains the 3rd largest active force in the world. The Indian Army is a well-trained and well-equipped military service, with a troop strength of over a million. It is a completely voluntary service, the military draft never having been imposed in India. The army has rich combat experience in diverse terrains, considering India's diversity on this front, and also has a distinguished history of serving in United Nations peacekeeping operations. The force is headed by the Chief of Army Staff, currently General J.J. Singh. The highest rank in the Indian Army is Field Marshal, but it is a largely ceremonial rank and appointments are made by the President of India, on the advice of the Union Cabinet of Ministers, only in exceptional circumstances. Field Marshal S.H.F.J Maneckshaw and the late Field Marshal K.M. Cariappa are the only two officers who have attained this rank.

Indian Art Cinema : In addition to commercial cinema, there is also high-minded Indian art cinema, known to film critics as "New Indian Cinema" or sometimes "the Indian New Wave". Most people in India simply call such films "art films" as opposed to mainstream commercial cinema. From the 1960s through the 1980s, the art film was usually government-supported cinema. Aspiring directors could get federal or state government grants to produce non-commercial films on Indian themes. Many of these directors were graduates of the government film school (FTII or Film and Television Institute of India). Their films were showcased at government film festivals and on the government-run TV station, Doordarshan. These films also had limited runs in art house theatres in India and overseas.

The art directors owed much more to foreign influences, such as Italian Neo-Realism or French New Wave, than they did to the genre conventions of commercial Indian cinema. The best known New Cinema directors were Bengali: Satyajit Ray, Ritwik Ghatak, and Bimal Roy. The best known films of this genre include the Apu Trilogy (Bengali) by Ray, Meghe Dhaka Tara (Bengali) by Ghatak and Do Bigha Zameen (Hindi) by Roy. Satyajit Ray was the most successful of the "art" directors. Many Indians knew his name and took pride in his numerous foreign awards. Prestige, however, did not translate to large-scale commercial success. His films played primarily to art-house audiences (students and intelligentsia) in the larger Indian cities, or to film buffs on the international art-house circuit.

However, many cinematographers, technicians and actors started in art cinema and moved to commercial cinema. The actor Naseeruddin Shah is one notable example. He has never achieved matinee idol status, but he has turned out a solid body of work as a supporting actor and a star in independent films such as Mira Nair's Monsoon Wedding. Art cinema was also well-supported in the state of Kerala. Malayalam movie makers like Adoor Gopalakrishnan, G. Aravindan, T. V. Chandran, and M. T. Vasudevan Nair were fairly successful. Starting the 1970s, Kannada film-makers from Karnataka state produced a string of serious, low-budget films. But virtually only one director from that period continues to make off-beat films — Girish Kasaravalli.

In the film markets of South India, particularly the Tamil film industry, directors such as K. Balachander, Bharathiraja, Balu Mahendra, Bapu, Puttanna, Siddalingaiah, Dr.K.Vishwanath, and Mani Ratnam have achieved box-office hits whilst balancing elements of art and popular cinema. Films from the South that balance art and commercial styles, that went on to receive acclaim nationally and internationally include "Nayagan" and "Kannathil Muthamittal". Independent films may be the future of art cinema in India, which has to a great extent lost its government patronage. The Indian film market will likely consist of big-budget mass-market films with big stars, and independent films made on a shoestring by aspiring auteurs — much like today's Western film market.

Indian Blackbuck Antelope : The Blackbuck (Antilope cervicapra), also called Indian Blackbuck antelope or Sasin, is a small antelope native to India and parts of Nepal.

They were originally found in Pakistan too but were hunted to extinction.

A few herds can be found straggling over the border, shared with India. They are also seen in parts of Texas, USA where they were released in 1932. During the '70 and '80 small groups of Blackbuck were reintroduced into Pakistan and now there are small captive populations of Blackbuck in 3-4 locations. Blackbuck are listed as endangered, due to poaching and habitat destruction. They are also hunted for sport, their flesh and skin. The remaining populations are under threat from inbreeding.

Indian Botanical Garden : The Indian Botanical Garden was founded in 1786 beside the Hooghly river in Shibpur, Howrah. It is spread across an area of 273 acres. It is the country's largest and oldest Botanical Garden. The major tourist attraction of the garden is a 250-year-old, 98 feet high, banyan tree (Ficus Bengalhensis) with 600 arial roots and the largest girth of any banyan tree ever recorded (1300 feet). The garden contains 12,000 living perennial plants and over two and half million driedout plant specimens in the herbarium, collected from all over the world.

Indian Breads : Indian breads are one of primary item in the daily menu of the Indian food. Basically they are made of finely milled wheat flour and water. Depends upon the ingredients and way of preparation the Indian breads can be classified as Chapati, Phulka, Roti, Paratha, Naan etc.

Most of these are cooked on a flat pan except Naan. A special oven called Tandoor is used for cooking Naan directly over the flame.

Indian Caste System : The Indian caste system is a social system in which people are divided into separate endogamous groups, known in English as castes, and in Hindi as jati (birth unit), biradari (fraternity) etc. Indian classes called varna, literally, "colour", and commonly known as "castes" in English. There were five major castes in Indian society in ancient times. There are now several thousand castes and subcastes in India. A caste is defined by the mutual interaction among the members of the caste. The two of the most common bonds are:"Roti" (bread): dining together and "beti" (daughter): intermarrying together.

In the past some individuals were excommunicated out of the caste (thus becoming an "outcaste") if they committed some unpardonable offences. They were denied the privilege of mingling socially with the rest of their former caste. The Indian caste system has been in use for many years. Still today the values of the caste system are held strongly. It has kept a sense of order, and peace among the people. There are five different levels of the system: Brahman, Kshatriya, Vaishya, Shudra, and Harijans. Within each of these categories are the actual "castes" or jatis within which people are born, marry, and die. They all have their own place among each other and accept that it is the way to keep society from disintegrating to chaos. This system has worked well for Indian people and still has a major role in modern India.

Indian Certificate of Secondary Education (ICSE) : ICSE examination is an examination conducted by the Council for the Indian School Certificate Examinations for class 10, i.e., grade 10. It has been designed to provide an examination in a course of general education, in accordance with the recommendations of the New Education Policy 1986 (India), through the medium of English. The examination allows secure suitable representation of Governments responsible for schools (which are affiliated to it) in their States/Territories. Most schools affiliate to either the ICSE or the CBSE examinations as the results of these exams are considered a benchmark all over the country. Private candidates are not permitted to appear for this examination.

Indian Classical Music : The word music in India means 'Sangeeta', which traditionally meant performing the art of singing, playing of instruments and dancing.

Indian classical music originated from Vedic chants or Sama music. This music chiefly consisted of chanting of hymns in praise of the Vedic gods. The musical structure of the chants was characterised by descending order of notes, initially two to five which later was increased to seven notes. Gradually various developments took place and this culminated in the Raga tradition.

The Raga (structure of melody) and Tala (structure of rhythm) are the two major characteristics of Indian Classical music. The melody deals with the rise and fall of sounds and the latter deals with the pattern of time beats of Ragas.

Tala is the pulse of Indian music. The term Tala is derived from the Sanskrit word 'Tal' which means to strike with palms. Early musicians may have employed claps or palm-strokes to mark time in dance and music which later developed into a complicated system of 108 talas of classical music. It is a time cycle that remains fixed through out a particular rendering. Tala, binds music together and offer a regularity that calms the mind.

Raga is the basic scale or note-pattern of a melody formed by selecting notes from the thirteen tonal intervals, conventionally established in the octave space. The notes are selected from ascending as well as descending progressions. They are Sa, Re, Ga, Ma, Pa, Dha, Ni in the ascending order and Sa, Ni, Dha, Pa, Ma, Ga, Re, Sa in the descending order. Frameworks, thus provided by the selected notes function as the ground-plan. Musicians can elaborate Ragas on the basis of this plan and create more tonal patterns pleasing to the ears of the listeners.

Ragas in the South mostly have Sanskrit names, unlike in the North, where their names often comes from specific region or from the dialects of regions.

Tala and raga varies in each composition. Sometimes Tala is more active and controls the other or vise versa. This depends on the person performing the music.

Music is a universal art. The two cultures of the south and the north gave rise to the two modes of singing-Uttaradi and Dakshinadi or Hindustani and Karnatic.

North Indian Music offers a variety of forms of music like the Dhruvapada, Khyal, Thumari, Tappa and Ghazal. The dhruvapada is a strictly classical and a slow form. The khyal incorporates into this rigidity, the romanticism of yet another form, the thumari. All these forms follow the same basic tenets of the raga-tala system. The thumari is used quite extensively to accompany the dance Kathak. This is because it incorporates a high degree of emotional and aesthetic content, from the bottom of the heart. The tappa is a lighter form of classical music that is brisk and replete with a variety of phrases, which makes it particularly difficult to render without a good degree of virtuosity.

North Indian music has a wide range of ancient and beautiful instruments, each having a tone quite unique. Some of the more well known are the sitar, the sarod, the rudraveena, the santoor, the flute, the shehnai and the sarangi. Among the percussion instruments are the tabla and the pakhawaj. The tabla is used as an accompaniment to most music recitals. The pakhawaj has a deeper tone than the tabla.

Karnatic music has a deeper understanding of 'notal' values and their inter-relations. The musician of the south adheres very firmly to the tala cycle. Karnatic music is rigid and deeply spiritual. Thus, taste for Karnatic music has to be cultivated. The dominant element of Karnatic music is the 'Kriti'; a form of composition with three parts. The literary content of the Kritis or songs, are in the form of offerings.

The three great composers known as the trinity of Karnatic music are Shyama Sastry, Thyagaraja and Muthuswamy Dikshitar. Tyagaraja is the most popular among them. The music compositions, 'Tyagaraja Gana', 'Valmikiya Kavana' and 'Agumbeya Astamaya' are said to be unique for enrapturing the human heart. The flute, the violin, the veena, the nadaswaram and the gottuvadyam are among the most well known South Indian instruments.

Indian Coast Guard : The Indian Coast Guard is the paramilitary service created to guard Republic of India's vast coastline. It was created on 19 August 1978 as an independent entity as per the Coast Guard Act. Though a paramilitary force, the Indian Coast Guard is not a part of the Indian Paramilitary Force (PMF). The coast guard works closely with the Indian navy and the Indian Customs Department. India's coast guard has a large number of fast craft including hovercrafts and hydrofoils. They patrol the seas, river mouths and also lakes in Kashmir bordering China. The coast guard has performed a number of commendable tasks of rescuing distressed personnel as well as apprehending pirates on high seas. Heavy patrolling of sensitive areas such as Gujarat, West Bengal and Mumbai have resulted in a huge catch of smugglers and illegal immigrants.

Indian Cobra : The Indian Spectacled cobra (Naja naja naja) is a type of venomous snake native to the Indian subcontinent. The Indian cobra, like all other cobras, raises its hood when in danger. These snakes grow to be approx. 6 feet in length (2 meters).

Just like the Indian Krait, a cobra has neurotoxins. The major difference is that the cobra has a post-synaptic neurotoxins. The venom acts on the synaptic gaps of the muscle thus paralysing them. Which can lead to respiratory failure or cardiac arrest.

Indian Cuisine : Indian cuisine is very diverse and is a result of India's diverse population. Over the centuries, each new wave of settlers brought with them their own culinary practices which, with time, blended into the Indian cuisine as it is known today. Besides settlers from outside, Indian cuisine has been influenced by environmental, social, religious and political factors from within. Most Indian cuisines are related by significant usage of spices, and by the use of a larger variety of vegetables than most other culinary traditions. Within these recognizable similarities, there is an enormous variety of local styles.

Typically, North Indian meals consist of chapatis or rotis and rice as staples, eaten with a wide variety of side dishes like dals, curries, yoghurt, chutney and achars. South Indian dishes are mostly rice-based, sambhar, rasam and curries being important side dishes. Coconut is an important ingredient in most South Indian food.

Besides the main dishes, various snacks are widely popular in Indian cuisine, such as samosa and vada. Among drinks, tea enjoys heavy popularity, while coffee is mostly popular in South India. Nimbu pani (lemonade), lassi, and coconut milk are also popular, while India also has many indigenous alcoholic beverages like Fenny and Indian beer.

Several customs are associated with the way in which food is consumed. Traditionally, meals are eaten while sitting on the floor or on very low stools, eating with the fingers of the right hand.

Indian Emergency : The Emergency in India was a 18-month period between 1975 and 1977, when President Fakhruddin Ali Ahmed, upon advice by Prime Minister Indira Gandhi, declared a state of emergency under Article 352 of the Constitution of India, effectively allowing her to rule by decree, suspending elections and civil liberties. It was the most controversial period in the history of independent India.

Opponents had long made allegations that Indira's party, Congress, had practiced electoral fraud to win the 1971 elections. The Gandhian socialist Jaya Prakash Narayan (JP) had been agitating in Bihar for a change in provincial government, and increasingly sought to direct popular action against the government at the Centre through satyagrahas. JP and his supporters sought to unify students', peasants', and labour organisations in a 'Total Revolution' to nonviolently transform Indian society. Indira's party was defeated in Gujarat by a coalition of parties calling itself the Janata Party (People's Party), and even faced an all-party, no-confidence motion in Parliament.

On June 21, 1975, Justice Jagmohanlal Sinha of the Allahabad High Court found the Prime Minister guilty of using government machinery for election purposes, and ordered her to be removed from her seat in Parliament and banned from running for an additional six years. Her conviction was actually upon a small technicality—an official in the Prime Minister's Office had failed to submit his resignation in time before officially beginning work on Indira's election campaign in 1971. However, strikes in labor and trade unions, student unions and government unions swept across the country. Protests led by Narayan and Morarji Desai flooded the streets of Delhi close to the Parliament building and the PM's residence.

President Fakhruddin Ali Ahmed declared a State of Emergency. Apart from being a political ally of Indira, the President in India acts mostly upon the advice of the Prime Minister. In her own words, Indira brought democracy "to a grinding halt". Elections for the Parliament and state governments were postponed. Invoking article 352 of the Indian Constitution, she granted herself extraordinary powers and launched a massive crackdown on civil liberties and political opposition. The Government cited threats to national security, as a recent war with Pakistan had just been concluded. The strikes and protests had paralyzed the government and hurt the economy of the country greatly. Indira herself had the right to appeal to the Supreme Court of India and had no legal obligation to resign until then. But in face of massive political opposition, desertion and disorder across the country, she took the advice of a few close party loyalists and her younger son Sanjay Gandhi, who had become a close political advisor.

As the constitution requires, Indira advised and President Ahmed approved the continuation of Emergency over every six-month period until her decision to hold elections in 1977. President Ahmed signed the decree, invoking a state of emergency under the Constitution. The Government used police forces across the country to arrest thousands of protestors and strike leaders. J.P. Narayan, Morarji Desai, Charan Singh, Jivatram Kripalani, Atal Bihari Vajpayee, Lal Krishna Advani and other protest leaders were immediately arrested. Organizations like the Rashtriya Swayamsevak Sangh and opposition political parties were banned.

Indira attempted to re-write the nation's laws with the help of the Parliament, where the Congress controlled over a two-thirds majority. She felt her powers were not amassing quickly enough, so she utilized the President to issue "extraordinary laws" that bypassed parliament altogether, allowing her to rule by decree. She constructed a 20-point economic program to increase agricultural and industrial production, improve public servics and fight poverty and illiteracy. Also, she had little trouble in making amendments to the constitution that exonerated her from any culpability in her election fraud case, declaring President's Rule in Gujarat and Tamil Nadu where anti-Indira parties ruled (state legislatures were thereby dissolved and suspended indefinitely), and jailing thousands of opponents.

On January 23, 1977, Indira Gandhi called fresh elections for March and released all political prisoners. Emergency officially ended on March 23, 1977. It is suggested that official intelligence sources told the Prime Minister that her administration was popular across the country. It has also been known that Indira feared that Field Marshall Sam Manekshaw, then Chief of Army Staff threatened to depose her if she did not immediately call elections, even though Maneckshaw denied any intentions in a later interview to The Times of India. The Janata Party alliance of political parties opposed to Indira swept the polls, winning a majority in Parliament. Many Congress Party loyalists deserted Indira, who herself lost her constituency seat. Morarji Desai became the first non-Congress Prime Minister of India.

The efforts of the Janata administration to try government officials and Congress politicians for Emergency-era abuses and crimes were largely a flop due to a disorganized, over-complex and politically-motivated process of litigation. Although special tribunals were organized and scores of senior Congress Party and government officials arrested and charged, including Indira and Sanjay Gandhi, police were unable to submit sufficient evidence for most cases, and only a few low-level officials were convicted of any abuses.

The people lost interest in the hearings owing to their continuous fumbling and complex nature, and the economic and social needs of the country grew more important to them. An impression was created that corruption and political subversion stalled the process of justice. The Emergency years were the biggest challenge to India's commitment to democracy, which proved vulnerable to the manipulation of powerful leaders and large parliamentary majorities.

Indian Film Industry : The Indian film industry is the largest in the world (1200 movies released in the year 2002). The industry is supported mainly by a vast film-going Indian public, though Indian films have been gaining increasing popularity in the rest of the world — notably in countries with large numbers of expatriate Indians. India is a large country where many languages are spoken. Each of the larger languages supports its own film industry: Urdu/Hindi, Bengali, Kannada, Tamil, Telugu, Malayalam.

1. The Hindi/Urdu film industry, based in Mumbai, formerly Bombay, is called Bollywood (a melding of Hollywood and Bombay).

2. The Tamil film industry is based in the Kodambakkam area of Chennai, South India, hence is sometimes called Kollywood.

3. Tollygunge is a metonym for the Bengali film industry, long centered in the Tollygunge district of Kolkata.

4. The Bengali language industry is notable as having nurtured the director Satyajit Ray, an internationally renowned filmmaker and a winner of many awards, among them the Bharat Ratna (India's highest civilian award), the Legion d'honneur (France), and the Lifetime achievement Academy Award.

5. Some people call the Kannada (Karnataka State) film industry (Sandalwood), as Karnataka is known for

sandalwood. This term does not seem to be in widespread use.

6. Some people call the Telugu film industry (Tollywood). The Bollywood industry is usually the largest in terms of films produced and box office receipts. Many workers in other regional industries, once established, also work in other film industries, nationally as well as internationally, owing to their talent, popularity and success. Commercial films, in whatever regional center they are made, tend to be:

— Long—three hours, with an intermission.

— Musical — action is periodically interruptedby song-and-dance routines. Good movies use the routines to move the story forward; mediocre movies have them only because the audience demands them. Songs are sung by professional play-back singers and lip-synched by dancing actors and actresses.

— Melodramatic, sentimental, of mixed genre — they mix romance, comedy, action, suspense, etc.

— Sometimes Indian-styled remakes of popular Hollywood movies, thus continuing a long film-making tradition (global in scope) of imitations and creative remixes.

Indian hairy-footed Gerbil : Indian hairy-footed gerbil, Gerbillus gleadowi is a species of Gerbil found mainly in Pakistan and northwestern India, They inhabit dry sandy and rocky country with sparse vegetation. Their burrows are often closed with sand. They feed nocturnally on seeds, roots, nuts, grasses and insects. They breed throughout the year. The gestation period is 20-22 days with litters of 4-5 naked pups. They young open their eyes at 16-20 days and they are weaned by their parents after a month.

Indian Independence Act 1947 : The Indian Independence Act 1947 was the legislation passed by the British Parliament that officially approved the independence of India and the partition of India. The legislation was designed by the administration of Prime Minister Clement Attlee, after Indian political parties came to an agreement on the transfer of power and the Partition of India with Viceroy Lord Mountbatten according to what has come to be known as the 3rd June Plan or Mountbatten Plan.

Indian Independence Movement : The Indian Independence Movement was a series of revolutions empowered by the people of India put forth to battle the British Empire for complete political independence, beginning with the Rebellion of 1857, reaching its climax with Mahatma Gandhi's Quit India Movement (1942-1945), and Subhash Chandra Bose's Indian National Army invasion of British India during World War II, culminating eventually in full freedom on August 15, 1947.

India's struggle for freedom is characterized by many unique and historic efforts, including the world's first and largest mass, non-violent civil resistance movement pioneered by Mahatma Gandhi, involving over 50 million people from 1918 to 1945, and Bose's daring creation of an Army of Indian POWs and indentured laborers. Its leadership is colored by some of the wealthiest and poorest, the most anglicized and Westernized, to the most orthodox, religious nationalist.

Indian Institute of Science (IISc) : The Indian Institute of Science (IISc) is one of the premier post-graduate institutions of research and higher learning located in Bangalore, India. It offers postgraduate and doctoral research programmes to over 2,000 active researchers working in 37 specialized departments — ranging from aerospace engineering to molecular biophysics. IISc is the best in India in terms of research output by the journal Current Science. It also ranks first among Indian universities (and South Asian universities) in the "Academic ranking of world universities" conducted by the SJTU, China. It was in the news recently when India's finance minister, P. Chidambaram provided for a grant of a billion rupees ($25m) for the institute in the national budget—2005.

Indian Institutes of Management (IIMs) : The Indian Institutes of Management (IIMs) are the premier management schools of India, located in the cities of Ahmedabad, Bangalore, Indore, Kolkata, Kozhikode and Lucknow. They award post-graduate diplomas in Management with various specializations. The CAT (Common Admission Test) conducted by the IIMs is a very competitive test conducted for admission to the numerous graduate programs in Management at the six campuses, and is usually considered one of the most competitive exams in the world, with a success rate of less than one in a hundred. Each institute conducts group discussions and personal interviews to evaluate the students shortlisted after the test.

Indian Institutes of Technology (IIT) : The Indian Institutes of Technology or IITs are a group of seven autonomous engineering and technology oriented institutes established by the Government of India. They have been declared Institutes of National Importance by the Government of India and are known throughout the world for their degree programs. There are about 17,000 undergraduate and 13,000 graduate students in the seven IITs in addition to the research scholars. The IITs were established over a period of time starting with the establishment of IIT Kharagpur in 1951. These institutes were created to train the scientists and engineers needed by India just after getting independent from the British rule. The students and alumni of IITs are referred to as IITians.

The individual IITs are autonomous universities and are linked in the top of their organizational structure having common Visitor and IIT Council. They also have a common admission program, the Joint Entrance Examination (or IIT-JEE). Many IITians have proceeeded to successful careers in industry, resulting in the establishment of the IIT Brand, considered to be a benchmark of academic excellence in India, and recognized all over the world. The autonomy of IITs have helped them to create specialized degrees in technology at undergraduate level, and consquently award the Bachelor of Technology (BTech) degree as opposed to Bachelor of Engineering (BE) degree elsewhere in the country.

Indian Institutes of Technology (IITs) : The Indian Institutes of Technology (IITs) are tertiary educational institutes established by the Government of India to offer undergraduate, integrated postgraduate and postgraduate degrees and the Doctor of Philosophy in over 25 different engineering, technology and business/management disciplines. The emphasis is on undergraduate education rather than on research.

The seven IITs are located in:

1. Chennai—IIT Madras
2. Guwahati—IIT Guwahati
3. Kanpur—IIT Kanpur
4. Kharagpur—IIT Kharagpur
5. Mumbai—IIT Bombay
6. New Delhi—IIT Delhi
7. Roorkee—IIT Roorkee

The related Indian Institute of Science is a post-graduate institution focussed on research and advanced instruction. (There are also six Indian Institutes of Management.) There are about 2500 undergraduate and 1500 graduate students in each IIT (except Guwahati, which is presently half this size, but increasing every year). In modern age no other institution in India, except Presidency College, Calcutta, had such an immense influence on Indian mind, as does IIT. Students/alumni are informally referred to as IITians with several alumni organizations active all over the world, for example the IIT Alumni Association of North Texas.

Indian Kashmir Barrier : The Indian Kashmir barrier is a 550 km (330 mile) separation barrier along the 740 km disputed 1972 Line of Control (or ceasefire line) between Indian and Pakistani controlled Kashmir: Jammu and Kashmir, India and Azad Kashmir, Pakistan. The rest of the Line of Control is too inaccessible for construction of a barrier. Constructed by India, its stated purpose is to exclude arms smuggling and infiltration by Pakistani-based separatist militants or terrorists, who wish to bring Kashmir into Pakistan, or gain independence for Kashmir. The barrier itself consists of double-row of fencing and barbed wire eight to twelve feet in height, and is electrified in stretches where power supply is available. The small stretch of land between the rows of fencing is mined.

The construction of the barrier was begun in the 1990s, but slowed in the early 2000s as hostilities between India and Pakistan increased. After a November 2003 ceasefire agreement, building resumed and was accelerated, and completion is expected in mid-2004. Pakistan has objected to the construction of the barrier, saying it violates both bilateral accords and relevant United Nations Security Council resolutions on the region. In Pakistan's view the border between Jammu and Kashmir is undemarcated, and border fencing is not allowed.

Indian Long-eared Hedgehog : The Indian Long-eared Hedgehog (Hemiechinus collaris; alternative names might include Erinaceus collaris and Erinaceus blanfordi) is a relatively small hedgehog (~17 cm, 200-500 grams) native to India and Pakistan. Notable for extremely large ears. Due to this feature used to be considered a subspecies of long-eared hedgehog.

Indian long-eared hedgehog is notable for a quite complex mating ritual that involves "dancing" aroung female for several days before mating.

Indian Muntjac : The Common muntjac, also called Indian muntjac (Muntiacus muntjak) is the most numerous muntjac deer species. It has soft, short, brownish or greyish hair, sometimes with creamy markings. This species is omnivorous, feeding on fruits, shoots, seeds, birds' eggs as well as small animals and even carrion. It gives calls similar to barking, usually on sensing a predator (hence the common name for all muntjacs of barking deer).

The male Indian muntjac has small antlers which attain 15 cm in length and have only 1 branch. They grow annually from a bony stalk on the head. Males are extremely territorial and can be fierce for their size. They will fight each other for territory using their antlers or their (more dangerous) tusk-like upper canine teeth, and can defend themselves against predators such as dogs.

Indian Muslim Nationalism : Indian Muslim nationalism refers to the political and cultural expression of nationalism, founded upon the religious tenets and identity of Islam, of the Muslims of the Indian subcontinent. Rising from the first days of Islamic empires in India, this article endeavors to explore and trace Muslim nationalism through medieval India and into the events of the 20th and early 21st century, within the modern nations of India, Pakistan and Bangladesh. The Indian subcontinent's Muslim population numbers more than 400 million.

The historical foundations of Muslim nationalist thinking derives inspiration from the glorious years of the Delhi Sultanate and the Mughal Empire in northern and central India. Those were the years when Muslim kingdoms were the most powerful and military forces in India, and an elite Islamic society that descended from Central Asia, Afghanistan and the Middle East spread the religion amongst common Indians.

The first organized expressions began with Muslim scholars and reformers like Syed Ahmed Khan, Syed Ameer Ali and the Aga Khan. Expression of Muslim separatism and nationhood emerged from modern Islam's pre-eminent poet and philosopher, Sir Allama Muhammad Iqbal and political activists like Choudhary Rahmat Ali.

Some prominant Muslims politically sought a base for themselves, separate from Hindus and other Indian nationalists, who espoused the Indian National Congress. Muslim scholars, religious leaders and politicians founded the All India Muslim League in 1906. Muslims comprised 25% to 30% of (pre-partition) India's collective population. Some Muslim leaders felt that their massive cultural and economic contributions to India's heritage and life merited an significant role for Muslims in a future independent India's governance and politics.

But others, led by Allama Iqbal and Muhammad Ali Jinnah felt a separate homeland must be obtained for all of India's Muslims. They espoused the Two-Nation Theory, that India was in fact home to the Muslim and Hindu nations, who were distinct in every way.

Another section of Muslim society, led by Khan Abdul Ghaffar Khan, Dr. Mukhtar Ahmed Ansari and Maulana

Azad felt that participation in the Indian Independence Movement and the Indian National Congress was a patriotic duty of all Muslims. Religious leaders like Maulana Maudoodi preferred a single nation, but sought to propogate the religion and create an Islamic republic in India.

Muhammad Ali Jinnah led the Muslim League's call for Pakistan. Some historians have come to believe that Jinnah did not actually want the partition of the Indian subcontinent, but used it as a potent weapon to secure greater political power for Indian Muslims. However, as time went on, communal tensions rose and so partition won increasing support among many Muslims in Muslim-majority areas of the Indian subcontinent.

On August 14, 1947, Pakistan was created out of the Muslim majority provinces of British India, Sind, the west of Punjab, Baluchistan, the east of Bengal and the North West Frontier Province. Communal violence broke out and millions of people were forced to flee their homes and many lost their lives. Hindus and Sikhs fled from Pakistan to India and Muslims fled from India to Pakistan. However, because Muslim communities existed throughout the Indian subcontinent, partition actually left tens of millions of Muslims within the boundaries of the secular Indian state. Currently, approximately 12% of the population of India is Muslim.

Indian National Army (I.N.A) : The Indian National Army (I.N.A) or Azad Hind Fauj was an auxiliary force to the Imperial Japanese Army in its southern mainland campaign during the Second World War. It consisted mostly of Indian prisoners of war who, in the course of service in the Indian Army, had been captured by Axis forces, although a significant portion were recruited from Indian civilians in Japanese-controlled Malaya and Burma.

The focus of the I.N.A. was the idea that as I.N.A. troops entered India, they could convince Indian army troops in India to join the I.N.A.. Along with popular civilian support, they could ultimately loosen British control of India. The I.N.A. literally planned to march to Delhi from the India/Burma border and lead a popular uprising along the way. The Japanese supported this idea, at times more or less, but sufficiently to provide material support to the formation of the I.N.A. in Japanese controlled territory in Asia, notably Malaya and Burma. Although the Japanese had not seriously planned on invading India themselves, the idea that their western boundary would be controlled by a more friendly government was attractive. It was also reconciled with the idea that Japanese expansion into Asia was part of an effort to support Asian government of Asia, driving out Europeans, and was useful to support this propoganda.

The I.N.A. was formally the military of the Arzi Hukumat-e-Azad Hind, the Provisional Government of Free India.

Indian National Congress : Indian National Congress (also known as the Congress Party or Congress (I), abbreviated INC) is a major political party in India. Created in 1885, the Indian National Congress became the nation's leader in the Independence Movement, with over 15 million Indians involved in its organisations and over 70 million participants in its struggle against the British Empire. After Independence in 1947, it became the nation's dominant political party. In the 14th Lok Sabha (2004-2009), 145 INC members, the largest contingent amongst all parties, serve in the house. The party is currently the chief member of the ruling United Progressive Alliance coalition government supported by the Left Front.

The history of the Indian National Congress falls into two distinct eras: i) The pre-independence era, when the party was at the forefront of the struggle for independence; ii) The post-independence era, when the party has enjoyed a prominent place in Indian politics, ruling the country for 47 of the 59 years since independence in 1947.

Founded in 1885 with the object of obtaining a greater share in government for educated Indians, the Indian National Congress was initially not opposed to British rule. The Congress met once a year during the Christmas vacation. Indeed, it was a Scotsman, Allan Octavian Hume, who brought about its first meeting in Bombay, with the approval of Lord Dufferin, the then-Viceroy. Later, however, its demands became more radical in the face of constant opposition from the government, and the party became very active in the independence movement. During this period there were two camps in the Congress: the Garam Dal of Bal Gangadhar Tilak, or Extremists (literally "hot faction"), and the Naram Dal of Gopal Krishna Gokhale, or Moderates (literally "soft faction"), distinguished by their attitude towards the British.

After the First World War the party became associated with Mahatma Gandhi, who (although never even a member of the party) remained its unofficial, spiritual leader and mass icon even as younger men and women became party president. The party was in many ways an umbrella organisation, sheltering within itself radical socialists, traditionalists and even Hindu and Muslim conservatives.

The official flag of the Congress during the Independence struggle. In its time as the nation's leader in the freedom struggle, it produced the nation's greatest leaders. Before the Gandhi Era came leaders like Bal Gangadhar Tilak, Bipin Chandra Pal, Lala Lajpat Rai, Gopal Krishna Gokhale, Mohammed Ali Jinnah (later leader of the Muslim League and instrumental in the creation of Pakistan), all starting with the first legendary icon of Indians was Dadabhai Naoroji, the president of the sister Indian National Association and later MP in the House of Commons, the first Indian to win a seat there.

With the rise of Mahatma Gandhi's popularity and his Satyagraha art of revolution came Sardar Vallabhbhai Patel, Pandit Jawaharlal Nehru (the nation's first Prime Minister), Dr. Rajendra Prasad (the nation's first President), Khan Abdul Ghaffar Khan, Chakravarti Rajgopalachari, Jivatram Kripalani and Maulana Abul Kalam Azad. The Congress under Gandhi's influence became the first integrated mass organization in the country, bringing together millions of people by specifically working against caste differences, untouchability, poverty, religious and ethnic boundaries. With members from virtually every ethnic group, economic class, linguistic group and religion, the Indian National Congress became the true representative of the people. From being an elitist group of educated and pro-British Indians, it became the 15 million-strong leader of the revolution.

Indian National Satellite System (INSAT) : Indian National Satellite System (INSAT) is a series of multipurpose Geo-Stationary satellites launched by ISRO to satisfy the telecommunications, broadcasting, meteorology, search and rescue needs of India. Commissioned in 1983, INSAT is the largest domestic communication system in the Asia-Pacific Region. Active satellites of this series include INSAT-2E, INSAT-3A, INSAT-3B, INSAT-3C, INSAT-3E, KALPANA-1 (METSAT), GSAT-2, EDUSAT (GSAT-3) and INSAT-4A. INSAT satellites provide transponders (about 150) in various bands (C, S, Extended C and Ku) to serve the television and communication needs of India. Some of the satellites also have the Very High Resolution Radiometer (VHRR), CCD cameras for metrological imaging. The satellites also incorporate transponder(s) for receiving distress alert signals for search and rescue missions in the South Asian and Indian Ocean Region, as ISRO is a member of the Cospas-Sarsat programme.

Indian Nationalism : Indian nationalism refers to the political and cultural expression of patriotism by peoples of India, of pride in the history and heritage of India, and visions for its future. It also refers to the consciousness and expression of religious and ethnic influences that help mould the national consciousness.

Nationalism describes the many underlying forces that moulded the Indian independence movement, and strongly continue to influence the politics of India, as well as being the heart of many contrasting ideologies that have caused ethnic and religious conflict in Indian society. It should be noted that, although controversial, Indian nationalism often imbibes the consciousness of Indians that prior to 1947, India embodied the broader Indian subcontinent.

Indian Navy : The Indian Navy is the naval-arm of the Armed Forces of India and has the prime responsibility of conducting sea-based warfare. It is the world's fifth largest navy in terms of personnel and was established by Britain when India was its colony. The Indian Navy is relatively well-armed among other Indian Ocean navies and presently operates more than 180 vessels, including one aircraft carrier.

Indian Ocean : The Indian Ocean is the third largest body of water in the world, covering about 20% of the Earth's water surface. It is bounded on the north by southern Asia; on the west by the Arabian Peninsula and Africa; on the east by the Malay Peninsula, the Sunda Islands, and Australia; and on the south by the Southern Ocean. It is separated from the Atlantic Ocean by the 20° east meridian running south from Cape Agulhas, and from the Pacific by the 147° east meridian. The northernmost extent of the Indian Ocean is approximately 30°north latitude in the Persian Gulf. This ocean is nearly 10,000 km wide at the southern tips of Africa and Australia; its area is 73,556,000 km^2, including the Red Sea and the Persian Gulf. The ocean's volume is estimated to be 292,131,000 km^3. Small islands dot the continental rims. Island nations within the ocean are Madagascar, the world's fourth largest island; Comoros; Seychelles; Maldives; Mauritius; and Sri Lanka. Indonesia borders it. The ocean's importance as a transit route between Asia and Africa has made it a scene of conflict. Because of its size, however, no nation had successfully dominated until the early 1800s when Britain controlled much of the surrounding land.

The African, Indian, and Antarctic crustal plates converge in the Indian Ocean. Their junctures are marked by branches of the Mid-Oceanic Ridge forming an inverted Y, with the stem running south from the edge of the continental shelf near Mumbai, India. The eastern, western, and southern basins thus formed are subdivided into smaller basins by ridges. The ocean's continental shelves are narrow, averaging 200 km in width. An exception is found off Australia's western coast, where the shelf width exceeds 1,000 km. The average depth of the ocean is 3,890 m. Its deepest point, in the Java Trench, is estimated to be 7,450 m. North of 50° south latitude, 86% of the main basin is covered by pelagic sediments, of which more than one-half is globigerina ooze. The remaining 14% is layered with terrigenous sediments. Glacial outwash dominates the extreme southern latitudes

The Indian Ocean provides major sea routes connecting the Middle East, Africa, and East Asia with Europe and the Americas. It carries a particularly heavy traffic of petroleum and petroleum products from the oilfields of the Persian Gulf and Indonesia. Large reserves of hydrocarbons are being tapped in the offshore areas of

Saudi Arabia, Iran, India, and western Australia. An estimated 40% of the world's offshore oil production comes from the Indian Ocean. Beach sands rich in heavy minerals and offshore placer deposits are actively exploited by bordering countries, particularly India, South Africa, Indonesia, Sri Lanka, and Thailand.

The warmth of the Indian Ocean keeps phytoplankton production low, except along the northern fringes and in a few scattered spots elsewhere; life in the ocean is thus limited. Fishing is confined to subsistence levels. Its fish are of great and growing importance to the bordering countries for domestic consumption and export. Fishing fleets from Russia, Japan, South Korea, and Taiwan also exploit the Indian Ocean, mainly for shrimp and tuna.

Indian Ocean Earthquake (2004): The 2004 Indian Ocean earthquake, known by the scientific community as the Sumatra-Andaman earthquake, was an undersea earthquake that occurred on December 26, 2004. According to the United States Geological Survey, the earthquake and its tsunami killed more than 283,100 people, making it one of the deadliest disasters in modern history. The disaster is known in Asia and the media as the Asian Tsunami and also known in Australia, Canada, New Zealand, and the United Kingdom as the Boxing Day Tsunami because it took place on Boxing Day.

Various values were given for the magnitude of the earthquake, ranging from 12.9 to 181.43), though authoritative estimates now put the magnitude at 9.15.

In May 2005, scientists reported that the earthquake itself lasted close to ten minutes when most major earthquakes last no more than a few seconds; it caused the entire planet to vibrate at least a few centimetres. It also triggered earthquakes elsewhere, as far away as Alaska.

The earthquake originated in the Indian Ocean just north of Simeulue island, off the western coast of northern Sumatra, Indonesia. The resulting tsunami devastated the shores of Indonesia, Sri Lanka, South India, Thailand and other countries with waves up to 30 m. It caused serious damage and deaths as far as the east coast of Africa, with the furthest recorded death due to the tsunami occurring at Port Elizabeth in South Africa, 8,000 km away from the epicentre.

The plight of the many affected people and countries prompted a widespread humanitarian response.

Indian Ocean Island States : Indian Ocean Island States is the name given to those island states in the Indian subcontinent which lie in the Indian Ocean. These include:

1. Democratic Socialist Republic of Sri Lanka
2. Andaman Islands (administrative territory of the Republic of India)
3. Nicobar Islands (administrative territory of the Republic of India)
4. Lakshadweep (administrative territory of the Republic of India)
5. Republic of Maldives
6. Chagos Archipelago (British Indian Ocean Territory)

Indian Oil Corporation Limited (IOC) : Indian Oil Corporation Limited or IOC is an Indian company. It is India's largest commercial enterprise and the only Indian company to be among the world's top 200 corporations according to Fortune magazine. It is also among the 20 largest petroleum companies in the world.

Indian Painting : Indian painting is a form of Indian art. The earliest Indian paintings were the rock paintings of pre-historic times, the petroglyphs as found in places like Bhimbetka, and some of them are older than 5500 BC. Such works continued and after several millennia, in the 7th century, carved pillars of Ellora, Maharashtra state present a fine example of Indian paintings, and the colors, mostly various shades of red and orange, were derived from minerals. Thereafter, frescoes of Ajanta and Ellora caves appeared. India's Buddhist literature is replete with examples of texts which describe that palaces of kings and aristocratic class were embellished with paintings, but they have largely not survived. But, it is believed that some form of art painting was practiced in that time.

In western India from the 16th to 18th century miniature painting developed. These small paintings were part of manuscripts written at the time and illustrate the subjects of the manuscripts.

Indian Pangolin : The Indian Pangolin (Manis crassicaudata) is a pangolin or scaly ant-eater that is found in many parts of India. Like other pangolins they have large, overlapping scales on the body which act like armour. They can also curl themselves as self defence against predators, namely the tiger. They are insectivores and feed on ants and termites, digging them out of their mounds using their long claws that are as long as their forelimb. They live mainly in burrows and are known to climb trees. They are also considered to be curious animals and have been killed for so-called medicinal value.

Pangolins are amazing creatures, as the scales are not skelatal, yet tiny hairs all squashed together to make scales.

Indian Paramilitary Forces : Indian Paramilitary Forces are those agencies of the Ministry of Defence or the Ministry of Home Affairs which act as armed forces auxiliaries and are considered part of the Indian Armed

Forces. The Indian Paramilitary Forces (PMF) are regarded as the world's largest and most formidable paramilitary force. In 2002, the total strength of the paramilitary force stood at 1.3 million personnel. The PMF is made up of twelve organisations

Indian Peafowl : The Indian Peafowl, Pavo cristatus, is a species of bird in the peafowl genus Pavo of the pheasant family, Phasianidae. The Indian Peafowl is a resident breeder in India and Sri Lanka. The species is found in dry semi-desert grasslands, scrub and deciduous forests. It forages on the ground and nests on the ground but roosts on top of trees. It eats mainly seeds, but also some insects, fruits and reptiles.

The male is called a peacock, the female a peahen. The Indian Peacock has beautiful iridescent blue-green plumage. The upper tail coverts are enormously elongated and ornate with an eye at the end of each feather. The female plumage is a mixture of dull green, grey and iridescent blue, with the greenish-grey predominating. In the breeding season, females can be told apart from the lack of the long 'tail' also known as the train. Peahens can be distinguished from males in the non-breeding season by the green colour of the neck as opposed to the blue on the males.

Indian Plate : The India or Indian Plate is a minor tectonic plate. Part of the major Indo-Australian Plate, it contains the subcontinent of India and a portion of the basin under the Indian Ocean. About 90 million years ago, in the late Cretaceous Period, the India Plate split from Madagascar off the east coast of Africa. It began moving north, at about 15 cm/yr (6 in/yr), and began colliding with Asia between 50 and 55 million years ago, in the Eocene epoch of the Cenozoic Era. During this time, the India Plate covered a distance of 2,000 to 3,000 km (1,200 to 1,900 mi), and moved faster than any other known plate.

The collision with the Eurasian Plate along the boundary between India and Nepal formed the orogenic belt that created the Tibetan Plateau and the Himalaya Mountains, as sediment bunched up like earth before a plow. The India Plate is currently moving northeast at 5 cm/yr (2 in/yr), while the Eurasian Plate is moving north at only 2 cm/yr (0.8 in/yr). This is causing the Eurasian Plate to deform, and the India Plate to compress at a rate of 4 mm/yr (0.15 in/yr).

Indian Porcupine : The Indian Porcupine (Hystrix indica) is a member of the Old World porcupines.

It is quite an adaptable rodent, found throughout southern Asia and the Middle East. It is tolerant of several different habitats: mountains, tropical and subtropical grasslands, scrublands, and forests. This is a large rodent, growing more that three feet long and weighs 32 pounds (this may be small to us, but keep in mind that most other rodents are smaller than this). It is covered in multiple layers of quills.

The longest quills grow from its shoulders to about a third of the animal's length. Its tail is covered in short, hollow quills that can rattle when threatened. It has broad feet and long claws for digging. When attacked, the Indian porcupine raises its quills and rattles the hollow quills on its tail.

Indian Railways (IRY) : Indian Railways (IRY) is the state-owned railway company of India. Indian Railways has a monopoly on the country's rail transport. It is also one of the largest and busiest rail networks in the world, transporting just under five billion passengers and almost 350 million tonnes of freight annually. IR is the world's largest commercial or utility employer, with more than 1.6 million employees.

The railways traverse through the length and width of the country covering a total length of 63,940 km (39,230 miles). As of 2005 IR owns a total of 216,717 wagons, 39,936 coaches and 7,339 locomotives and runs a total of 14,244 trains daily, including about 8,002 passenger trains.

Railways were first introduced to India in 1853. By 1947, the year of India's independence, there were forty-two rail systems. In 1951 the systems were nationalised as one unit, becoming one of the largest networks in the world. Indian Railways operates both long distance and suburban rail systems.

Indian Rebellion of 1857 : 1857–1858 was a period of armed uprising as well as rebellions in mostly northern and central India against British occupation of the subcontinent. The war brought about the end of the British East India Company's regime in India, and led to almost a century of direct rule of the Indian subcontinent by Britain: the British Raj. The events of this period are known to many Indians as the First War of Independence and the War of Independence of 1857 and to the British, and many western historians, variously as the Indian Mutiny, the Sepoy Mutiny, the Sepoy Rebellion, the Great Mutiny and the Revolt of 1857.

On May 10, 1857, Indian soldiers of the British Indian Army, drawn mostly from Muslim units from Bengal, mutinied in Meerut, a cantonment eighty kilometers northeast of Delhi. The rebels marched to Delhi to offer their services to the Mughal emperor, and soon much of north and central India was plunged into a year-long insurrection against the British.

The uprising, which seriously threatened British rule in India, has been called many names by historians, including the Sepoy Rebellion, the Great Mutiny, and the

Revolt of 1857; many people in South Asia, however, prefer to call it India's first war of independence. Undoubtedly, it was the culmination of mounting Indian resentment toward British economic and social policies over many decades. Until the rebellion, the British had succeeded in suppressing numerous riots and "tribal" wars or in accommodating them through concessions, but two events triggered the violent explosion of wrath in 1857. First, was the annexation in 1856 of Oudh, a wealthy princely state that generated huge revenue and represented a vestige of Mughal authority. The second was the British blunder in using cartridges for the Lee-Enfield rifle that were allegedly greased with animal fat, which was offensive to the religious beliefs of Muslim and Hindu sepoys. The rebellion soon engulfed much of North India, including Oudh and various areas once under the control of Maratha princes. Isolated mutinies also occurred at military posts in the center of the subcontinent. Initially, the rebels, although divided and uncoordinated, gained the upper hand, while the unprepared British were terrified, and even paralyzed, without replacements for the casualties. The civil war inflicted havoc on both Indians and British as each vented its fury on the other; each community suffered humiliation and triumph in battle as well, although the final outcome was victory for the British. The last major sepoy rebels surrendered on June 21, 1858, at Gwalior (Madhya Pradesh), one of the principal centers of the revolt. A final battle was fought at Sirwa Pass on May 21, 1859, and the defeated rebels fled into Nepal.

The spontaneous and widespread rebellion later fired the imagination of the nationalists who would debate the most effective method of protest against British rule. For them, the rebellion represented the first Indian attempt at gaining independence. This interpretation, however, is open to serious question.

Indian Remote Sensing Satellites (IRS) : Indian Remote Sensing satellites (IRS) are a series of Earth Observation satellites, mostly built, launched and maintained by Indian Space Research Organisation of India as part of the Indian space program. The IRS series provides remote sensing services and are composed of the 1 (A,B,C,D). The future versions are named based on their area of application including OceanSat, CartoSat, ResourceSat. Some of the satellites have alternate designations based on the launch number and vehicle (P series for PSLV).

Indian Rhinoceros : The Indian Rhinoceros or the Great One-horned Rhinoceros, Rhinoceros unicornis, is found in Nepal and in Assam, India. It is confined to the tall grasslands and forests in the foothills of the Himalayas. The Indian Rhinoceros is an excellent swimmer. It can also run up to a speed of 55 km/h for short times. It has excellent hearing and smell but poor eyesight.

Indian rhinos are poached for their horn, which some cultures in East Asia believe has healing and potency powers. Less than 2500 individuals remain in the wild, and the species is an endangered one. Major steps have been taken by the Indian and Nepalese governments with the help of World Wildlife Fund or WWF for their protection. The Kaziranga National Park and Manas National Park in Assam and Royal Chitwan National Park in Nepal are the homes for the endangered animal.

Indian Rupee : The Indian Rupee is the official currency of India. The issuance of the currency is controlled by the Reserve Bank of India. The most commonly used symbol for the Rupee is Rs. The ISO 4217 code for the India Rupee is INR.

In most parts of India, the Rupee is known as the Rupee, Rupaye, Rubai, or one of other terms derived from the Sanskrit rupya, meaning silver. However, in the Bengali and Assamese languages, spoken in Assam, Tripura, and West Bengal, the Rupee is known as a Taka, and is written as such on Indian banknotes

Indian School Certificate (**ISC**) **:** The Indian School Certificate (ISC) is an examination conducted by the Council for the Indian School Certificate Examinations for Grade 12, i.e. year 12. A student attempts this examination after first completing the Indian Certificate of Secondary Education in Grade 10, although the completion of a recognised equivalent level of education is normally sufficient. The Examination has been designed to provide an examination in a course of general education, in accordance with the recommendations of the New Education Policy 1986 (India), through the medium of English. This system gives great emphasis to application and practical means of education instead of learning by rote. Importance is also given to Socially Useful and Productive Work as a requirement to be achieved by all candidates in order to receive Pass Certificates. In accordance with a Supreme Court of India directive, Environmental Education, is now a compulsory subject for all candidates. Candidates therefore have to attempt the subjects of English and Environmental Education, and must also attempt, two, three or four other subjects that may be chosen by the candidate from a wide range of subjects ranging from Fashion Designing to Political Science. Schools generally offer a limited number of these subjects depending upon their logistical requirements.

Indian Space Program : The Indian space program has been set up by the government of India for the advancement of space science and technology and its application in assisting in all-round development of the nation. The program involves developing satellites (mainly communication, remote sensing, meteorological) and launch capability for placing them in orbit (now polar and geostationary). The principal agency conducting the space program is the Indian Space Research Organisation (ISRO), under the aegis of the Department of Space, Government of India.

Indian Space Research Organisation (ISRO) : The Indian Space Research Organisation (ISRO) is India's national space agency. With its headquarters in Bangalore, the ISRO employs approximately 17,000 people. Its mandate is the development of technologies related to space and their applications towards India's development. The current Chairman of ISRO is G. Madhavan Nair. The ISRO is the only organisation in South Asia dedicated to space research and the launching of satellites. In addition to domestic payloads, it offers international launch services. ISRO is regarded as one of the top 5 space agencies in the world.

ISRO was founded in 1969 under the Department of Atomic Energy and continued under the Space Commission and Department of Space, created in June of 1972. India's and ISRO's first foray into space began with the launch of its satellite Aryabhata in 1975 by a Soviet booster. The first domestic launch was in 1980. Dr. Vikram Sarabhai is the founding father of the ISRO and thus the Indian space program. The ISRO has a long history of cooperation with Russian Federation. By the 1990's, ISRO had planned to acquire booster technology from the Russian space organization Glavkosmos. The United States opposed the technology transfer on non-proliferation grounds and imposed sanctions against the ISRO in May, 1992.

Under pressure, Glavkomos halted the transfer of associated manufacturing and design technology to India, but agreed to sell some hardware. Consequently, India developed its own robust booster technology and research capability. ISRO still uses some Russian technology for cryogenic stages on the GSLV, but this is being replaced by their own designs

Indian Space Research Organisation (ISRO) : The Indian Space Research Organisation (ISRO) is India's national space agency. With its headquarters in Bangalore, the ISRO employs approximately 17,000 people. Its mandate is the development of technologies related to space and their applications towards India's development. The current Chairman of ISRO is G. Madhavan Nair. The ISRO is the only organisation in South Asia dedicated to space research and the launching of satellites. In addition to domestic payloads, it offers international launch services. ISRO is regarded as one of the leading space agencies in the world.

ISRO was founded in 1969 under the Department of Atomic Energy and continued under the Space Commission and Department of Space, created in June of 1972. India's and ISRO's first foray into space began with the launch of its satellite Aryabhata in 1975 by a Soviet booster. The first domestic launch was in 1980.

Indian Standard Time : Indian Standard Time (IST) is the time zone for India. It is 5 hours and 30 minutes ahead of GMT/UTC (UTC+5:30). The entire country shares the same time. Although using one time universally has its advantages, the drawback is that in places in the far east, the sun rises very early and sets very early, while in the west it rises late and sets late. The Indian Standard Time is calculated from the Allahabad observatory. Allahabad has 82.5 °E longitude which corresponds to an exact 5 hours and 30 minutes difference between India and Greenwich, the reference point for GMT. India's time zones were established in 1884. However at that time there were two standard time zones, Bombay Time and Calcutta Time. The IST came into effect in 1905. However, Bombay still persisted with its own time zone, 39 minutes behind IST, until 1955.

Indian Subcontinent : The Indian subcontinent is a peninsular landmass of the Asian continent occupying the Indian Plate and extending into the Indian Ocean, bordered on the north by the Eurasian Plate.

Geographically, the Indian subcontinent can be divided into the following regions:

1. the Himalayas/Himalayan states
2. the Peninsular India/Deccan Plateau
3. the Indian Ocean states

Indian Union Muslim League : Indian Union Muslim League is a political party in India. The foremost stronghold of the party is northern Kerala, where the party is the leading political force in many areas. Note that since the name 'Indian Union Muslim League' is registered at the Electoral Commission by a splinter-group of the party, the party contests elections as the 'Muslim League Kerala State Committee'. The party has roots in the Muslim League of Jinnah. IUML was founded on March 10, 1948. IUML claims to be the political organization of all Indian muslims, but only a fraction of the Muslim masses of the country supports the party.

The party participated in the overthrow of the first communist government in Kerala in 1959. In 1960 the party took part in the formation of a coalition government in the state, consisting of the Indian National Congress, Praja Socialist Party and IUML. That government didn't last long. In the elections in Kerala in 1967 the party had entered a united front led by the Communist Party of India (Marxist). The other members of the front were Communist Party of India, Revolutionary Socialist Party, Karshaka Thozhilali Party (Peasants and Workers Party), Kerala Socialist Party and Samyukta Socialist Party. Muslim League had two ministers in the state government of that front.

In 1969 the party left the CPI(M)-led government and participated in the formation of a new government, led by Communist Party of India leader Achutha Menon as Chief Minister, together with CPI, RSP, KSP and Kerala Congress.

After the 1970 elections Menon became elected Chief Minister for the second time. Members of the governing coalition were Indian National Congress, IUML, RSP and PSP. The Menon government lasted until the downfall of the Indira Gandhi regime in 1977 (no state elections were held in this period). In the chaos that followed the IUML leader C.H. Mohammed Koya held the post of Chief Minister for a brief period in 1979. When two political fronts, United Democratic Front and Left Democratic Front, crystalized ahead of the 1980 elections two different sections of IUML landed up in opposite camps. A break-away faction, the All India Muslim League joined LDF and the Indian Union Muslim League joined UDF. The two groups reunited in 1985 under the name IUML and as members of UDF.

After the demolition of the Babri Mosque in Ayodhya in 1992 IUML was split. The Indian National Congress which then held government at centre were considered as co-responsible for the destruction and a faction led all India president Ibrahim Sulaiman Sait wanted to break the political bond with INC but the majority opposed it and rejected his appeal (they were governing Kerala as part of a UDF government). The party expelled the factionalist from its folder and stand firmly for the benefit of community. The Kerala State Committee gained recognition as a "State Party" IUML, the party has roots in outside kerala, especially in Tamilnadu and some other states.

The party youth wing is called Muslim Youth League and their students wing is called Muslim Students Federation. The Party has a women's political wing too—it is called Muslim Women's League. In Kerala the party has a separate trade union organization, Swatantra Thozhilali Union (S.T.U., Independent Workers Union), and a peasants union, Swathanthra Karshaka Sangam (Independent Peasants Union) and KMCC for Gulf employees. The party is today part of the United Progressive Alliance central government and party secretary E. Ahmed is a minister in that government. The president of the party is G.M. Banatwalla.

Indira Gandhi : Indira Gandhi was the first women Prime Minister and an important world stateswoman. She was born in Allahabad, in the state of Uttar Pradesh. She was the only child of Jawaharlal Nehru, the first Prime Minister of India. She was a great crusader of world peace. When she was just 13 years old, Indira organized a 'Monkey Army' (Vanar Sena) comprising of young teenagers which proved her intention to fight for the independence of her country.

In 1942, she got married to Feroze Gandhi. Two sons were born to her- Rajiv Gandhi and Sanjay Gandhi. Indira Gandhi became the third Prime Minister of India on January 24,1966 and remained in this post up to 1977. In 1975, her election to Parliament was declared invalid and she declared internal emergency, which led to her defeat in 1977 elections. Indira Gandhi returned to power in 1980 with an overwhelming majority.

She was one of the most efficient Prime Ministers of India and is credited with great achievements. Noteworthy among them are nationalization of banks, liberation of Bangladesh and 20 point programme for the upliftment of the poor. She was honoured with 'Bharat Ratna' in 1971. Mrs. Gandhi, met her tragic end on 31st October 1984, when she was brutally assassinated by her own guards.

Indira Gandhi International (IGI) Airport : Indira Gandhi International (IGI) Airport (IATA: DEL, ICAO:

VIDP), located in the city of Delhi, India is one of India's main domestic and international gateways. The airport has been named after former prime minister Indira Gandhi, the daughter of Jawaharlal Nehru. Earlier known as Palam airport, it was renamed IGI airport with the inauguration of a new international building (Terminal 2) on 2 May 1986. The older Palam airport (Terminal 1) is exclusively used for domestic operations. Delhi has two runways: the main runway 10-28 (12,500 ft) and an auxiliary runway 09-27 (9,229 ft). Runway 10-28 is one of the few runways in Asia equipped with CAT III-B Instrument Landing System. On 31 March 2006, it became the first Indian airport operating two runways simultaneously following a test run involving a SpiceJet plane landing and a Jet Airways plane taking off at the same time.

Indira Gandhi National Park : The park covers an area of 118sq.km. in the district of Coimbatore. The nearest airport is Coimbatore, 80 km from the park. The rail head pollachi is 35 km from the park. The forests of the park are from tropical deciduous type to semi-evergreen and evergreen containing teak, rosewood and other tropical species. The wild life species found in the park are elephant, tiger, leopard, lion tailed macaque, civet, sloth bear, gaur, nilgiri languor, crocodile, python, peafowl etc. The best season for visiting the park is October to May. The park had guest houses accommodation.

Indira Gandhi Zoological Park : The park covers an area of 625 acres. It is presently one of the largest zoo located in the natural settings of a reserve forest about 4 km. from the Visakhapatnam railway station on the National High Way.

Indira Point : Indira Point (formerly known as Pygmalion Point and for a brief period of time as India Point) is situated on the island of Great Nicobar in the Nicobar Islands, eastern Indian Ocean, and it represents the southernmost point of land in the territory of India. The point is located in the Union Territory of Andaman and Nicobar Islands.

Although Kanyakumari is the southernmost tip of the Indian subcontinent itself, Indira Point was the furthest south on Indian soil until the tsunami generated by the 2004 Indian Ocean earthquake reclaimed most of its area submerged into the sea. Geologists however have stated that the sea is slowly starting to retreat back to the original position, which would enable the resurfacing of Indira point where the lighthouse is partially submerged under sea.

Indo-Aryan Languages : The Indo-Aryan languages form a subgroup of the Indo-Iranian languages, thus belonging to the Indo-European family of languages. The term Indic refers to the same group without the negative connotations of "Aryan". Note that in opposition to the generic adjective Indian, Indic is the term used in the context of Indo-European linguistics, and is not strictly a geographical term, so that non-Indo-European languages spoken in India are not included in the term, while the Mitanni, on the other hand, probably were speakers of an Indic language without ever having settled on the Indian subcontinent.

The earliest attestations of the group are in Vedic Sanskrit, the language used in the oldest scriptures of India, the foundational canon of Hinduism known as the Vedas. The language of the Mitanni is of similar age, but is only attested fragmentary. In ca. the fifth century BC, the Sanskrit language was codified and standardized by the grammarian Panini; this led (in about 200 BC) to what is now known as 'Classical' Sanskrit. However, although this preserved the integrity of written language for a long time, the spoken language continues to evolve, and by the sixth century, Sanskrit as a spoken language was rare, being by and large replaced by its descendants, the Prakrits. All the Prakrits share a common ancestry, but they are not necessarily mutually intelligible.

Apabramsa was the next modification in the spoken language, in a period broadly lasting from the fifth to the tenth century. Increasing numbers of literary texts begin to appear in Apabhransha languages, and the Sravakachar of Devasena (dated to the 930s) is now considered to be the first Hindi book.

The next major milestone occurred with the Muslim invasions of India in the 13th, 14th, 15th and 16th centuries. Under the flourishing Mughal empire, Persian became very influential as the language of prestige of the Islamic courts. However, Persian was soon displaced by Urdu. This Indo-Aryan language is a combination of Persian and Arabic in its vocabulary with the grammar of the local dialects.

The two largest languages that formed from Apabhransa were Bengali and Hindi; others include Gujarati, Marathi and Punjabi.

In the Hindi-speaking areas, the main form was Braj-bhasha, which is still spoken today, but was replaced in the 19th century by the Khari Boli dialect. However, a large amount of modern spoken Hindi vocabulary is derived from Perso-Arabic.

This state of affairs continued until the Partition of India in 1947. Hindustani (mixture of Urdu & Hindi) was replaced by 'Hindi' as the official language of India, and soon the Perso-Arabic words of Urdu began to be excised from the official Hindi corpus, in a bid to make the language more 'Indian'. A throwback to Hindi poets like Tulsidas resulted in what is known as a Sanskritization of the language. Arabic or Persian words in common parlance were slowly replaced by Sanskrit words, sometimes borrowed wholesale, or in new compounds. In contemporary times, there is a continuum of Hindi-Urdu, with heavily-Persianized Urdu at one end and Sanskritized Hindi at the other, although the basic grammar remains identical. Most people speak a blend of the two, a dialect known as Hindustani.

Indo-Aryan Migration : Indo-Aryan migration refers to the migration and expansion of the Indo-Aryans during the 2nd millennium BC or earlier. Archaeological and philological data indicates that there was a shift of settlements from the northwestern part of India to the Gangetic valley and to the south during the second millennium BCE, but does not clearly support a migration of Indo-Aryan people into India. Based on linguistic data, many scholars have argued that Indo-Aryan speakers migrated to India in the second millennium BCE. This corresponds to the first wave of expansion of the Indo-Iranians beyond Central Asia, notably into the Indian Subcontinent.

Indo-Aryans : The Indo-Aryans are the ethno-linguistic descendents of the Indo-Aryan branch of the Indo-Iranians. The earliest records of Indo-Aryans are in the Rigveda, and in references to the Mitanni rulers. The Indo-Aryans inhabiting northern India, the bearers of the Vedic civilization are sometimes called Vedic Aryans, precursors of modern Hinduism. The term derives from the Sanskrit word "Arya".

The separation of Indo-Aryans proper from Proto-Indo-Iranians is commonly dated, on linguistic grounds, to roughly 1800 BC. The Nuristani languages probably split in such early times, and are either classified as remote Indo-Aryan dialects, or as an independent branch of Indo-Iranian. It is believed that by 1500 BC, Indo-Aryans had reached Assyria in the west and the Punjab in the east.

The spread of Indo-Aryan languages has been connected with the spread of the chariot in the first half of the second millennium BC. Some scholars trace the Indo-Iranians (both Indo-Aryans and Iranians) back to the Andronovo culture (2nd millennium BC). Other scholars like Brentjes (1981), Klejn (1974), Francfort (1989), Lyonnet (1993), Hiebert (1998) and Sarianidi (1993) have argued that the Andronovo culture cannot be associated with the Indo-Aryans of India or with the Mitannis because the Andronovo culture took shape too late and because no actual traces of their culture (e.g. warrior burials or timber-frame materials of the Andronovo culture) have been found in India or Mesopotamia (Edwin Bryant. 2001). The archaeologist J.P. Mallory (1998) finds it "extraordinarily difficult to make a case for expansions from this nothern region to northern India" and remarks that the proposed migration routes "only gets the Indo-Iranian to Central Asia, but not as far as the seats of the Medes, Persians or Indo-Aryans" (Edwin Bryant. 2001).

Other scholars like Asko Parpola (1988) connect the BMAC with the Indo-Aryans. But although horses were known to the Indo-Aryans, evidence for the presence of horse in form of horse bones is missing in the BMAC (e.g. Bernard Sergent. Genèse de l'Inde. 1997:161 ff.). Asko Parpola (1988) has argued that the Dasas were the "carriers of the Bronze Age culture of Greater Iran" living in the BMAC and that the forts with circular walls destroyed by the Indo-Aryans were actually located in the BMAC. Parpola's hypothesis has been criticized by K.D. Sethna (1992) and other scholars.

Indo-European Languages : The Indo-European languages are a group of several hundred languages and dialects (specifically 443 according to the SIL estimate), including most of the major language families of Europe, as well as many languages of Asia, which belong to a single superfamily. Contemporary languages in this superfamily include Bengali, English, French, German, Hindi, Portuguese, Russian, and Spanish (each with more than 100 million native speakers), as well as numerous smaller national or minority languages. Indo-European is the largest family of languages in the world today, with its languages spoken by approximately 3 billion native speakers; the second largest family of tongues is Sino-Tibetan. There are other, controversial supergroupings

Indo-Gangetic Plain : The Indo-Gangetic Plain is a rich, fertile and ancient land encompassing most of northern and eastern India, the most populous parts of Pakistan, and virtually all of Bangladesh. The Plains get their names from the rivers Ganges and Indus. It stretches from: Kashmir in the north; the Punjab region of Pakistan and ·Aravalli Range, Rajasthan in the west; and Himalayan foothills in the east and the Deccan Plateau in the south. The fertile Terai region is the Nepalese extension of the Plain. The rivers encompassed are the Ganga (Ganges), Indus, Beas, Yamuna, Gomti, Ravi, Chambal, Sutlej, Chenab. The soil is rich in silt, making the plain one of the most intensely farmed areas of the world. Even rural areas here are densely populated.

Farming on the Indo-Gangetic Plain primarily consists of rice and wheat grown in rotation. Other crops include maize, sugarcane, and cotton. The main source of rainfall is the southwest monsoon, which is normally sufficient for agriculture except for occasional droughts. The many rivers flowing out of the Himalayas provide water for major irrigation works.

The region is also known for the Indus Valley Civilisation and is responsible for the birth of ancient India. The flat and fertile terrain has facilitated the repeated rise and expansion of empires, including Magadha and the Maurya empire, the Gupta empire, Kanauj, the Sultanate of Delhi, and the Mughal Empire, all of which had their demographic and political centres in the Indo-Gangetic plain. Both British and independent India also have their centres here.

Indo-Gangetic Tradition : Indo-Gangetic Tradition refers to the continuation of the Indus Valley Tradition. The geographical extent of the Indo-Gangetic Tradition is larger and comprises the Gangetic, Yamuna and the Greater Indus Valley. The Painted Gray Ware culture (ca 1200-800 BCE) and the Northern Black Polished Ware culture (ca 700-300 BCE) belong to the Regionalization Era of the Indo-Gangetic Tradition. The Integration Era of the Indo-Gangetic Tradition begins in ca. 300 BCE. Chandragupta Maurya and Ashoka belong to this era.

Indo-Iranian : The term Indo-Iranian includes all speakers of the Indo-Iranian languages, i.e., Indo-Aryans, Iranians and the speakers of the Nuristani languages. The historic term for these cultures is Aryan.

The near-universally cited candidate for the homeland of the Proto-Indian-Iranian culture is the Andronovo Archaeological Complex. A commonly given date for the last period of Proto-Indo-Iranian linguistic unity is approximately 2000 BCE, perhaps a little later, preceding both the Vedic and Iranian cultures. The earliest recorded forms of these languages, Vedic Sanskrit and Gathic Avestan, are remarkably similar. The origin and earliest relationship between the Nuristani languages and that of the Iranian and Indic groups is unrecoverably obscure

Indo-Pak Mushaira : The Indo-Pak Mushaira in December brings together poets from India and Pakistan. The significance of this event is felt especially by the older generation whose memories go back to the years before the partition of India. For the younger generation it brings home the deep commonalties of language and culture that unite the people of two nations.

Indo-Pakistani War of 1947 : The Indo-Pakistani War of 1947 sometimes known as the First Kashmir War was a war fought between India and Pakistan over the region of Kashmir from 1947 to 1949. It was the first of the many wars fought among the two newly independent nations The state of Jammu and Kashmir was one of a number of Indian states that recognised British paramountcy. Prior to the withdrawal of the British from India, the state came under pressure from both India and Pakistan to join them. The Maharaja of Kashmir, Hari Singh wanted to remain independent and tried to delay the issue. However at the time of British withdrawal the state was invaded by a concentrated force of Pro-Pakistan Tribals from North West Frontier Province (NWFP) and regular Pakistani soldiers. This forced him to accede Kashmir to India who promptly rushed into Kashmir and thus the war had started. The accession is still questioned by the Pakistanis. AZK (Azad Kashmir) forces (Azad in Urdu means liberation or freedom) are the local militia supported by the Pakistan. The AZK had several advantages in the war, notably:

1. Prior to the war the Jammu and Kashmir state forces had been spread thinly around the border as a response to terrorist activity, and so were badly deployed to counter a full scale invasion.

2. Some of the state forces joined Indian forces.

3. The AZK were also aided by regular Pakistani soldiers who manned some of their units, with the proportion increasing throughout the war.

4. British officers may have helped the Pakistanis plan the attack.

As a result of these advantages the main invasion force quickly brushed aside the Jammu and Kashmir state forces. But the attacker's advantage was not vigorously pressed and the Indians saved the country by airlifting reinforcements. This was at the price of the state formally seceding to India. With Indian reinforcements the Pakistani / AZK offensive ran out of steam towards the end of 1947. The exception to this was in the High Himalayas sector where the AZK were able to make substantial progress until turned back at the outskirts of Leh in late June 1948. Throughout 1948 many small-scale battles were fought. None of these gave a strategic advantage to either side and the fronts gradually solidified. Support for the AZK forces by Pakistan became gradually more overt with regular Pakistani units becoming involved. A formal cease-fire was declared on 31 December, 1948.

Indo-Pakistani War of 1965 : The 1965 war between India and Pakistan, also known as the Second Kashmir War, was the culmination of a series of skirmishes that occurred between April 1965 and September 1965. It is generally accepted that the war began following failed infiltration attempts by Pakistan in Jammu and Kashmir. The fighting ended in a stalemate on September 23. Fighting broke out between India and Pakistan in an area known as the Rann of Kutch, a barren region in the Indian state of Gujarat. Initially involving the border police from both nations, the disputed area soon witnessed intermittent skirmishes between the countries' armed forces firstly on March 20 and again in April 1965.

After its successes in the Rann of Kutch, Pakistan, under the leadership of General Ayub Khan is said to have believed that the Indian Army was unwilling or unable to defend itself against a quick military campaign in the disputed territory of Kashmir, following a loss to China in 1962. Pakistan believed that the population of Kashmir was generally discontented with Indian rule and that a resistance movement could be ignited by a few infiltrating saboteurs. This was codenamed Operation Gibraltar. For its part, Pakistan claimed to have been concerned by the attempts of India to absorb Kashmir—a state that Pakistan claims as "disputed", into the Indian union by way Articles 356 and 357 of the Indian Constitution allowing the President of India to declare President's Rule in the disputed state.

On August 15, 1965, Indian forces crossed the ceasefire line and launched an attack on Pakistan administered Kashmir, marking an official beginning to the war.

Indo-Pakistani War of 1971 : The Indo-Pakistani War of 1971 was a military conflict between India and Pakistan. The war is closely associated with Bangladesh Liberation War (sometimes also referred to as Pakistani Civil War). There is an argument about exact dates of the war. However, war on India's Western front during the period between 3 December 1971 and 16 December 1971 is called the Indo-Pakistani War by both the Bangladeshi and Indian Armies. The War ended in a crushing defeat for Pakistan Military in just a fortnight.

The Indo-Pakistani conflict was sparked by the Bangladesh Liberation War, a conflict between the traditionally dominant West Pakistanis and the majority East Pakistanis. The war ignited after the 1970 Pakistani election, in which the East Pakistani Awami League party won 167 of 169 seats in East Pakistan, thus securing a simple majority in the 313-seat lower house of the Pakistani parliament. Awami League leader Sheikh Mujibur Rahman presented Six Points and claimed the right to form the government. After the leader of the Pakistan People's Party, Zulfikar Ali Bhutto, refused to give premiership of Pakistan to Sheikh Mujib, President Yahya Khan called in the military, which was made up largely of West Pakistanis.

Mass arrests of dissidents began, and attempts were made to disarm East Pakistani soldiers and police. After several days of strikes and non-cooperation movements, Pakistani military cracked down on Dhaka on the night of

March 25, 1971. The Awami League was banned; many members fled into exile in India. Mujib was arrested and taken to West Pakistan. On 26 March 1971, Ziaur Rahman, a rebellious major in the Pakistani army, declared the independence of Bangladesh on behalf of Sheikh Mujib. In April, exiled Awami League leaders formed a government-in-exile in Boiddonathtola of Meherpur. The East Pakistan Rifles, an elite paramilitary force, defected to the rebellion. A guerrilla troop of civilians, the Mukti Bahini, was formed to help the Bangladesh Army.

Indo-Pakistani Wars : Since both nations achieved independence in August 1947, there have been three major wars and one minor war between India and Pakistan. All the wars fought between the two nations were over the disputed area of Kashmir with the only exception being in 1971, where the cause of friction between the two nations was over the Genocide and the resulting problems in East Pakistan (now Bangladesh). The root of most conflicts and the mutual hatred lies in Kashmir and in the manner in which its political alignment was decided by the two countries following partition in 1947. Kashmir was ruled by a Hindu Maharajah ruling a largely muslim population who tried to make Kashmir an independent state. But following an invasion by Pakistani tribals and some regulars he acceeded to India. Immediately afterwards the First Kashmir War broke out between the two nations over the mountainous region of Kashmir when Indian and Pakistani troops fought against each other. The war lasted for more than a year with both nations making significant advances into each other's territory. As the war was ended by a UN ceasefire, India had managed to secure just under three-fifths of Kashmir and importantly the most fertile part of it including the Kashmir Valley.

The Second Kashmir War again involved the issue of Kashmir with Pakistan infiltrating and starting a rebellion in Jammu and Kashmir, India. The plan was a non-starter and India reacted by launching a formal attack on Pakistan igniting the war. The war ended in stalemate. The third war was unique in that it did not involve the issue of Kashmir but was entirely about East Pakistan and the crisis brewing there. After months of internal conflict India decided to help the Bengalis in East Pakistan much to the consternation of West Pakistan. Within just a fortnight the Indian Military had decisively defeated Pakistan with the aid of the rebels and forced a surrender upon Pakistan.

The latest war, the Kargil War, is considered a minor war though it produced stirring emotions between the two nations involved coming at a time of increased media and electronic coverage. The war ended in a multi-pronged victory for India. The withdrawal of Pakistan from its occupation was seen both as a politico-diplomatic triumph as much as a military success. Apart from the aforementioned wars, there have been skirmishes between the two nations from time to time. Some have bordered on an all out war whilst others were pretty limited in conflict. The nations were expected to fight each other in 1955 after war-like posturing of both nations, though it was neutralised. In 1984 there was an issue as both nations attempted to control the Siachen Glacier.

Further clashes erupted in the glacial area in 1987 as Pakistan sought to oust India from its stronghold without success. The very next year Operation Brasstacks was conducted by India. This miliatry exercise—the largest of its kind in South Asia—raised eyebrows in Pakistan and was feared to lead to another war between the two neighbours. Tensions were high again in 1990 after the Kashmir militacy start exploding. The 2002 parliamentary attacks by terrorists fighting for the Kashmiri cause prompted India on a military and diplomatic offensive and was believed by many military analysts as the push towards a war.

The casualties suffered by both nations in all the wars have often been difficult to pinpoint given the mix of partisans who have fought with the armies of both countries at one time or the other. However, based on some relevant data, it is estimated that the war casualties of the conflict in 1947-48; 1965; 1971 and 1999 (Kargil) have been 8,733 for India and 13,896 for Pakistan. This does not include the losses in minor skirmishes and areas like Siachen.

Indore : Indore is the commercial capital of the Malwa region and the central Indian state of Madhya Pradesh (MP). It is situated on the Malwa plateau, just south of the Satpura Range. It is the largest city of Madhya Pradesh. Indore is the administrative headquarters of Indore District and Indore Division, and formerly served as the capital of the former princely state of Indore and the summer capital of the erstwhile state of Madhya Bharat.

Indore was formerly ruled by the Maratha Maharajas of the Holkar dynasty. The dynasty's founder, "Malhar Rao Holkar", (1694-1766), was granted control of Maratha armies in Malwa in 1724, and in 1733, he was installed as the Maratha governor of the region. By the end of his reign, the Holkar state was de facto independent. His daughter-in-law "Ahilyabai Holkàr", succeeded him, ruling from 1767 to 1795. She ruled from a palace-fort at Maheshwar, south of Indore on the Narmada River. Ahilya Bai Holkar was an architectural patron, who donated Hindu temples across India. In 1818, the Holkars were defeated by the British in the Third Anglo-Maratha War, and the Holkar kingdom became part of the British Raj. As a result of this loss in the Battle of Mahidpur, the treaty of Mandsaur was signed and the Cantonment town of Mhow was handed over to the British. It was as a result of this treaty that the capital of Holkar state shifted from Maheshwar to Indore.

After India's independence in 1947, Indore, together with a number of neighboring princely states, became part of the Indian state of Madhya Bharat. Indore was designated the summer capital of this newly created state. On November 1, 1956, Madhya Bharat was merged into Madhya Pradesh, with Bhopal as the capital city.

Indrani Rehman : One of the greatest dancers of our time, Indrani Rehman was among the luminous names of the sixties and seventies who carried the glory of Indian classical arts to all corners of the world, through her varied performances imbued with grace of body and spirit, and her mastery over several dance forms.

Having settled in the United States, Indrani Rehman had become a distant legend for dance enthusiasts in India, though she continued to work actively in the USA. Indrani Rehman helped in the revival and popularization of Odissi dance. She was awarded Padma Shri in 1969 and Sahitya Kala Parishad award in 1973.

Indraprastha : The city of Indraprastha (City of Indra) was a major northern city in ancient India that was the capital of the kingdom led by the Pandavas in the Mahabharata epic. It is located upon the banks of the river Yamuna and extremely close to the modern national capital of Delhi. Indeed, it is said to have been "the first city of Delhi".

Indraprastha : The city of Indraprastha (City of Indra) was a major northern city in ancient India that was the capital of the kingdom led by the Pandavas in the Mahabharata epic. It is located upon the banks of the river Yamuna and extremely close to the modern national capital of Delhi. Indeed, it is said to have been "the first city of Delhi".

When Yudhisthira, the eldest of the five Pandava brothers is given the kingdom of Khandavaprastha, a region northwest to the city of Hastinapura, a land cursed with barren and arid soils, diseased and dangerous forests and famine. However Lord Krishna summons Indra, the king of the Devas to help Yudhisthira, who in turn summons the Deva architect Vishwakarman.

Performing sacred ceremonies to bless the land, Vishwakarman builds a glorious new city, which becomes the capital. Millions of people flock to this new city, and soon prosperity and health spread across Khandavaprastha, thanks to the perfectly pious rule of Yudhisthira and his brothers.

After the Kurukshetra War, Yudhisthira, now king of Hastinapura retains control of his city. Archaeological evidence suggests that Indraprastha once stood where Purana Quila is today. A village called Indrapat existed in Delhi until the beginning of the 19th century; the village was levelled and the British city of New Delhi was made. The excavations of the ancient mound of Indraprastha, capital of the Pandavas, located within Purana Quila revealed evidence of continuous habitation of the site for almost 2,500 years.

Indravati National Park : This park was established in 1978 in Bastar district on the banks of river Indravati, after which is named. It is spread over and area of 1258 sq km away from the park which also serves as the railhead. The nearest air port is Rai pur 486km away.

The park comprises tropical deciduous forest with teak, amaltas, anjan, arjun, amlabaheda and palas. There is profuse growth of bamboos also. The deep forests are interspersed with grasslands and the trees are covered with climbers. It is an ideal habitat for diverse fauna. The common mammals found in the park are chital, sambar, chausingha, blue bull, black buck, chinkara, barking deer, swamp deer, wild buffalo, sloth bear and wild boar. Tiger, leopard, wolf, jackal, hyena and python are important carnivora.

Indroda Dinosaur and Fossil Park : The Indroda Dinosaur and Fossil Park in the Gandhinagar in the state of Gujarat, India, contains the second largest hatchery of dinosaur eggs in the world. The Park was set up by the Geological Survey of India and is the only dinosaur museum in the country.

The Park is run by the Gujarat Ecological and Research Foundation (GEERI) and is widely regarded as India's Jurassic Park. Several fossilised dinosaur eggs and skeletal parts have been found here. The fossils which were found in Upper Cretaceous formations in the region date back 65 million years ago. The eggs are of different sizes, some the size of cannon balls. Fossil trackways of these gargantuan animals are also on display in the park.

Dinosaurs that are on display include Tyrannosaurus rex, Megalosaurus, Titanosaurus, Barapasaurus, Brachiosaurus, Antarctosaurus, Stegosaurus and Iguanodon. The park displays life-size models of the dinosaurs along with details of each period in which they existed and characteristics of the animals.

The fossils were found in the Songhir Bagh Basin, the Himatnagat basin of Balasinor, south-eastern parts of Kheda, Panchamahals and Vadodara districts of the state.

Indus Highway : Indus Highway In 1988, the government of Pakistan announced its program of construction of Indus Highway (N-55): 1250km designated to provide alternative to existing National Highway (N-5): 1650 km linking Karachi with Peshawar via Lahore. Besides reducing the distance and lessening the pressure on the traffic on the National Highway, the Indus Highway would be instrumental in bringing socio-economic progress to other wise backward areas, which lie in the proposed path.

Indus River : The Indus, (known Sanskrit and Hindi as the Sindhu) is the longest and one of the most important rivers in South Asia. Originating in the Tibetan plateau in the vicinity of Lake Mansarovar, the river runs a course through Kashmir in both India and Pakistan, and in a southernly direction along the entire length of Pakistan to merge into the Arabian Sea. Figures for the total length of the river vary between 2,900 and 3,200 kilometres. The river has a total drainage area exceeding 450,000 miles. The river's estimated annual flow stands at around 207 billion cubic metres. Beginning at the heights of the world with glaciers, the river feeds the ecosystem of temperate forests, plains and arid countryside. Together with the rivers Chenab, Ravi, Sutlej, Jhelum, Beas and the extinct Sarasvati River, the Indus forms the Sapta Sindhu (Seven rivers) delta in the Sindh province of Pakistan. It has 20 tributaries.

The Indus was the primary support and base of the Indus Valley Civilization—one of the earliest in world history—which arose along its course. The Rigveda (c. 1500 BCE) first mentions the river. The Indus is the English name derived from Sinthos in Greek, and Sindus in Latin. The name India is derived from the root of the river's name. The region through which it passes prior to entering the sea is named Sindh—home to ancient kingdoms, now a province in Pakistan. The river is considered sacred in Hinduism—the term Hindu itself is derived from Sindhu—and is worshipped by Hindus. The Indus provides the key water resources for the economy of Pakistan—especially the breadbasket of Punjab province, which accounts for most of the nation's agricultural production, and Sindh. It also supports many heavy industries and provides the main supply of potable water in Pakistan.

Indus River Delta : The Indus River Delta occurs where the Indus River flows into the Arabian Sea in Pakistan. The delta covers an area of about 16,000 square miles (41,440 sq km), and is approximately 130 miles across where it meets the sea. Unlike many other deltas, the Indus River Delta consists of clay and other infertile soils, and is very swampy. The delta receives between 10 and 20 inches of rainfall in a normal year.

Pakistans fifth largest city, Hyderabad, lies about 130 miles north of the mouths of the Indus. Towns are found throughout the delta, but there are no large cities on the delta south of Hyderabad. Karachi, Pakistan's largest city, lies west of the delta on the coast of the Arabian Sea.

Average temperatures for the delta region in July range from 70 - 85°F, and 50 - 70°F in January. The Indus River Delta is an important region for migrating water birds, and is an area rich in freshwater fauna. Fish found in the delta include the Hilsa, Indus baril, Indus garua, the giant snakehead, golden mahaseer and the Rita catfish.

Indus Valley Civilization : The Indus Valley Civilization, 3300 BCE–1700 BCE, was an ancient civilization thriving along the lower Indus River and the Ghaggar-Hakra river in what is now Pakistan and Gujarat (western India). Among other names for this civilization is the Harappan Civilization, in reference to its first excavated city of Harappa. In India it is known as the Indus-Sarasvati Civilization because most of the more than 1000 sites of this civilization were discovered at the banks of the Sarasvati River. According to the Indo-Aryan migration hypothesis, Gujarat and Pakistan were the first settlements for Indo-Aryans.

Settlements have been found, mainly in the general region of the Hakra-Ghaggar river and its tributaries. Among the settlements were the major urban centers of

Harappa and Mohenjo-daro, as well as Lothal, Dholavira, Ganweriwala, Kalibanga, and Rakhigarhi. Additionally, there is some disputed evidence indicative of another large river, now long dried up, running parallel to and east of the Indus. The dried-up river beds overlap with the Hakra channel in Pakistan, and the seasonal Ghaggar river in India. Over 500 ancient sites belonging to the Indus Valley Civilization have been discovered along the Hakra-Ghaggar river and its tributaries (S.P. Gupta 1995: 183). In contrast to this, only 90 to 96 of the over 800 known Indus Valley sites have been discovered on the Indus and its tributaries.

The Indus civilization was predated by the first farming cultures in south Asia, which emerged in the hills of what is now called Balochistan, to the west of the Indus Valley. The civilization's mature Harappan period began from 2600 BC.

Indus civilization agriculture must have been highly productive; after all, it was capable of generating surpluses sufficient to support tens of thousands of urban residents who were not primarily engaged in agriculture. It relied on the considerable technological achievements of the pre-Harappan culture, including the plough.

Indus civilization people practiced rainfall harvesting, a powerful technology that was brought to fruition by classical Indian civilization but nearly forgotten in the 20th century. It should be remembered that Indus civilization people, like all peoples in South Asia, built their lives around the monsoon,a weather pattern in which the bulk of a year's rainfall occurs in a four-month period.

Well over 400 Indus symbols have been found on seals or ceramic pots and over a dozen other materials, including a 'signboard' that apparently once hung over the gate of the inner citadel of the Indus city of Dholavira. Typical Indus inscriptions are no more than four or five characters in length, most of which (aside from the Dholavira 'signboard') are exquisitely tiny; the longest on a single surface, which is less than 1 inch (2.54 cm) square, is 17 signs long; the longest on any object (found on three different faces of a mass-produced object) carries only 26 symbols.

Around 1900 BC, signs of a gradual decline begin to emerge. People started to leave the cities. Those who remained were poorly nourished. By around 1800 BC, most of the cities were abandoned. In the aftermath of the Indus civilization's collapse, regional cultures emerged, to varying degrees showing the influence of the Indus civilization. In the formerly great city of Harappa, burials have been found that correspond to a regional culture called the Cemetery H culture. At the same time, the Ochre Coloured Pottery culture expands from Rajasthan into the Gangetic Plain.

Indus Valley Desert : The Indus Valley Desert is a desert ecoregion of northern Pakistan. The Indus Valley desert covers an area of 19,500 square kilometers (7,500 square miles) in northwestern Punjab Province, lying between the Chenab and Indus rivers. The Indus Valley Desert is drier and less hospitable than the Northwestern thorn scrub forests that surround it.

Indus Waters Treaty : The Indus Waters Treaty is a water-sharing treaty between India and Pakistan. The treaty was signed in Karachi on September 19, 1960 by the then Indian Prime Minister Jawaharlal Nehru and the then President of Pakistan Field Marshal Mohammad Ayub Khan. The World Bank (then the International Bank for Reconstruction and Development) is a signatory as a third party.

The Indus System of Rivers comprises three Eastern Rivers—the Sutlej, the Beas and the Ravi; and three Western Rivers—the Indus, the Jhelum and Chenab. With minor exceptions, the treaty gives India exclusive use of all of the waters of the Eastern Rivers and their tributaries before the point where the rivers enter Pakistan. Similarly, Pakistan has exclusive use of the Western Rivers. Pakistan also received one-time financial compensation for the loss of water from the Eastern rivers.

The countries agree to exchange data and co-operate in matters related to the treaty. For this purpose, treaty creates the Permanent Indus Commission, with a commisioner appointed by each country.

Institute of Indology : Located near the Gujarat University campus, the museum has an important collection of illustrated manuscripts and miniatures and one of the finest collections relating to Jainism in India. It is open daily from 11.30 am to 5.30pm except Sunday.

Institute of Space Technology : Institute of Space Technology is located at Islamabad, Pakistan. Institute of Space Technology is affiliated with UET,Lahore. Institute of Space Technology offers degree programs in Aerospace Engineering and Communication System Engineering.It is the first and only institute of its kind that is offering higher education in the fields of Aerospace and Communication Systems Engineering in the country. An institute where one can find large oppertunities for research and persuing career in these advance fields of engineering.

Institute of Water Modelling : The Institute of Water Modelling (IWM) is a Bangladesh based key player in the water modelling sector. It commands about 90% of the jobs in this area. The headquarter of the organisation is located at the New DOHS, Dhaka, Bangladesh. IWM had been established in December 1996 as a TRUST of the Government of Bangladesh to function as a center of excellence and learning in the field of Computational Hydraulics, Water Modelling and Allied Science. IWM offers a wide range of specialist services in the fields of Water Resources Planning and Management as well as Hydrometric Measurements, Hydrographic and topographic surveys and monitoring. The applications of IWM modelling tools cover a wide range of water related areas such as: flood control, flood forecasting, irrigation and drainage, river morphology, salinity and sediment transport, coastal hydraulics, port, coast and estuary management, environmental impact assessment, bridge hydraulics and related infrastructure development

Intelligence Bureau (IB) : The Intelligence Bureau is India's internal intelligence agency. It was recast as the Central Intelligence Bureau in 1947 under the Ministry of Home Affairs. The reason for the perception may be because in 1885, Major General Sir Charles Metcalfe MacGregor was appointed Quartermaster General and head of the Intelligence Department for the British Indian Army at Shimla. The objective then was to monitor Russian troop deployments in Afghanistan, fearing a Russian invasion of British India through the North-West during the late 19th century. In 1921, a new state-run surveillance and monitoring agency — Indian Political Intelligence (IPI) — was established, in reaction the development of Indian anarchist activities in England. IPI was run jointly by the India Office and the Government of India and reported jointly to the Secretary of the Public and Judicial Department of the India Office, and the Director of Intelligence Bureau (DIB) in India, and maintained close contact with Scotland Yard and MI5.

Responsibilities of IB are: shrouded in secrecy, the IB is used to garner intelligence from within India and also execute counter-intelligence and counter-terrorism tasks. The intelligence bureau is comprised of employees from law enforcement agencies mostly Indian Police Service officers as well as from the military. The current chief of the IB is Ajit Kumar Doval, who replaced K. P. Singh. In addition to domestic intelligence responsibilities, the IB is particularly tasked with intelligence collection in border areas, following the 1951 recommendations of the Himmatsinhji Committee (also known as the North and North-East Border Committee), a task entrusted to military intelligence organizations prior to independence in 1947. The IB was also tasked with other external intelligence responsibilities as of 1951.

Understanding of the arcane workings of the IB is largely speculative. One known task of the IB is to clear licenses to Ham radio enthusiasts. The IB also passes on intelligence between other Indian intelligence agencies and the police. The IB also grants the necessary security clearances to Indian diplomats and judges before they take the oath. On rare occasions, IB officers interact with the media during crises. The IB is also rumoured to intercept and open around 6,000 letters daily. The Bureau is also authorised to conduct wiretapping without a warrant. This clause is mostly misused by ruling governments to spy on their political opponents, sometimes indicting them on false criminal charges. The IB also has numerous authors who write letters to various newspapers and magazines to support the government's perspective.

International Gandhi Peace Prize : The International Gandhi Peace Prize, named after Mahatma Gandhi, is awarded annually by the government of India for outstanding work and contribution to social, economic and political transformation through non-violence and other Gandhian methods.

Recipients have included Nelson Mandela, John Hume, Baba Amte, Vaclav Havel, Sir Shridath Ramphal, Shri Ramakrishna Mission (in 1999, received by its president Swami Ranganathananda) and the International Red Cross.

International Gita Society : The International Gita Society was founded in 1984 as The American Gita Society, by Dr. Ramananda Prasad. The aims and objectives of IGS include:

1. Publish and distribute, free if possible, The Bhagavad-Gita in simple and easy to understand languages, and put the Bhagavd-Gita in libraries, hotels, motels, schools, prisons and other public places.
2. Spread the basic non-sectarian universal teachings of the Bhagavad-Gita and other Vedic scriptures in easy to understand languages by establishing branches of the society in other countries.
3. Provide support and guidance in establishing Gita Study and Discussion (Satsang) groups, including a free Gita correspondence course.
4. Provide inspiration, cooperation, and support in the study and propagation of the Vedic knowledge, and other metaphysical sciences.
5. Highlight and focus on similarities amongst scriptures and religions to promote the universal brotherhood of humanity.

International Islamic University Islamabad : The International Islamic University Islamabad was founded as the Islamic University in Islamabad on the first day of the fifteenth century Hijrah (Muharram 1, 1401 or November 11, 1980). This landmark of the beginning of the new century symbolizes the aspirations and hopes of the Muslim Ummah for an Islamic renaissance. The desire to produce scholars and practitioners, imbued with Islamic learning, character, and personality, and the capablilities to meet the economic, social, political, technological, and intellectual needs of the Muslim Ummah was the purpose of this University.

International Kite Festival : The kitists from all over the world demonstrate unimaginable kite forms and skills at thin 4-day festival. Ahmedabad is a permanent venue, the festival rotates to other Gujarat cities every year.

Inter-Services Intelligence : The Directorate for Inter-Services Intelligence (also Inter-Services Intelligence or ISI) is the principal intelligence agency body of Pakistan. The ISI provided most of the operational and organizational leadership during the U.S.-funded insurgency in Afghanistan against the USSR. Perhaps the most spectacular success of the ISI came in Afghanistan, where it engineered a takeover of the country by the hardline Islamic Taliban regime. Before that, it funneled US aid selectively to hardline Islamic mujahideen groups, most notably that of Gulbuddin Hekmatyar.

ISI has been responsible for gathering information in and around Pakistan. Apart from gathering information, the ISI is also responsible for training spies, security of the Pakistan nuclear program and the security of top Pakistan army generals.

Inzamam-ul-Haq : Inzamam-ul-Haq (born 3 March 1970 in Multan) is a Pakistani cricketer. He is considered to be one of Pakistan's best batsmen and one of the best in the world today. He is currently the captain of the Pakistani team. He made his Test debut against England at Edgbaston in 1992.

He plays shots all round the wicket, is especially strong off his legs, and unleashes ferocious pulls and lofted drives. So far he has scored 25 Test 100s and Pakistan has won 17 of the matches in which he has scored 100s. Inzamam ul-Haq is well-known for his poor running between the wickets (as of May 2005, he has been run out a record 38 times in one-day internationals) and his ability to play shots around the ground.

Iqbal Bano : Iqbal Bano is a ghazal singer from Pakistan and singer both classical and modern ghazals. She won the Pride of Performance medal in 1974. She also sings thumri and dadra.

Irfan Khan Pathan : Irfan Khan Pathan (born October 27, 1984) is an Indian cricketer and member of the Indian national cricket team since 2003. He was born in Baroda in Gujarat. He made his international debut against Australia in Adelaide at the age of 19. Following some good performances at the under-19 level, Pathan was picked for India's 2003-2004 tour of Australia and the 2004 tour of Pakistan.

He has taken 5 wickets in an innings six times in Test cricket, and once in one-day internationals, against Zimbabwe in the 2005 Videocon Tri-Series. His spell in the final match against Pakistan in the 2004 tour was arguably his best performance in ODI cricket. His trademark weapon is an inswinger which darts into a right-hand batsman, and he also has the ability to reverse swing the old ball. In the ODI format, Pathan has been particularly impressive, frequently giving India early breakthroughs. He now consistantly ranks in or near the top 10 of the LG ICC cricket ratings.

Pathan was the inaugural winner of the ICC Emerging Player of the year award in 2004, and is being groomed as the spearhead of the Indian attack for years to come, as well as a potential captain. Following his strong performances in 2005, Pathan was promoted in December to an A-grade contract by the BCCI.

Iron Pillar : The iron pillar is one of the world's foremost metallurgical curiosities. The pillar, almost seven metres high and weighing more than six tonnes, was erected by Kumara Gupta I of the Gupta dynasty that ruled northern India 320-540. The pillar was originally located in the temple of Muttra, with the idol of Garuda at the top. It is the only piece of the Hindu temple remaining, which stood there before being destroyed by Qutb-ud-din Aybak to build the Qutub Minar and Quwwat-ul-Islam mosque. Qutub built around it when he constructed the mosque.

The pillar bears an inscription which states that it was erected as a flagstaff in honour of the Hindu god, Vishnu, and in the memory of the Gupta King Chandragupta II (375-413). Made up of 98% wrought iron of impure quality, it is 23 feet 8 inches (7.21 m) high and has a diameter of 16 inches (0.41 m). The pillar is a testament to the high level of skill achieved by ancient Indian iron smiths in the extraction and processing of iron. It has attracted the attention of archaeologists and metallurgists as it has withstood corrosion for the last 1600 years, despite harsh weather.

A fence was erected around the pillar due to the popularity of a tradition that it was considered good luck if you could stand with your back to the pillar and make your hands meet behind it.

Isa Khan : Isa Khan is the most famous of the twelve Bhuiyans of medieval Bengal. It is estimated that he was born in 1529. He was the ruler of a region that now comprises parts of the districts of Dhaka and Mymensingh in Bangladesh. His capital city was in Sonargaon, near present day Dhaka city. The most momentous moment of his life was repelling the forces of the legendary Mansingh, the great general of Akbar. This incident has come to represent the definace and love of freedom of the people of Bengal and has been celebrated in numerous plays, songs, ballads and novels.

Ishwar Chandra Vidyasagar : Ishwar Chandra Vidyasagar (26th September1820—29th July1891) was a polymath. Born in Midnapore, West Bengal, he is widely considered as one of the most significant figures of the Bengal Renaissance of 19th century. He was an academic, philosopher, educator, entrepreneur, writer, translator, reformer and philanthropist. The materialistic world of the West looks down on India as a poor nation. That assessment is and remains empirically valid, no doubt, even at the end of the twentieth century.

Although Vidyasagar cannot be judged as one of the best pure literary figures of Bengal, for he mostly devoted his time writing reformist literature and text books, his pioneering work in Bengali prose certainly deserves the very best of appreciation. His simplification of idiomatic expressions and clarification of the writing style provided the sound base on which latter Bengali writers like Tekchand Thakur, Pyarichand Mitra and Bankim Chandra Chatterjee built their literary superstructures.

Indeed, Tagore revered him as 'the father of modern Bengali prose'. Vidysagar's other contribution in this area was to translate the best of Sanskrit works to Bengali so that the ordinary person, who were not sufficiently versed with that language, could appreciate the immortal contribution by literary greats of India. He wrote biographical notes on numerous noteworthy personalities in the history of the world so that the young generation could be inspired by the great examples of their edurance, hard work, honesty, patience, perseverence, courage, determination and, above all, philosophy of life.

Iskander Mirza : Iskander Mirza (November 13, 1899 – November 13, 1969) was the first President of Pakistan and held that position from 1956 until 1958.

He was also the fourth Governor-General of Pakistan before it was replaced by the Presidency. Iskander Mirza was born in Murshidabad, Bengal in 1899 and grew up in

Bombay. After completing his early education, he was educated at the Royal Military Academy at Sandhurst, becoming the first Indian graduate at the academy, and commissioned into the British Indian Army in 1920. Mirza only served in the army for six years, after which he was the first Indian to be accepted in the elite Indian Politcal Service, eventually becoming a joint secretary in the Ministry of Defense of British India. In this position he was responsible for dividing the British Indian Army into the future armies of Pakistan and India.

Upon the formation of Pakistan, Mirza was made the Defense Secretary of the new nation, this appointment owed to Mirza's ranking as the highest Muslim civil servant in India at the time. In 1954 he was made governor of East Pakistan to bring order to a politically distressed region. This position was followed by his being appointed Minister of Interior and Frontier Regions in Prime Minister Bogra's cabinet. In 1955 he became acting Governor-General, before becoming the last Governor-General of Pakistan. Iskander Mirza was also a great advocate of the One Unit scheme and believed in the seperation of state and religion.

In 1956, Pakistan established its first constitution, and the position of Governor-General was replaced by that of President. The two were essentially the same, but Mirza was officially elected as President by the Assembly. During his presidency, Pakistan was politically unstable, this was marked by four different prime ministers in two years.

By 1958, realising that the 1956 Constitution was contributing to political instability, Mirza declared martial law on October 7th with the view to introducing a new constitution "more suited to the genious of the Pakistani people" in November. He appointed the commander-in-chief of the Pakistan Army, Ayub Khan as the martial law administrator. This move quickly backfired as Ayub Khan forced Mirza to step down within three weeks after the establishment of martial law and exiled him to England. Ayub Khan declared himself President on October 27th after a bloodless coup d'état.

Mirza lived in exile in London till his death in 1969. After Yahya Khan's military government refused to allow him to be buried in his own country, his body was flown to Tehran where the Shah of Iran gave him a State Funeral befitting a Head of State.

Islam : Islam is an Arabic word meaning both 'Submission to God' and 'peace'. The followers of Islam who are called Muslims are found all over the world. There are over 100 crores of Muslims all over the world and out of this around one-tenth live in India alone.

Islam is not only a religion but also a particular way of life. The followers of Islam are governed by their religious teachings. Muhammad, the prophet of Islam, was born in Mecca in about 570AD. In about 610 AD, God sent his first message to Muhammad. Messages came to him from god till his death in 632AD. These messages were recorded by the companions of Muhammad. The collection containing these messages is called the 'Quran', the holy book of Muslims. The sayings of Muhammad which were distinguished from the words of god, were collected and are known as 'Hadith', the second most important source of Islam.

The Arabs called Muhammad, 'Al-Amin' or 'The trustworthy man' and respected him greatly. But when god sent through him the first message of Islam, there was stiff opposition against Muhammad from all sides. The opposition kept mounting, so Muhammad was forced to leave Mecca in 622AD. It is from this year that the Muslim calendar starts. Muhammad arrived in Medina where people listened to Muhammad and accepted him as a true prophet. The people in other towns challenged those who had already become Muslims and war became inevitable. However, when Muhammad died in 632AD, not only the whole of Arabia had embraced Islam but also his religion called the Perfect Religion was fast spreading in many lands.

The death of the prophet of Islam posed the problem of succession. One group of Muslims wanted a person from the family of the prophet to be his successor. This group was known as the 'Shias'. The other group, the 'Sunnis', wanted the successor to be chosen by majority opinion. The majority went in favour of Abu Bakr, who was chosen as Caliph. The Sunnis won, but this brought about two broad divisions of Muslims. After Abu Bakr, two more caliphs-'Umar and Uthaman'-were chosen. Then Ali, the son-in-law of prophet Muhammad and a candidate chosen by the Shias from the very beginning, became the fourth Caliph of Islam. These four Caliphs are known in Islamic history as the Pious Caliphs.

Islam was revealed by god to the prophet of Islam at a time when Arabia was witnessing a period of ignorance and tribal wars. A common cause of wars was the dispute over which god was superior to the others. Each Arab tribe had its own god. Islam substituted one god in place of so many and brought the Arab tribes together under the supreme Islamic belief that there is only one god. From the belief in the unity of god, Islam went on to preach the unity of mankind.

The great force with which the message of the 'Quran' spread from Arabia to the whole of Mid-Asia and other far-off lands, gives proof that it had an easy appeal for the human beings. It was the Arabs who went for trade with various countries, carried the message of Islam forward along with their merchandise.

The great increase in knowledge in all fields that followed the birth of Islam was a result of the great emphasis laid by the 'Quran' and by the prophet, on the acquisition of knowledge from whatever source, was available. The 'Quran' states clearly the importance of people who seek knowledge when it asks: 'Say, shall those who have knowledge and those who do not have it be considered equal?'. The great contribution of Muslims to literature is to be seen in books like the 'Arabian Nights' and their contribution to art and architecture in many thousands of buildings, from the giant and majestic palace of Al-Hamra in Spain to the Taj Mahal in India.

The mystics of Islam, known as 'Sufis', played an important part in spreading the message of universal love and toning down the aggressive trends in Islam. Islam's spirit of brotherhood helped in loosening the rigidity of the caste system.

It will be observed that the cultures of the Muslims in various parts of the world have remained unchanged. This proves that Islam never attempted to uproot people from their own cultures. On the other hand, it has allowed them to nurture their culture within the broad framework of the basic beliefs and practices.

Every Muslim isrequired by Islam to hold certain beliefs and practice certain religious exercises. It is essential for a Muslim to believe that there is only one god, and that Muhammad was chosen by him as the last prophet ; that god has created angels, and has revealed his messages to prophets before Muhammad, and that all of us will have another life after death in which we shall be rewarded or punished according to our deeds on earth. The religious practices which every Muslim has to perform are Prayer (Namaz) five times a day, fasting (Roza) for one month-the month of Ramadan in a year, giving away one fortieth of one's wealth every year as charity, and going, if one has money, on Hajj at least once in his lifetime. The Hajj is a great assembly of Muslims from all parts of the world in Mecca, the birth-place of Muhammad. Here the Muslims visit Ka'aba, a place regarded holy since the time of Abraham, another prophet who lived long before Muhammad.

Islam introduces the fraternal feelings among the followers by brining them closer together in stages. The people who pray five times a day may pray either at home or in a local mosque. On Fridays the Muslims must offer their midday prayer in the central Mosque, called Jami' Masjid. Here one has the opportunity of meeting people from various parts of the city. This is the second stage in the promotion of collectivity. The first stage being coming together in a local mosque. The third and the last stage is coming together of people from various parts of the world in Mecca during the Hajj. The religion Islam tries to bring mankind together as one large family descended from one man and one woman. It does not allow any feeling of superiority on the basis of race or colour. Superiority, according to Islam, comes only through a man's virtues.

The literal meaning of Islam being 'submission to god', the life of Muslim is governed not by his desires and ambitions but according to the desires of god. The 'Quran' and the 'Hadith' together provide elaborate instructions for the Muslims on how to conduct themselves in their day to day life, at home and in their dealings with others.

Religion and the affairs of the world are both regulated in equal measure by the teachings of Islam. That is to say, it does not keep the church and the state separate as most nation sates of the world do today. The success of Islam as a socio-religions system can be measured from its contribution to humanity. With its simple, powerful and appealing doctrine of the unity of god it has been able to wean the people away from irrational and conflicting beliefs and practices. The great collectivization of men of different faiths and different races has been an important achievement.

Islam Pracharak : Islam Pracharak (literally, preacher of Islam) monthly magazine, first published in Bhadra 1298 (September 1891) from Kolkata and edited by Muhammad Reazuddin Ahmad. The policy of the magazine, as proclaimed in its epigraph, was to promote Islamic principles relating to religion, society, history and literature. Islam Pracharak published news, articles, poems, and stories to promote religious feelings, remove religious superstitions, and improve the traditional values of the Muslim community in Bengal. The writers also supported and inspired the rising sense of nationalism among Muslims. Islam Pracharak played an important role in translating the Quran, Tafsir and other religious books into Bangla.

Islamabad Capital Territory: Islamabad Capital Territory is the capital of Pakistan. It is located to the north of Punjab and to the south of North-West Frontier Province. Islamabad was designed and built to be a modern capital for Pakistan. It is located amongst the Margalla Hills at the northern end of Pothowar Plateau. It was established in 1960 by the orders of then President General Ayub Khan.

The capital is full of natural terraces and meadows and the southern plain drained by the Kurang River with the Margalla Hills in the north east.

Islamabad International Airport : Islamabad International Airport (IATA) is located in Islamabad, Pakistan. The current location of the airport is shared with the Chaklala airbase of Pakistan Air Force. The new location of the Islamabad International Airport has been selected at Fateh Jang, nearly 5 kilometers from Islamabad, and the construction will start in 2006.

Islamabad Stock Exchange : Islamabad Stock Exchange is the youngest of the three stock exchanges of Pakistan. It was incorporated on October 25, 1989 and it became fully operational on August 10, 1992. Islamabad Stock Exchange is centrally located in Anees Plaza, Fazal ul Haq Road, Islamabad. It can be accessed from East and West i.e. from both sides of Blue Area.

Islami Jamiat-e-Talaba (IJT) : Islami Jamiat-e-Talaba (IJT), is the largest student orgnization in Pakistan. Also known as the Jamiat ("jam-ee-at"), it is one oldest students' organization of Pakistan, founded on 23rd December 1947 in Lahore,Pakistan and after a tireless struggle of last 56 years has become the largest and the most organized students' organization in Pakistan. Jamiat has been striving for student rights and inviting students to practice Islam in their lives since its inception and its main emphasis has been at conversion of the society by preparing Islamic mindset among the nation, particularly in students.

Islamic Invasion of India : The Islamic invasion of India took place during the Rajput supremacy in north India, which lasted from the seventh to the twelfth centuries. The first effort toward invasion was made in 664 CE during the Umayyad caliphate, when Muslim forces led by Mohalib began launching numerous raids from Persia. Among the cities struck was Multan in the southern Punjab region in what is today Pakistan. Mohalib penetrated as far as the ancient capital of the Maili and returned with many prisoners of war. However, the Muslims did not come to conquer at this time, seeming only to make exploratory raids. It took several centuries for Islam to spread to parts of India. Hindus were converted to Islam by laws favoring Muslims, by force, by marriage, or voluntarily. Some of the ruling families and warrior castes of various Hindu kingdoms were forced to convert.

Islamic Oikyo Jote (IOJ) : IOJ was established in 1990 consisting of seven parties: Khelafat Majlis, Nezam-e-Islam, Faraizi Jamaat, Islami Morcha, Ulama Committee, a splinter group of NAP (Bhasani), and Islami Shashantantra Andolon. Its main objective is to steer a united political movement with a view to establishing an Islamic polity modeled upon the Khilafat. The organisation of the IOJ consists of a Majlish-e-Sura with five members from each of its component parties, and an advisory council. In the general elections held in 1996, IOJ won only one parliamentary seat.

Islamic Republic of Pakistan : The Islamic Republic of Pakistan, (Islami Jamhuriya i Pakistan) is a country located in South Asia that overlaps onto Central Asia. Its eastern provinces are located in the northwestern corner of the Indian subcontinent, while the western provinces are contiguous with the Iranian plateau. It borders Iran, Afghanistan, China, India, and the Arabian Sea. The name "Pakistan" in Urdu and Persian means Land of the Pure. It is the sixth most populous country and the second largest Muslim country.

Pakistan has a total area of 803,940 square kilometres or 310,403 square miles (land area of 778,720 km^{2}or 300,666 sq. mi), approximately the combined land areas of France and the United Kingdom. The State comprises four provinces, two territories, and also administers parts of Kashmir. The provinces are further subdivided into a total of 105 districts.

The name is believed to have been coined by Choudhary Rahmat Ali. He devised the word and first published it on January 28, 1933 in the pamphlet Now or Never. He saw it as an acronym formed from the names of the "homelands" of Muslims in South Asia. P for Punjab, A for Afghania, the Afghan areas of the region, K for Kashmir, S for Sindh and tan for Baluchistan, thus forming 'Pakstan'. An 'i' was later added to the English rendition of the name to ease pronunciation, producing Pakistan.

Pakistan is a member of the United Nations, the World Trade Organisation, the Organisation of the Islamic Conference, the Economic Cooperation Organisation, the Commonwealth of Nations, and the South Asian Association for Regional Cooperation.

As one of the cradles of human civilisation, the Pakistani region has long been at the crossroads of history. It was the birthplace of some of the most ancient civilisations and a strategic centre of historic trade routes, including the Silk Road. Pakistan was the site of one of the first town in the world at Mehrgarh and later much of the Indus Valley Civilisation. Modern Pakistan was subsequently settled by many groups, including Dravidians, Aryans, Persians, Greeks, Greco-Bactrians, Kushans, White Huns, Scythians and Arabs. This period saw the country advance in trade and culture to a level where the Gandhara region and the great city of Taxila (Takshashila) became a great centre of learning and development. Modern Pakistan region was invaded by great conquerors such as Assyrian Queen Semiramis, Alexander the Great from Macedonia and Umayyad general Muhammad bin Qasim.

Pakistan is a federal republic with a semi-presidential system, with four autonomous provinces, two territories, and de facto control of two regions in the northernmost part of the country. The bicameral legislature comprises a 100-member Senate and a 342-member National Assembly. The president is the Head of State and the Commander in Chief of the Armed Forces. Elections for the president are determined by the outcome of an electoral college. The prime minister is usually the leader of the largest party in the National Assembly. Each province has a Provincal Assembly, which in turn selects a Chief Minister and a Provincial Governor nominated by the Chief Minister.

Ismail Gulgee : Ismail Gulgee (born 1926) is an award winning globally famous Pakistani artist. Qualified engineer in USA and self-taught abstract painter. Before 1959, he painted the entire Afghan Royal Family. His paintings are bright and full of color, but the paint is put on with greater sensitivity and paintings vibrate with intense feeling. Areas sing with luxminous thin color, thick blobs of paint pulsate with fiber-glass tears, the brush swirls strong and free. The total effect is very gray, yet considered and well thought out. They work enormously well, because it is all orchestrated with great care and concentration.

Ismail Merchant : Ismail Merchant was born in Mumbai in 25th December in the year 1935 as Ismail Noormohamed Abdul Reh. In his career spanning three and a half decades, he has made some 40 feature films. Many of them made with the collaboration of his pal, director James Ivory and writer Ruth Prawer Jhabvala.

The famous Merchant- Ivory duo has made a mark of their own in the film world. Adaptation of E. M. Forster's 'A room with a view', Kazuo Ishiguro's 'Remains of the Day', 'Rose Land' and 'Heat & Dust' are some of the best Merchant-Ivory movies. Vanessa Redgrave, Isabelle Adjani, Christopher Reeve, Anthony Hopkins, Paul Newman, Emma Thompson, Isabelle Adjani, Paul Newman are a few well known actors who have featured in his films. They all crave to work with him knowing that he will pay them only a little more than his attention.

Besides film making, Merchant was also a renowned chef and the author of several books on quality cooking.

He passed away at the age of 68. He was unmarried and had no children.

Israr Ahmed : Dr. Israr Ahmed is a well-known religious figure in Pakistan, India, the Middle East, and the North America. He is the founder of the Tanzeem-e-islami, an off-shoot of the Jamaat-e-Islami. He was born on April 26, 1932 in Hisar District (a district of East Punjab, now a part of Haryana) in India.

Istor-o-Nal : Istor-o-Nal is the second highest mountain in the Hindu Kush. It is the second highest mountain outside of the Himalayas and the 36th highest mountain in the world. It is actually a range of mountains with 11 peaks at more than 7000 meters each. Istor-o-Nal is either 7403 m or 7398 m high depending on which source you rely upon. Istor-o-Nal is in Chitral, Pakistan. It is located behind Terichmir, which is the highest mountain in the Hindu Kush. Because Istor-o-Nal is located behind the higher peak of Terichmir, it cannot be seen and therefore is not well known.

Ita Fort : This historical fort in Arunachal Pradesh of an irregular shape, built mainly with bricks is situated at the heart of the capital complex in Papum Pare district. There are three gates on three sides viz; Eastern, Western and Southern, which is said to be built by Ahom rulers. It is estimated that more than 80 lakhs of bricks, 45 cubic metres of stone and 46,300 man-days were required to build the fort.

Itanagar : Itanagar is the capital of Arunachal Pradesh. Itanagar is situated at the foothills of Himalayas. It comes administratively under Papumpare district. The Nishi, also known as the Nishing, is the major tribe in Itanagar area. As a capital town, Itanagar is well connected with the rest of the country by road and air communications. Pawan Hans provides helicopter service between Guwahati and

Naharlagun (Itanagar). Deluxe buses are available from Guwahati.

Interesting places around are historical fort called Itafort which dates back to the 15th century (after which the city is named), legendary Ganga Lake or Gyakar Sinyi and the new Buddhist temple known as Buddha Vihar consecrated by the Dalai Lama. Fundamentalist Baptist missionaries have converted about one-fifth of the town population to Christianity. As of today, Itanagar has two churches.

Itanagar Sanctuary : Itanagar Wildlife Sanctuary, spread over an area of about 140.30 sq. km was established in 1978 and is situated in the Lower Subansiri district. With evergreen forests, the wild life present here are elephant, barking deer, tiger, leopard, serow, birds & orchids.

ITC Sangeet Sammelan : ITC Sangeet Sammelan started in 1971 has been showcasing the best in Indian Classical music annually since more than 3 decades. A substantial cash award is given to one of the oldest living musicians of stature during this Sammelan. This award is recognized as a great honour in the world of Indian classical music. The festival has a participation of eminent musicians and is appreciated by music lovers across the country. The Sammelan conducted by the ITC Sangeeth research Academy is held in different places in India.

Itihasa : Itihasa is the word for History. The word is also used in most other Indian languages, with the same meaning. The word is often used within India to refer to Hindu Epics such as the Ramayana, the Mahabharata and sometimes the puranas. Some historians may also accept this use, with a view to attribute historic veracity to such legends. This usage is eschewed by most historians because the dating of events alluded to in these legends, as also the substantiation of their historic veracity and accuracy, is generally impossible.

Ittefaq : The Daily Ittefaq is one of the Bangladesh's most published and circulated newspapers. It's written in Bangla. It has great contribution to country's independence and fall of military rule in present Bangladesh in 1990s. The Ittefaq, first published as weekly 24 December 1953 by Tofazzal Hossain Manik Mia although for first few years Maulana Abdul Hamid Khan Bhasani mentioned on the top of the paper as its founder. In colonial era it widely published the negligence and colonial mind of Pakistan leaders to East Pakistan. Hence government used to take action against its editors and journalists.

Tofazzal Hossain's post editorial column 'Rajnaitik Mancha' (political platform) earned great popularity in East Pakistan. Ittefaq had a significant role in the general elections of 1954 and contributed victory of the United Front. Ittefaq always strongly opposed all military rule of Pakistan starting from Ayub Khan to Yahya Khan. The Ittefaq supported to the Six Point Program of Awami League in mid 60 and played important role to publish the idea into people. Quickly Ittefaq emerged as the voice of the East Pakistan citizens. President Ayub Khan censored its publication from June 17th to July 11th,1966, and then again from July 17th,1966 to February 9th,1969. Tofazzal Hossain, was imprisoned several times. Tofazzal Hossain died on June 1st, 1969, and paper was managed by his two sons; Mainul Hosein and Anwar Hossain.

Ittefaq Office was burnt down by the Pakistan army on 25 March 1971, and publication of the paper ceased. However, it published again from 21st May, 1971 under direct control of Pakistani ruler. The Ittefaq was nationalized on 17 June 1975. Nurul Islam Patwary was made the chief editor and was published from New Nation Press at 1 Ramkrishna Mission Road, Dhaka. Ownership was returned to Manik Mia's sons on 24 August 1975. Mainul Hossain is now chairman of the editorial board while Anwar Hossain is its editor.

Iyengar Yoga : Iyengar Yoga, created by B.K.S. Iyengar, is a form of yoga known for its use of props, such as belts and blocks, as aids in performing asanas. It is firmly based on the traditional eight limbs of yoga as expounded by Patanjali in his Yoga Sutras, emphasizing the development of strength, stamina, flexibility and balance, as well as concentration (Dharana) and meditation (Dhyana).

Iyengar Yoga is characterized by great attention to detail and precise focus on body alignment. Iyengar pioneered the use of "props" such as cushions, benches, blocks, straps, and even sand bags, which function as aids allowing beginners to experience asanas more easily and fully than might otherwise be possible without several years of practice. Props also allow tired or ill students to enjoy the benefits of many asanas via fully "supported" methods requiring less muscular effort.

Standing poses are emphasized in Iyengar Yoga. They build strong legs, increase general vitality, and improve circulation, coordination and balance, ensuring a strong foundation for study of more advanced poses. Unlike more experiential approaches where students are encouraged to independently "find their way" to the asanas by imitating the teacher, an Iyengar Yoga class is highly verbal and didactic, with misalignments and errors actively corrected. Iyengar has trained thousands of teachers, who complete 2-5 years of rigorous training for the introductory level of certification (higher-level certification may take a decade or more). The center of Iyengar Yoga is the Ramamani Iyengar Memorial Yoga Institute located in Pune, India.

